AF262784

Gardens AND Imagination

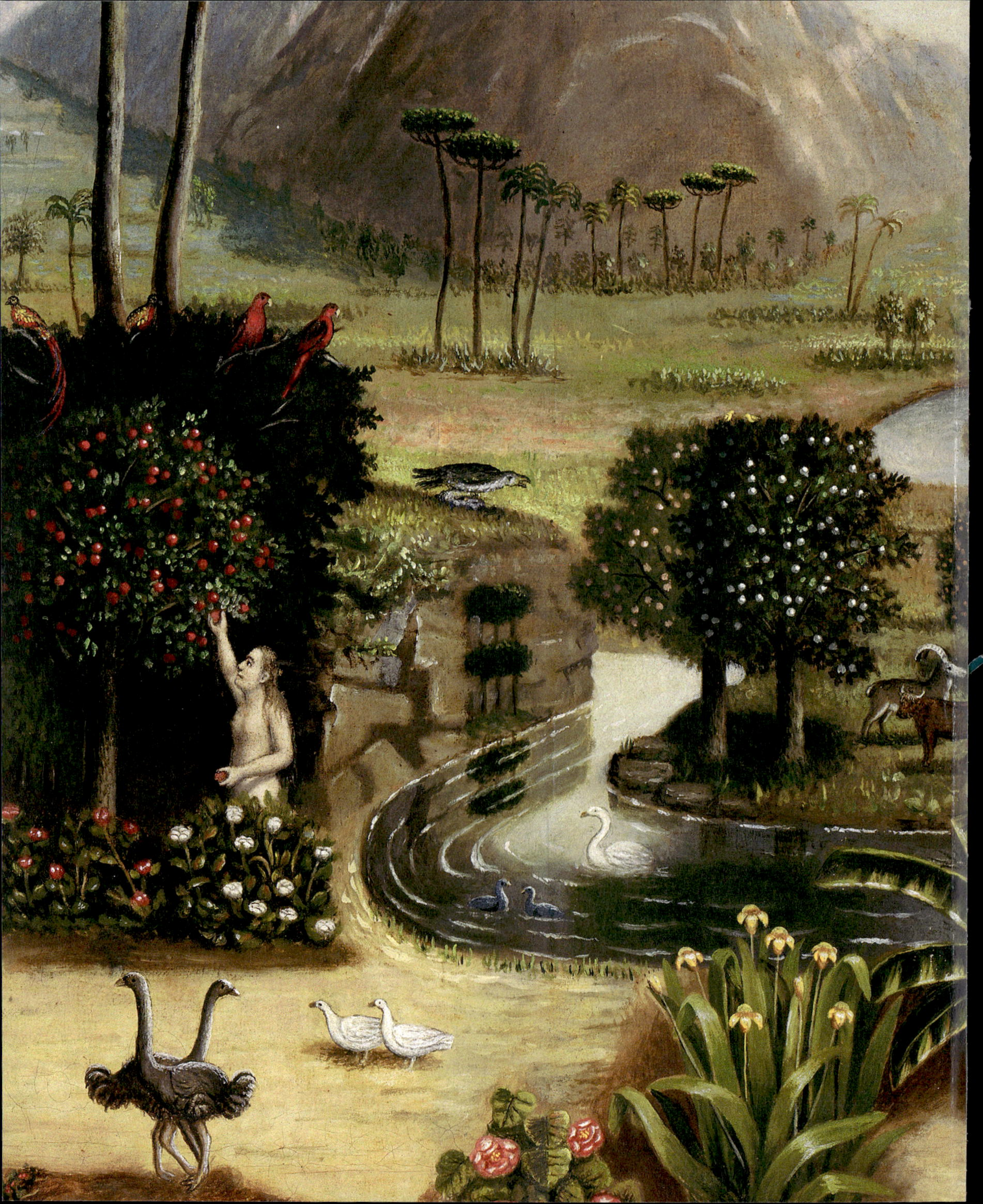

Gardens AND Imagination

FRAMING NATURE IN ART

Elizabeth Dospěl Williams, Karen E. Haas,
Courtney Leigh Harris, and Meghan Melvin

MFA PUBLICATIONS
MUSEUM OF FINE ARTS, BOSTON

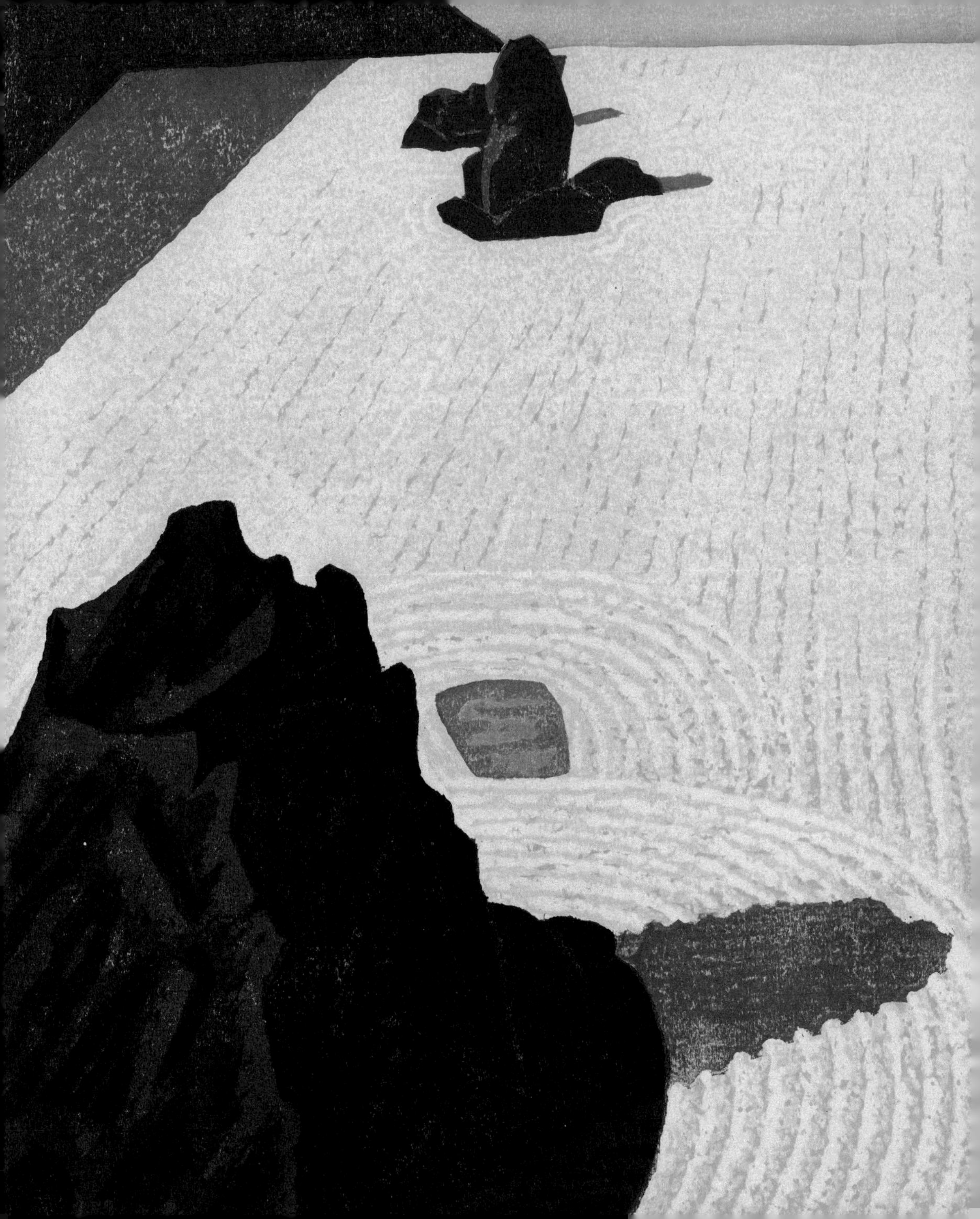

CONTENTS

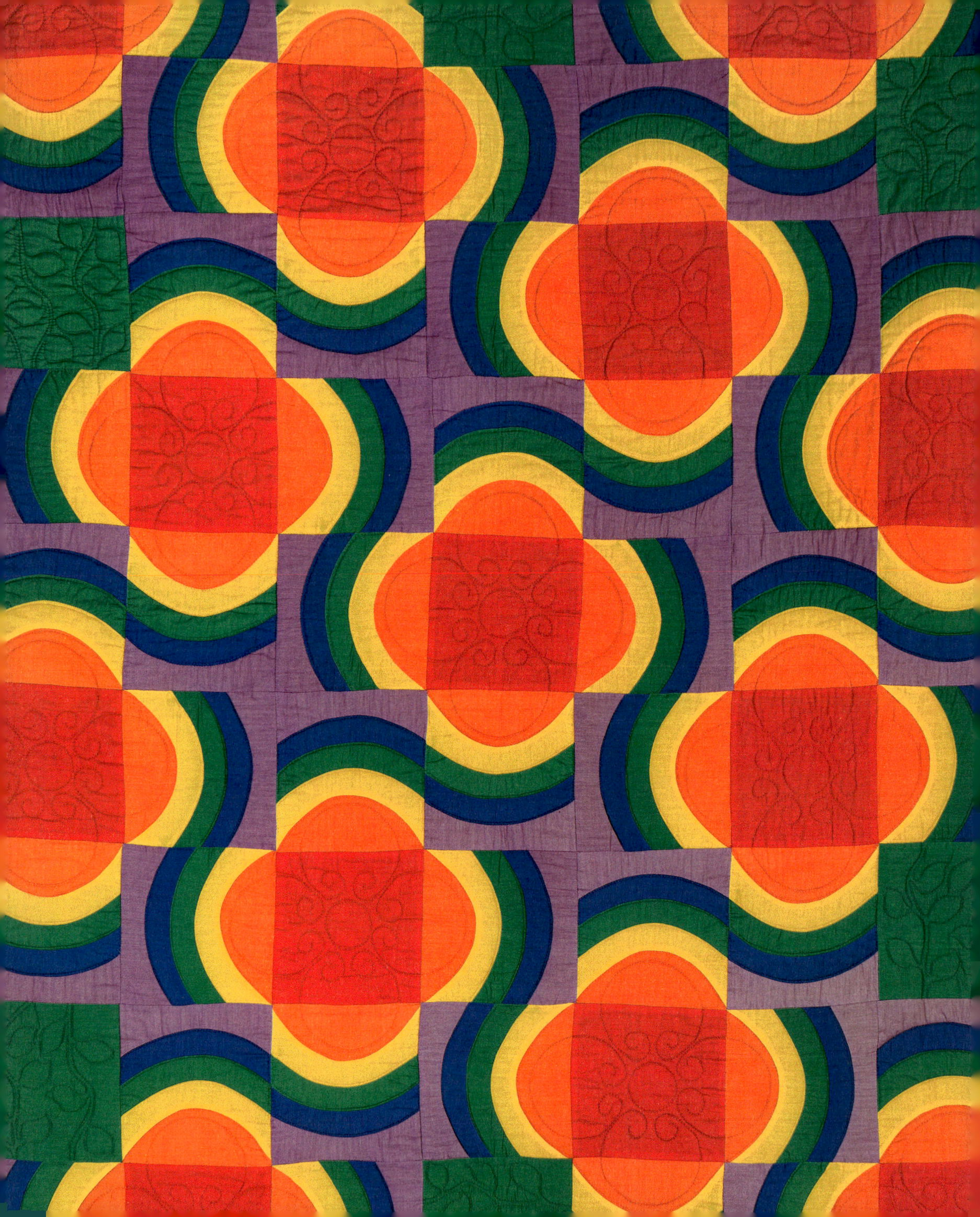

A garden may be a gathering place of shared seeds and tools for a community just as much as a humble plot in one's private backyard. In appearance it can exude the formality of a vast royal park, dense with manicured hedges and formal pathways, or take the form of an arid landscape of succulents and rocks. In short, gardens have evidently meant many different things across space and time, and served as places of solace, labor, growth, and introspection.

Gardens and Imagination considers the many ways gardens have inspired human creativity and ingenuity. Drawing from the Museum's collection, this publication and the exhibition it accompanies explore how gardens have found a place in the visual arts, and how they also have been works of art in their own right. Plants, rocks, and water features are raw materials for artistic expression; shovels and hoes are among the tools to give it shape; and soil is a ubiquitous canvas. By considering the creative dimension of gardens through a range of perspectives, the essays included in this book invite us to examine our relation, as individuals and as communities, to a longstanding focus of human interest and activity, and also cast a new light on works of art that span two millennia in our collection.

Generous support for this exhibition is provided by Penny Vinik. Additional support is provided by the Laura and Tait Nielsen Exhibition Fund, the James & Virginia Welch Foundation, the Loring Textile Gallery Exhibition Fund, the Wendy Lipsey Ecker and Family Exhibition and Publication Fund for Fashion, Textiles and Jewelry, the Patricia B. Jacoby Exhibition Fund, and the Ellen and Robert Jaffe Fund. This publication is made possible with generous support from the MFA Associates/Senior Associates Tribute Fund in Memory of Past Members. Additional support is provided by the Anne Poulet European Decorative Arts and Sculpture Publication Fund.

PIERRE TERJANIAN
Ann and Graham Gund Director
Museum of Fine Arts, Boston

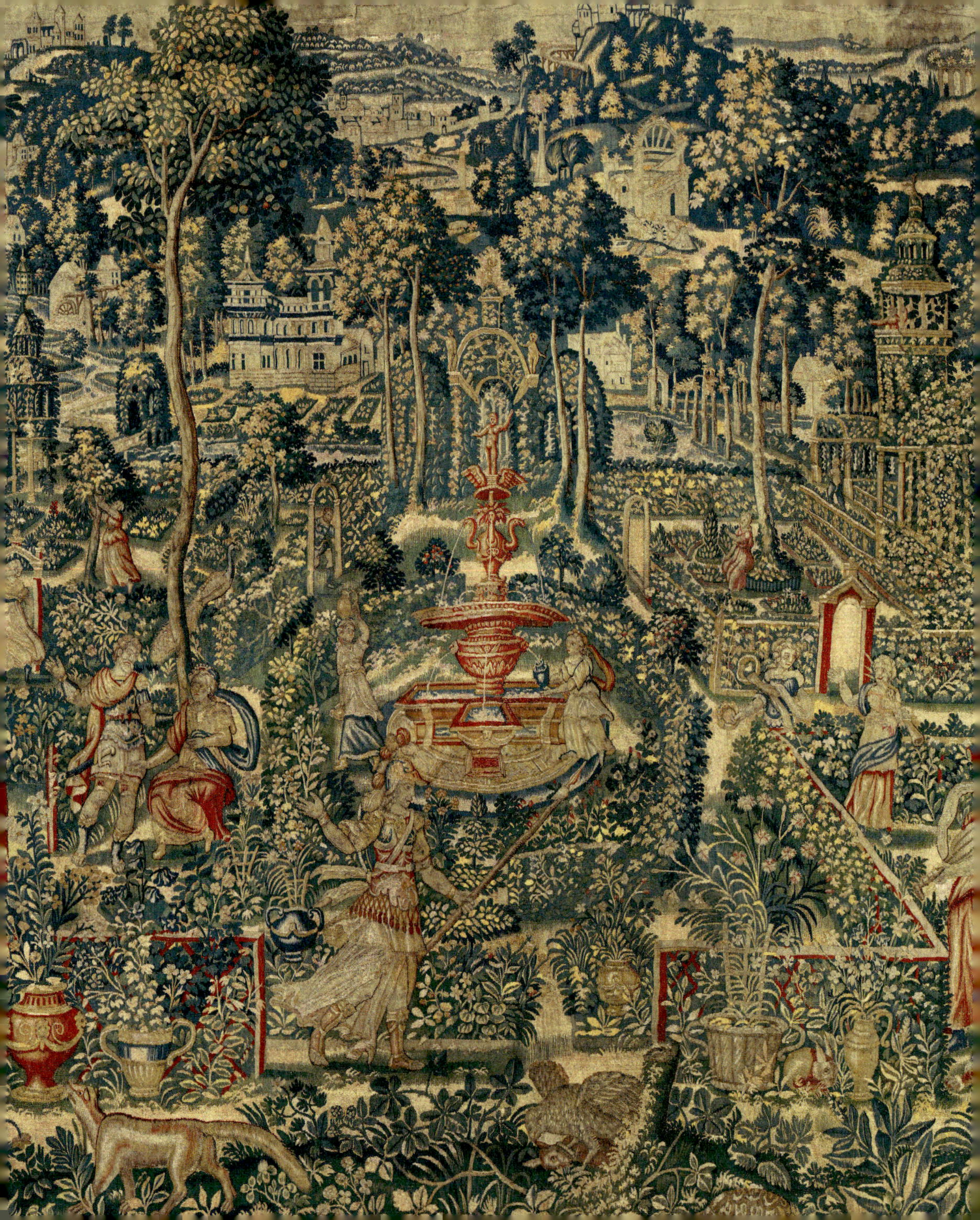

Gardens and People

On the surface, gardens might appear a straight-
forward theme for reaching across an encyclopedic
museum's global historic and contemporary collections. After all, depictions of the plants, animals, and
structures associated with gardens pervade artworks of
all kinds, past and present, from European tapestries to
Impressionist paintings, from contemporary photography
to ceramics from the ancient Americas. Such representations of gardens at first glance convey messages about universal phenomena shared across cultures concerning the
joys and frustrations, necessities and pleasures of gardens.
But go deeper and the topic of gardens proves elusive,
the theme reflecting not so much common experiences of
nature, as the particulars of any given moment and place.
So while ideas about tending the natural world in gardens
find analogous expression across cultures and periods,
gardens' meanings remain deeply personal to individuals
and communities, in a manner demanding careful attention
to detail.

Against this background, the gardens presented in
art throughout this book might be defined not by shared
characteristics, forms, or practices, but rather through the
unique ways they reflect humankind's impulses to dominate,
intervene in, or live alongside nature. Instead of looking
for converging trends, one is better prompted to consider

the dazzling array of difference found in artistic expression around the garden theme. This is because what looks like a garden to one person might look quite different, or even unrecognizable, to another. Some gardens consist of plants and others of rocks, some gardens splendid with greenery and others parched perfectly for succulents, some carefully cultivated and others seemingly overgrown, yet all might be considered gardens in the eyes of their beholders. For this reason, gardens must be understood in relation to the people who care for them, enjoy them, and even struggle to maintain them. To consider gardens in a global, transhistorical framework is thus to prompt self-reflection about one's own expectations of what defines a garden, and to consider how others see and understand gardens differently.

Like gardens, museums too are places for people, filled with artworks that people care for, containing collections meant to be enjoyed by all. It is thus not surprising that the permanent collections of the Museum of Fine Arts, Boston, house many artworks depicting garden themes, reflecting both the depths of the Museum's holdings and the special place gardens hold in the hearts of the city's people. Beyond artworks of the kinds brought together in the pages of this book, the MFA itself has been home to many living gardens over the course of its history. Gardens featured in the Museum's galleries at an early date, where green spaces prompted visitors to take a mental pause from the human-made forms of paintings, sculpture, and other artworks. Building on this tradition, the MFA opened its own Japanese-style garden, *Tenshin-En* (The Garden of the Heart of Heaven) in 1988, a tranquil place in warm weather even today. More recently, *A Garden for Boston* project in 2021 placed indigenous traditions and community gardens in dialogue with the permanent structures of the Museum itself. And bringing together gardens, art museums, and people finds its most enduring expression in the MFA's annual Art in Bloom celebration, established in 1976, where the region's garden clubs turn to the Museum's permanent galleries to translate beloved artworks into ephemeral bouquets for all to enjoy.

The tension between the permanent and the transitory represents perhaps the most consistent feature connecting gardens, people, and museums. Gardens change and grow, as seeds transform into plants, as weeds take over carefully tended plots, as seasons shift with increasing unpredictability. So too do human beings, who see in gardens metaphors for life's ups and downs, its cycles of aging, decay, renewal, and rebirth. The enduring preservation of museums, as places stewarding artworks for future generations, might seem in opposition to the mutability inherent in gardens and human lives. Yet in staging temporary exhibitions that reinterpret artworks for ever-changing audiences, museums, too, are places for change and imagination across time and place.

As an example, consider a magnificent tapestry with park scene, woven in Flanders in the late sixteenth or early seventeenth century (6). Entering the MFA's collections in 1942 (certainly passing by where the Museum would start a Victory Garden in 1943), the artwork was left quietly in storage, a seed-like dormancy, for decades. The tapestry's massive scale invites an immersive looking experience, a constant moving back and forth from the big picture to the tiny details, a perfect metaphor for the play between the universal and the particular inherent in any garden theme. And while the viewer today can get easily lost in this tapestry garden's meandering paths and carefully managed plantings, it is the people represented in the tapestry who arguably attract our care-filled attention. The tapestry is indeed replete with all manner of people: people at work, people at play, people enjoying music, people laughing and living, all set within the idealized space of a timeless garden. In this way, the tapestry speaks to us across the centuries, inviting us to enter the garden as visitors and to imagine ourselves there, too. — EDW

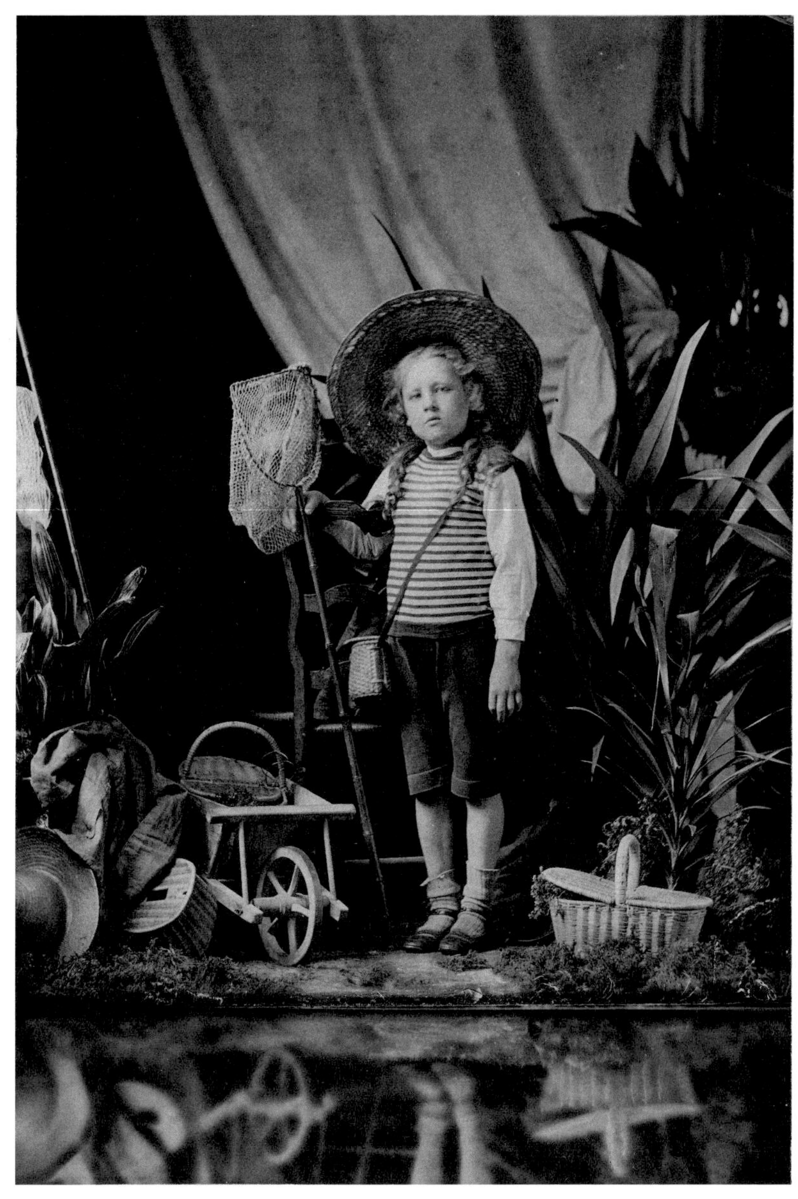

— 1 —

Emmanuel de La Villéon, The photographer's son, 1890s

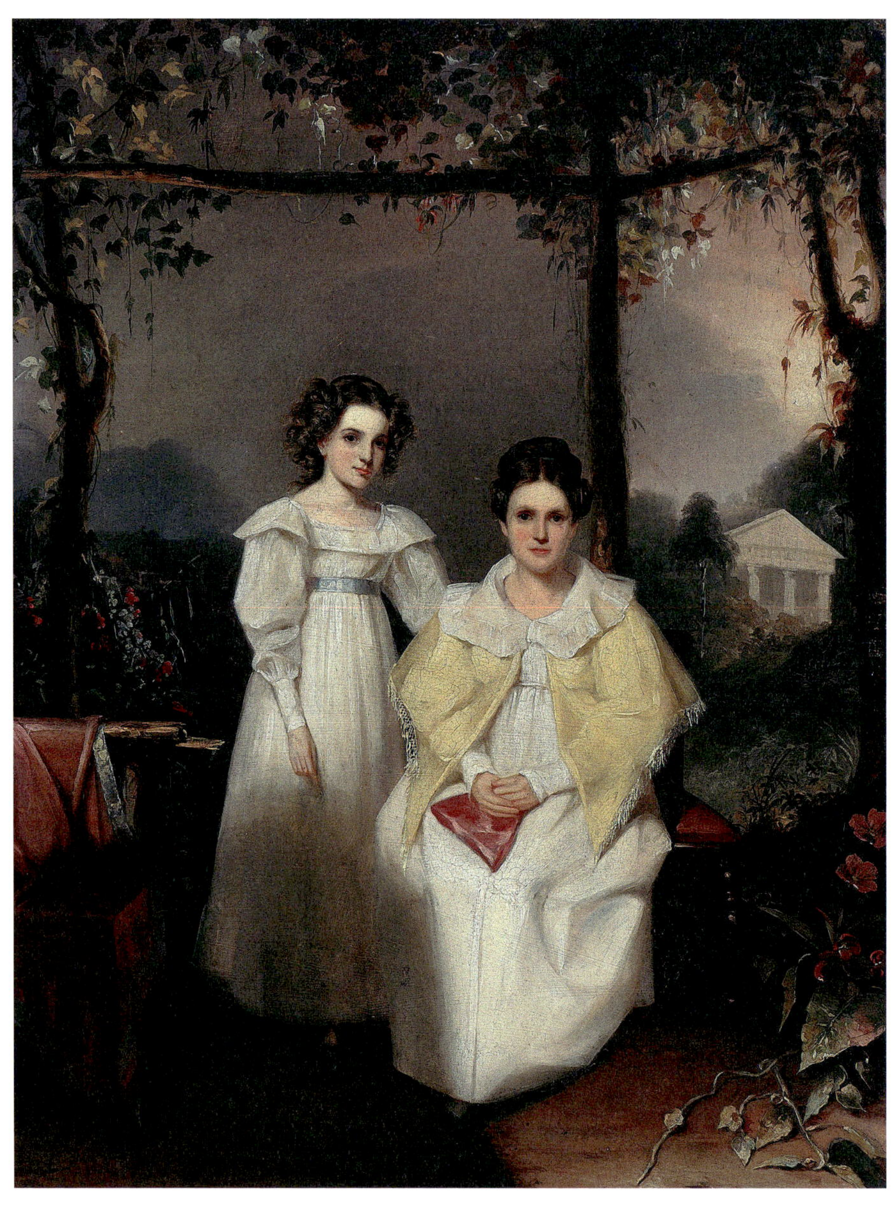

— 2 —

William James Hubard, *Margaret Oliver Colt and Mary Devereux Colt
in the Gardens at "Green Mount," Baltimore*, 1830

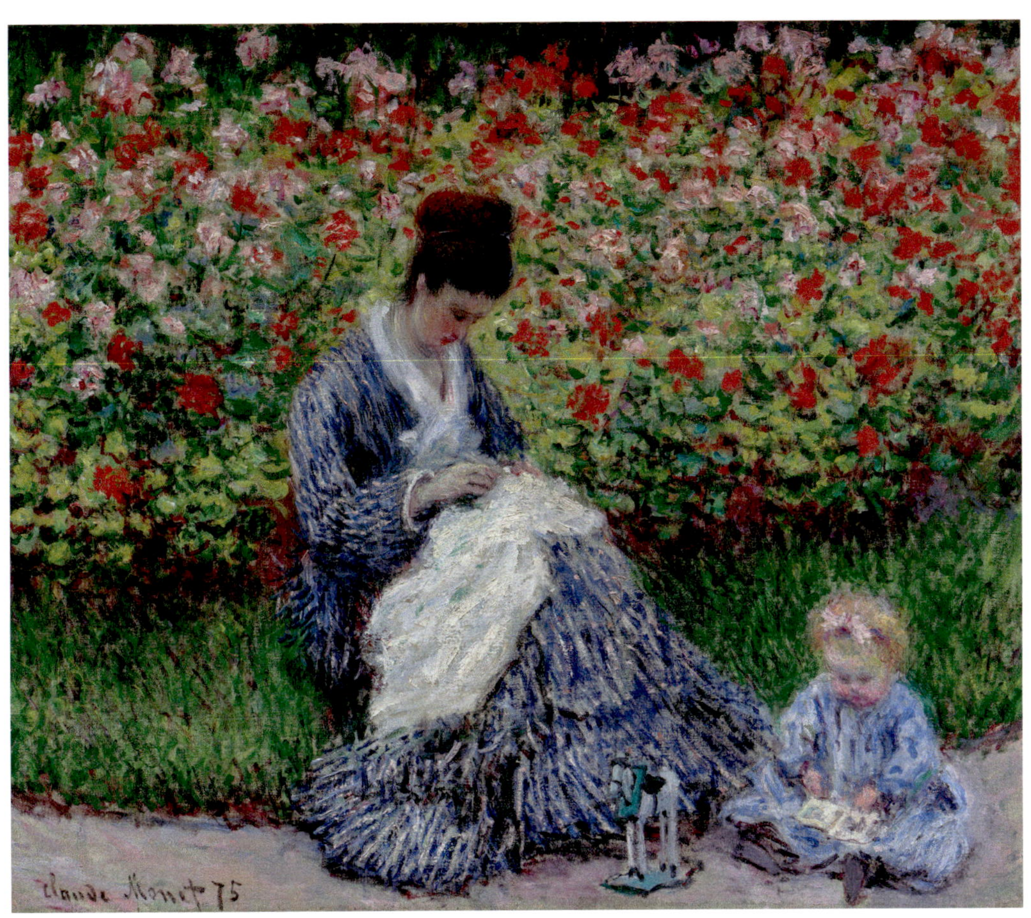

— 3 —

Claude Monet, *Camille Monet and a Child in the Artist's Garden in Argenteuil*, 1875   17

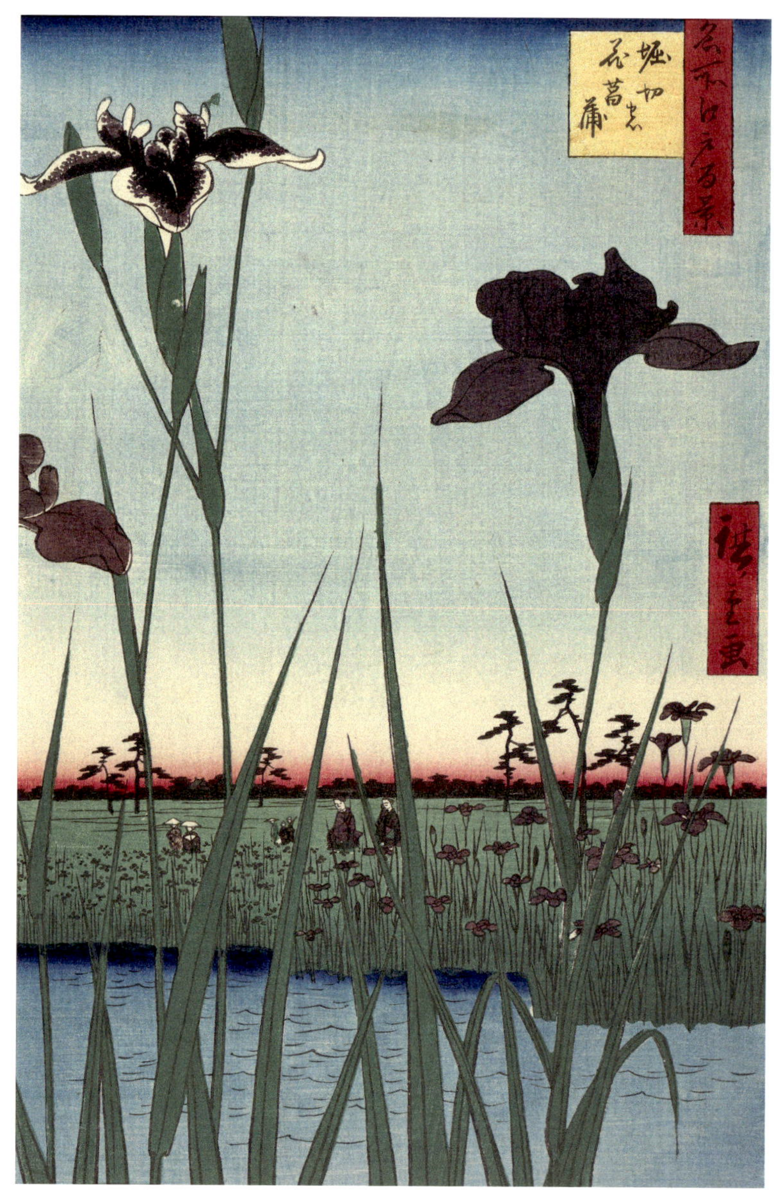

— 4 —

Utagawa Hiroshige I, *Horikiri Iris Garden*, 1857

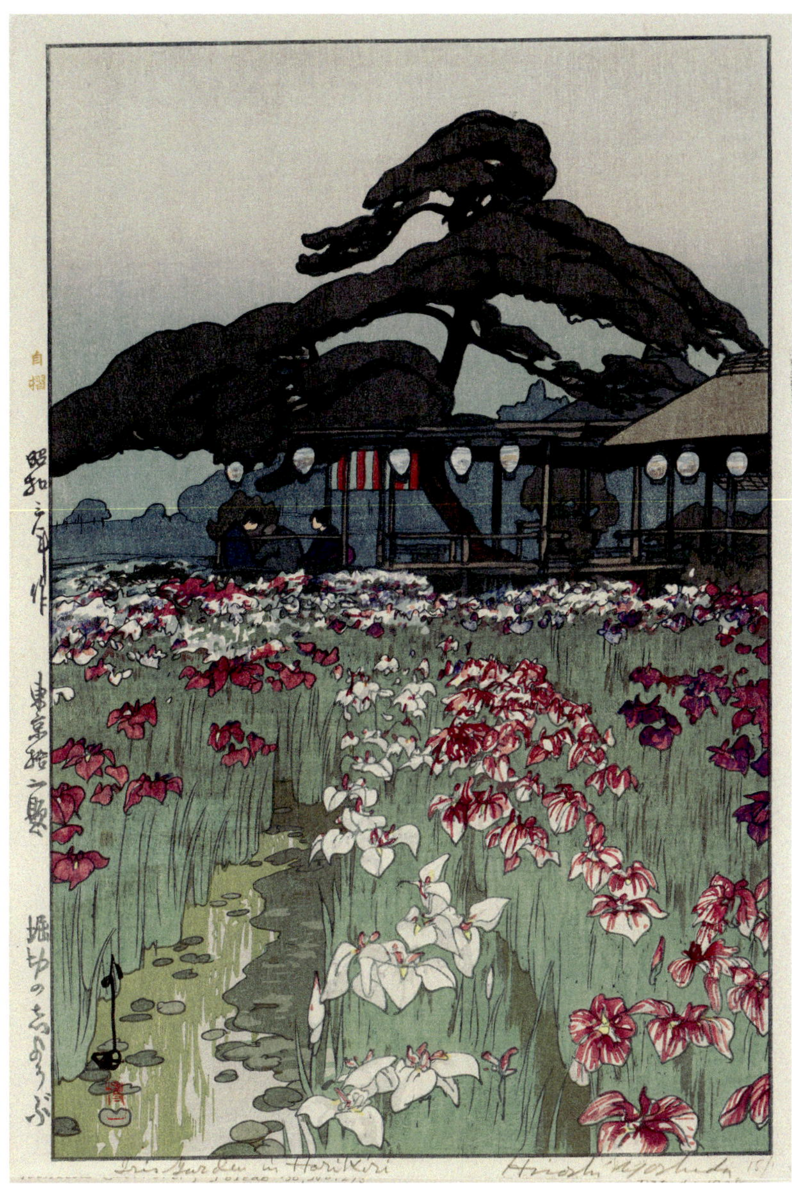

Yoshida Hiroshi, *Iris Garden in Horikiri*, 1928

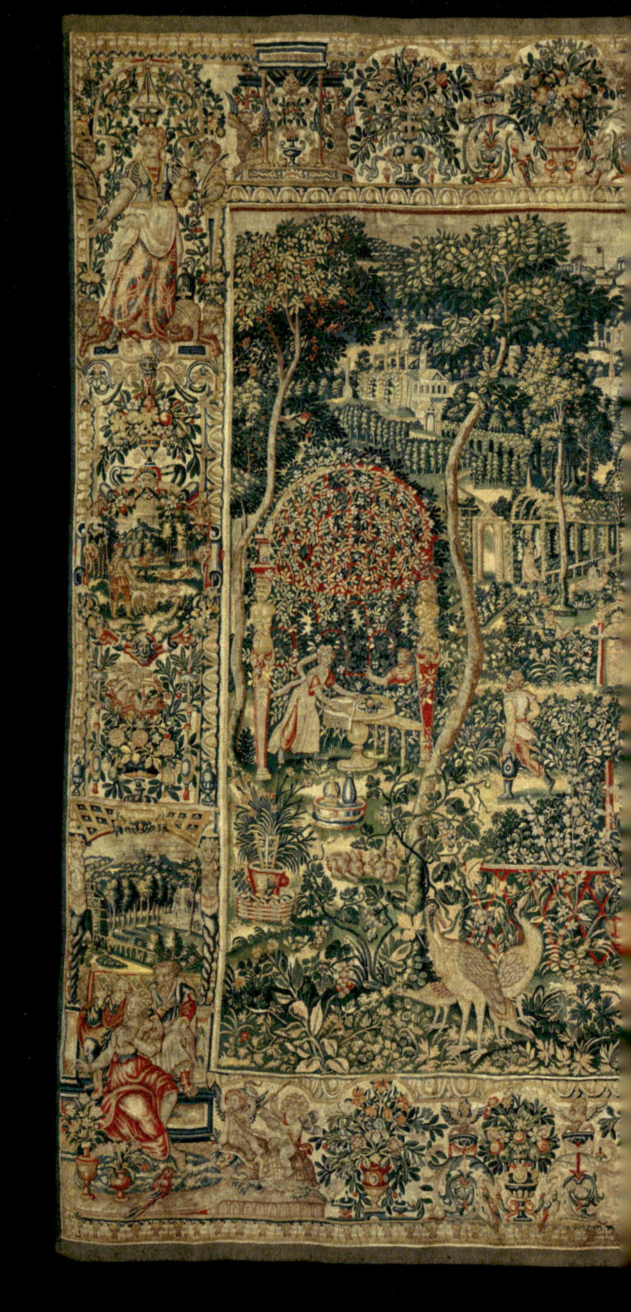

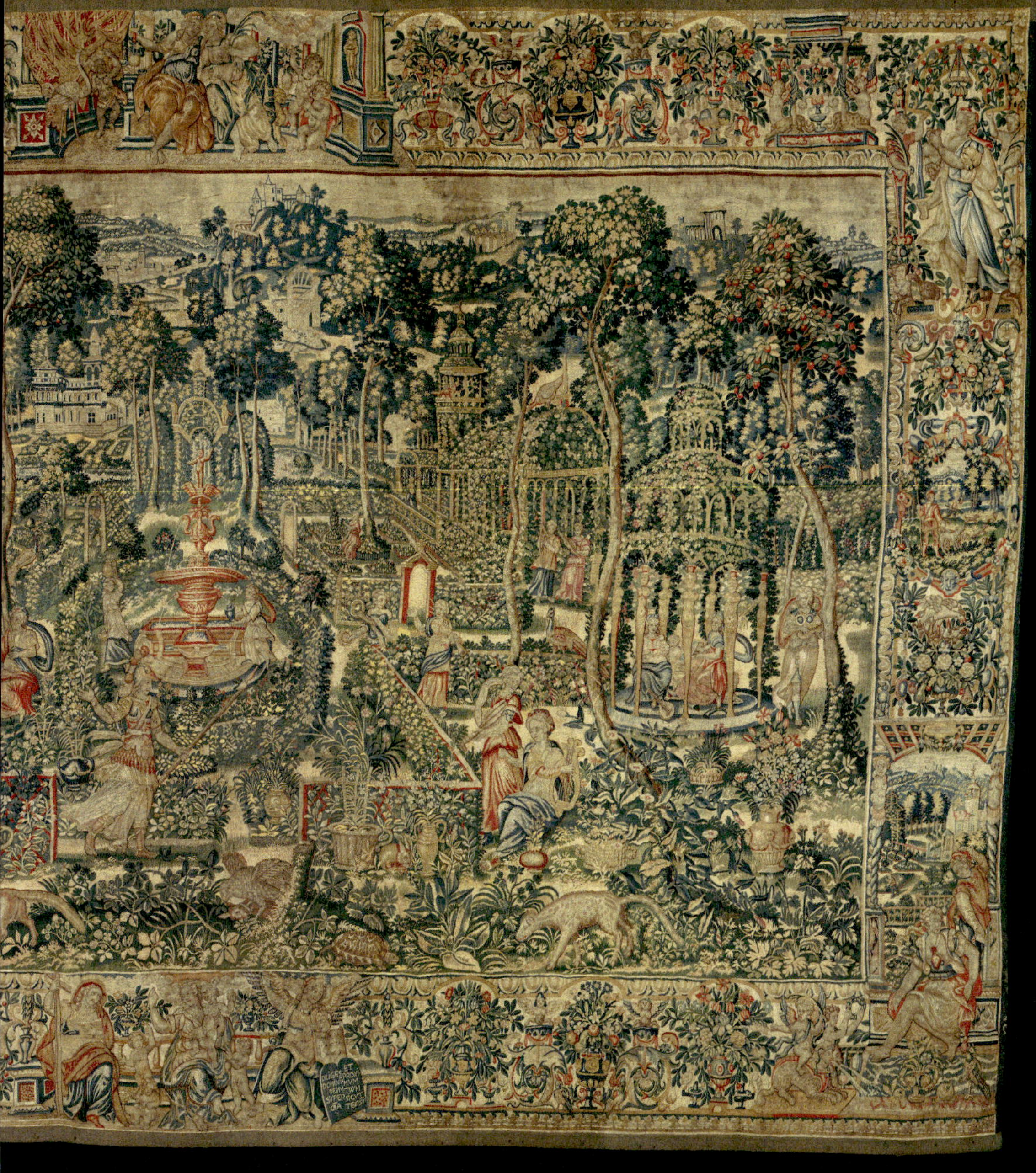

Tapestry with park scene, Flemish, late 16th–early 17th century

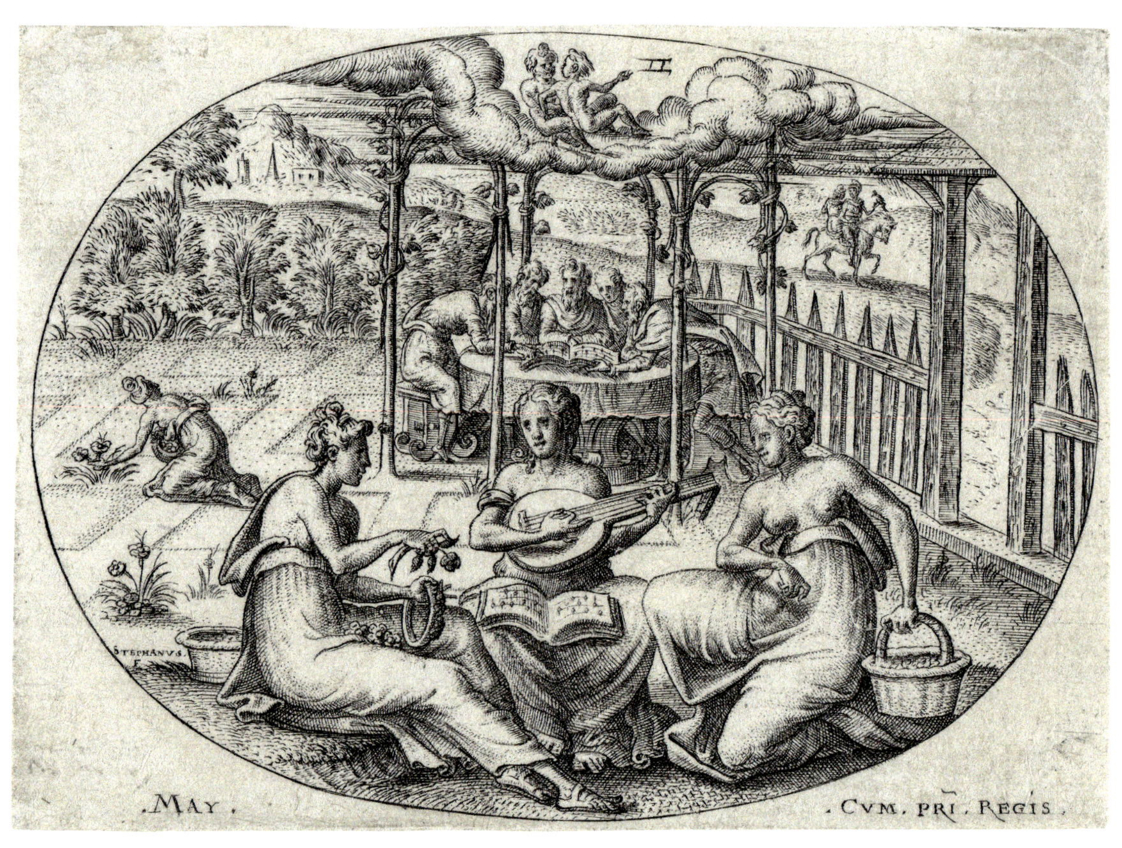

— 7 —

Étienne Delaune, *Making Music*, 1568

— 8 —

Prince and Lady under Flowering Branch,
Timurid, about 1420–40

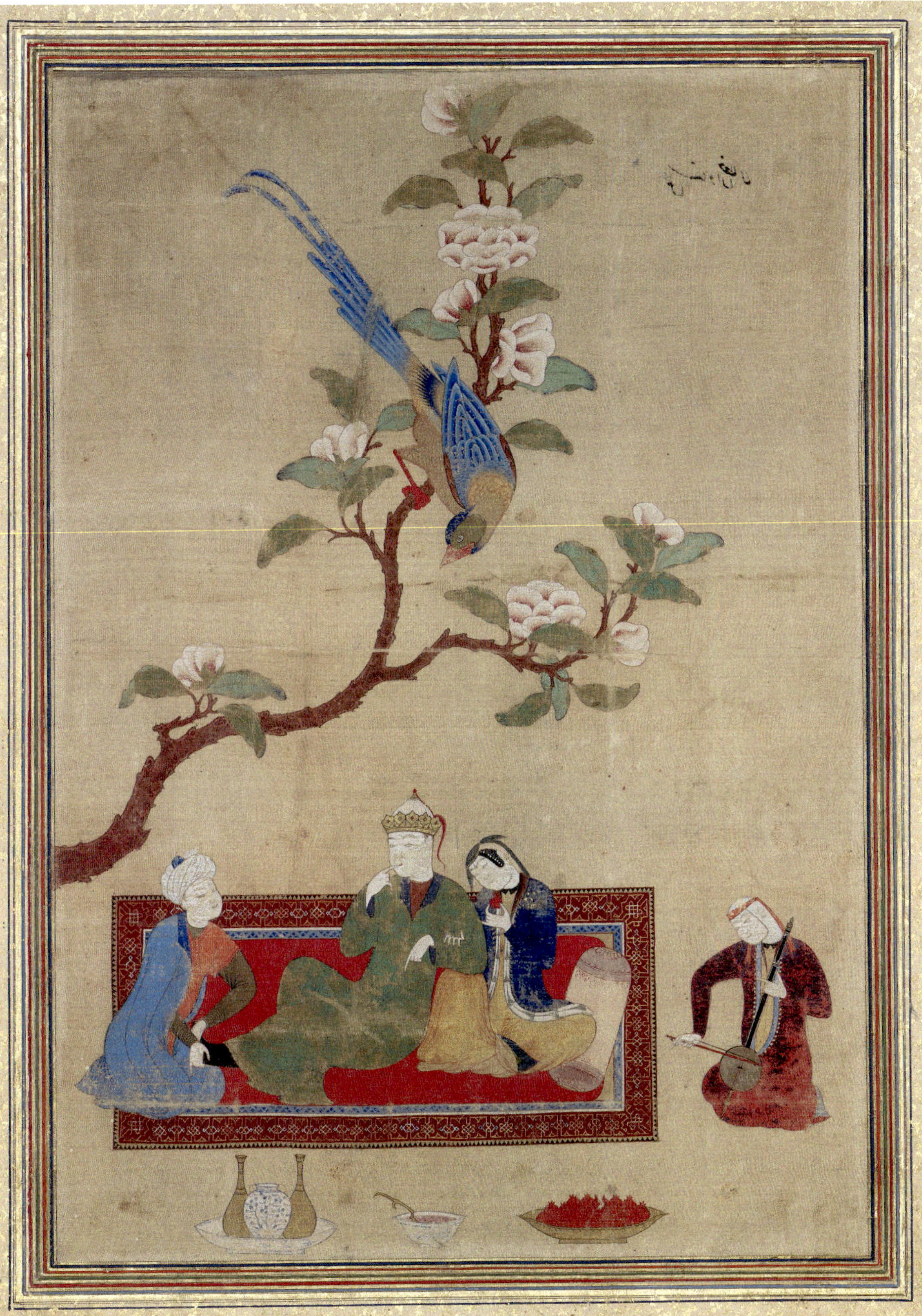

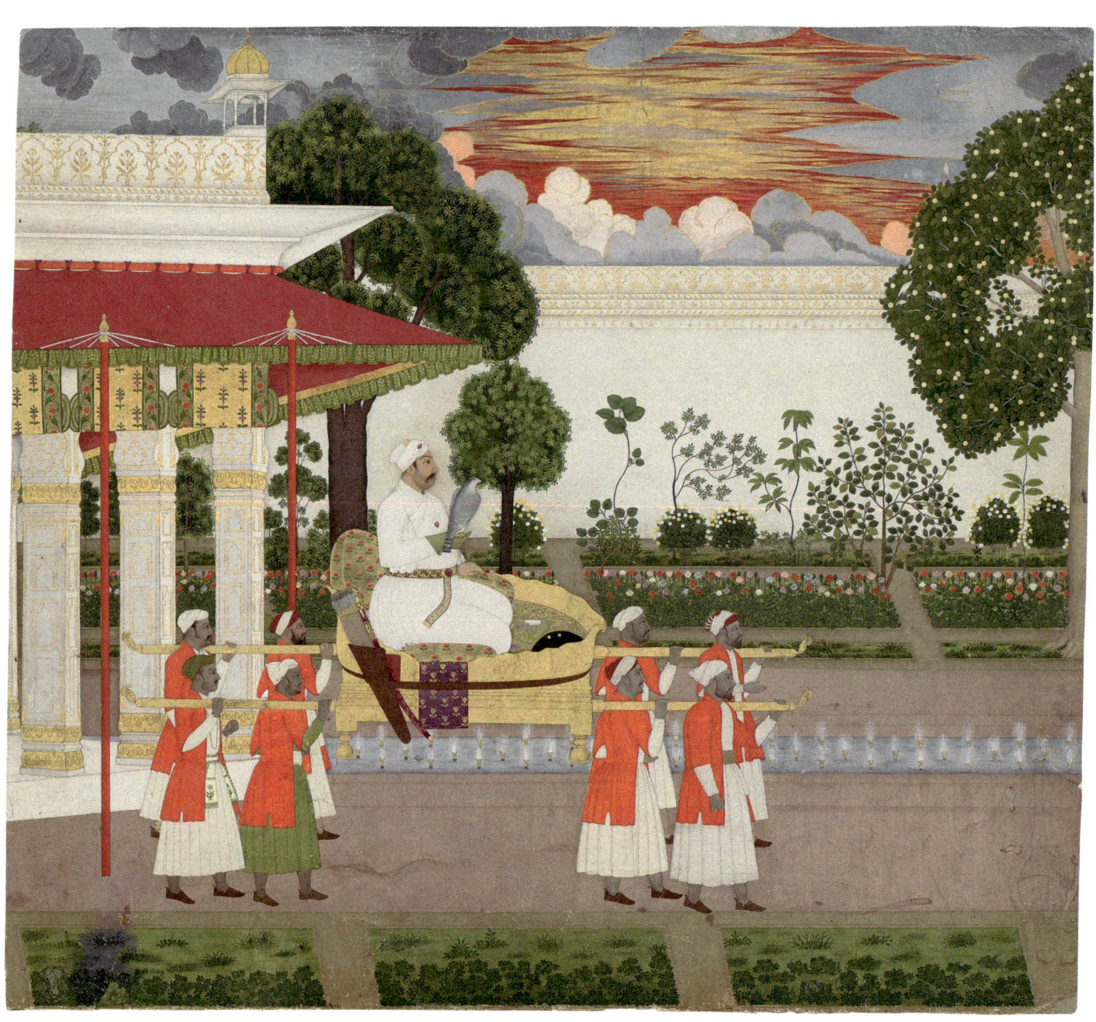

— 9 —
Attributed to Muhammad Ali, Scholar in a garden, about 1610–15

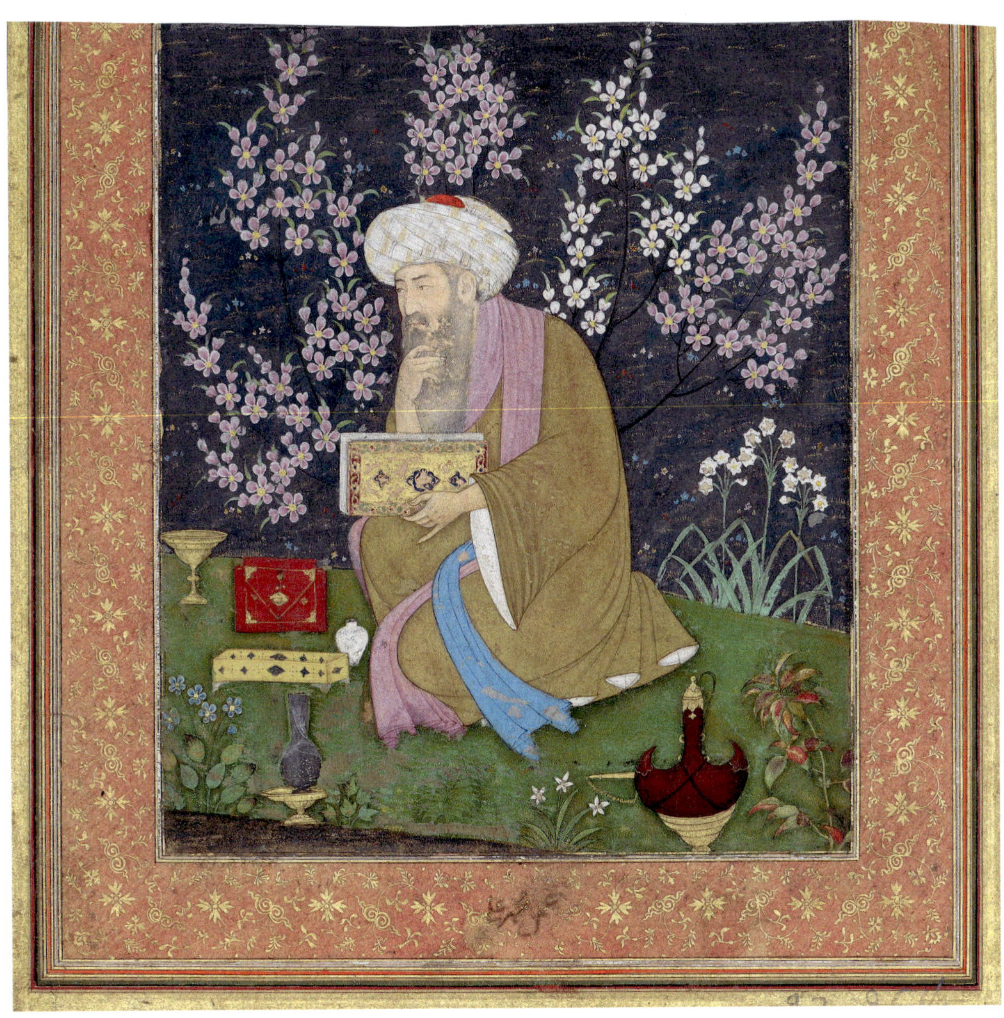

Attributed to Chitarman, Muhammad Shah in a garden, about 1730–40

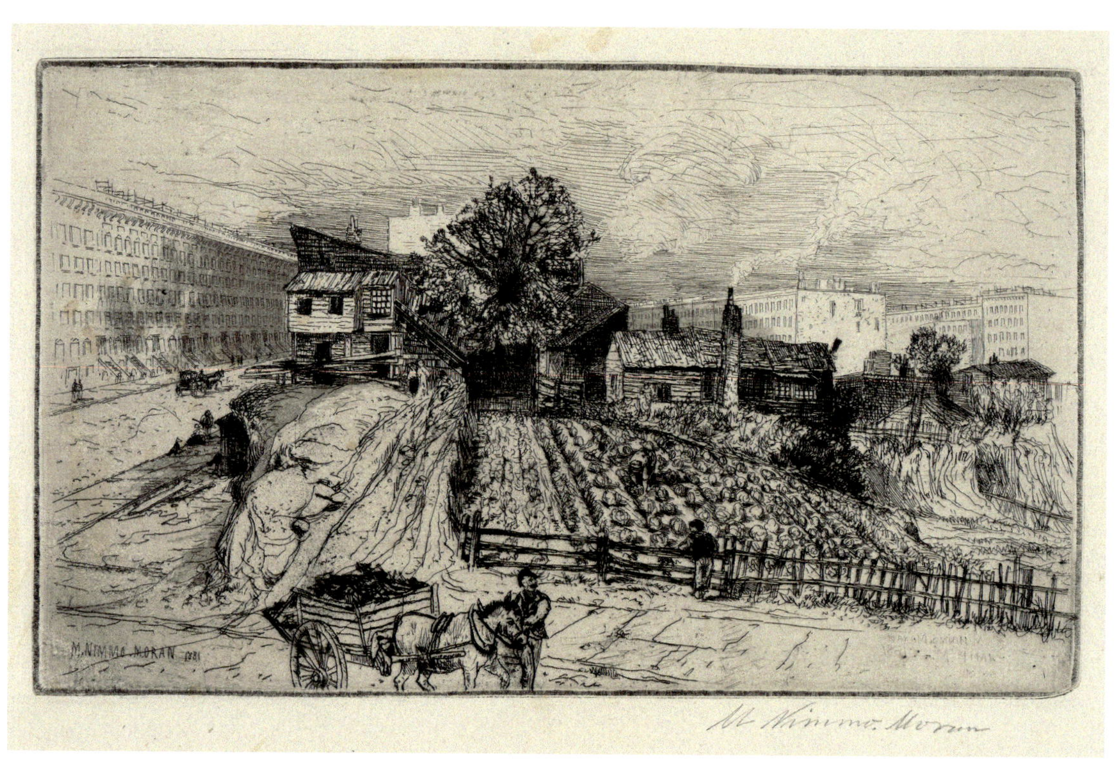

— 11 —

Mary Nimmo Moran, *A City Farm—New York*, 1881

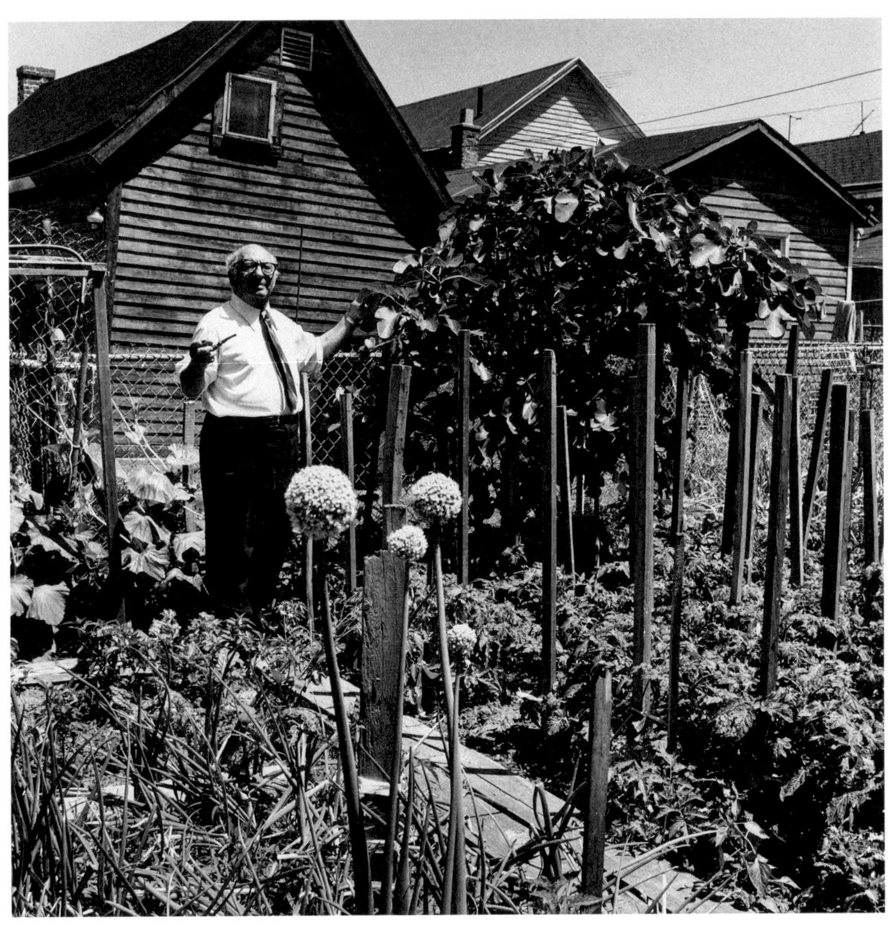

Milton Rogovin, *Lower West Side, Buffalo (Joe and Garden)*, 1974

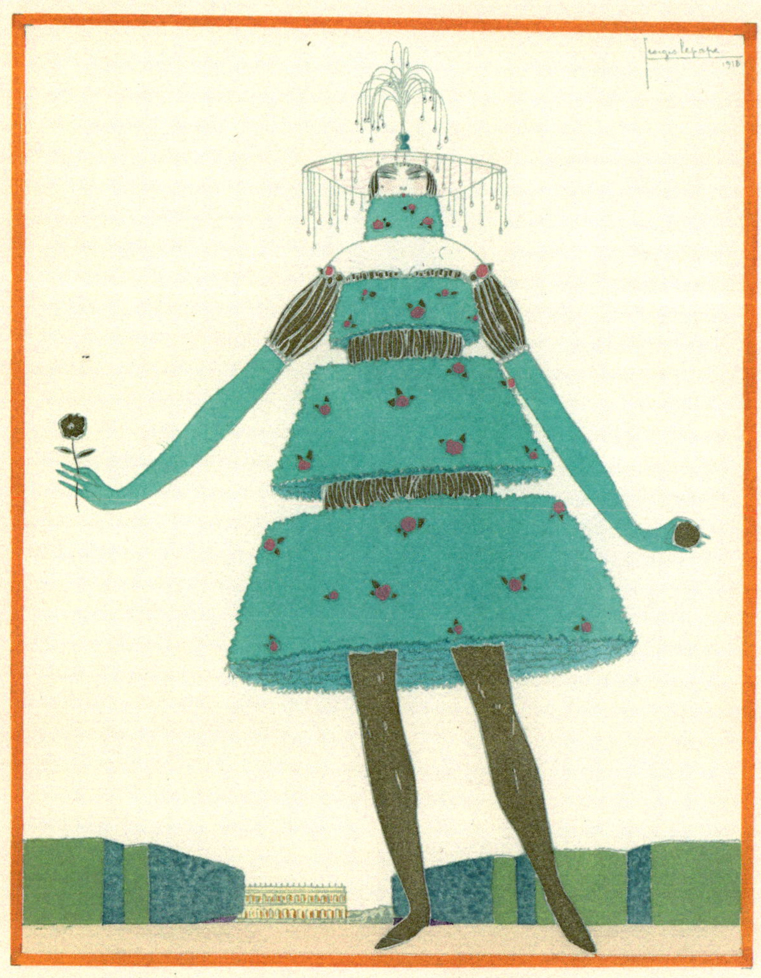

LES JARDINS DE VERSAILLES

Costume de Paul Poiret dans le goût Louis XIV

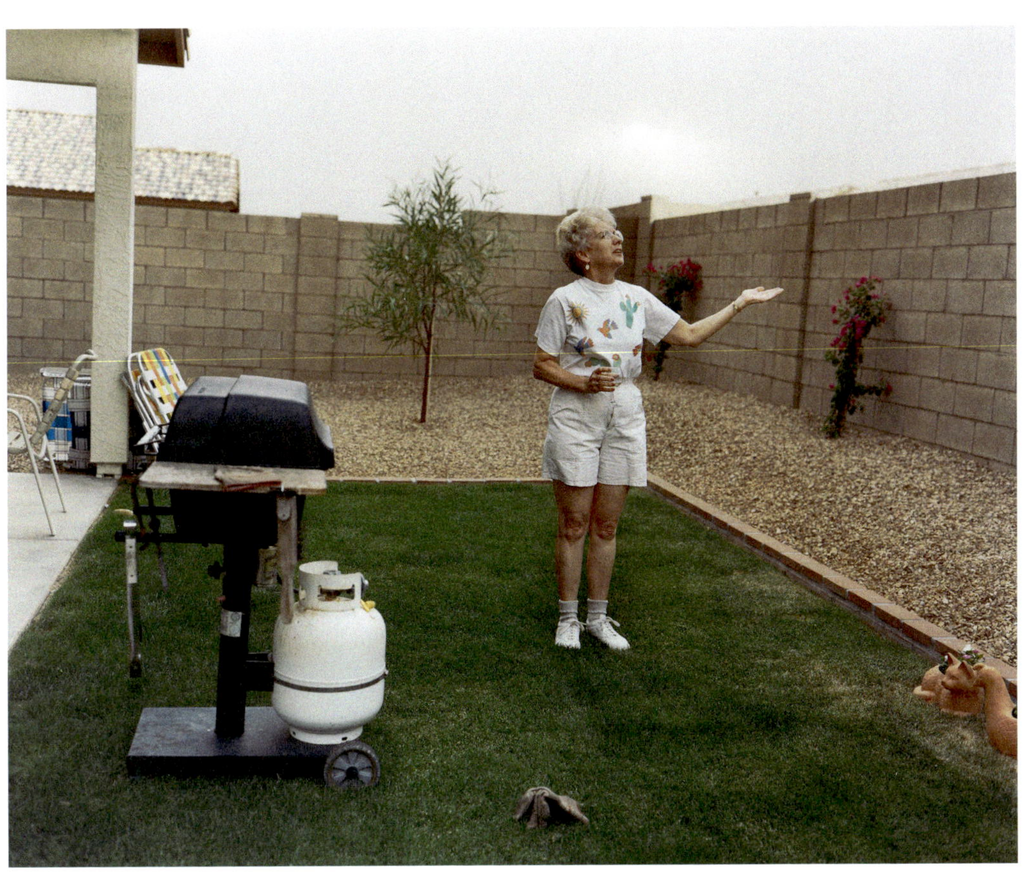

— 13 —
Paul Poiret and Georges Lepape,
"Les Jardins de Versailles," 1913

— 14 —
Justin Kimball, *Phoenix, Arizona*, 1997

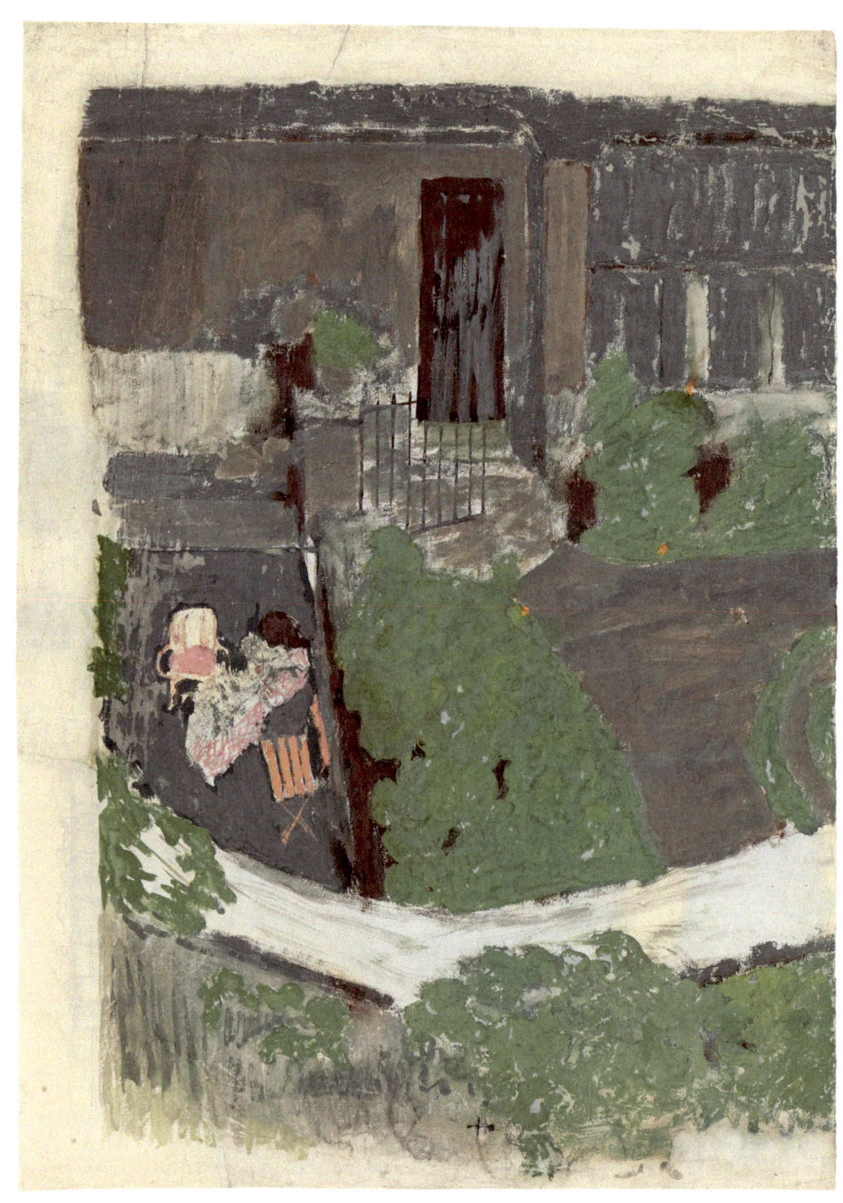

— 15 —

  Edouard Vuillard, *Le jardin devant l'atelier*, about 1901

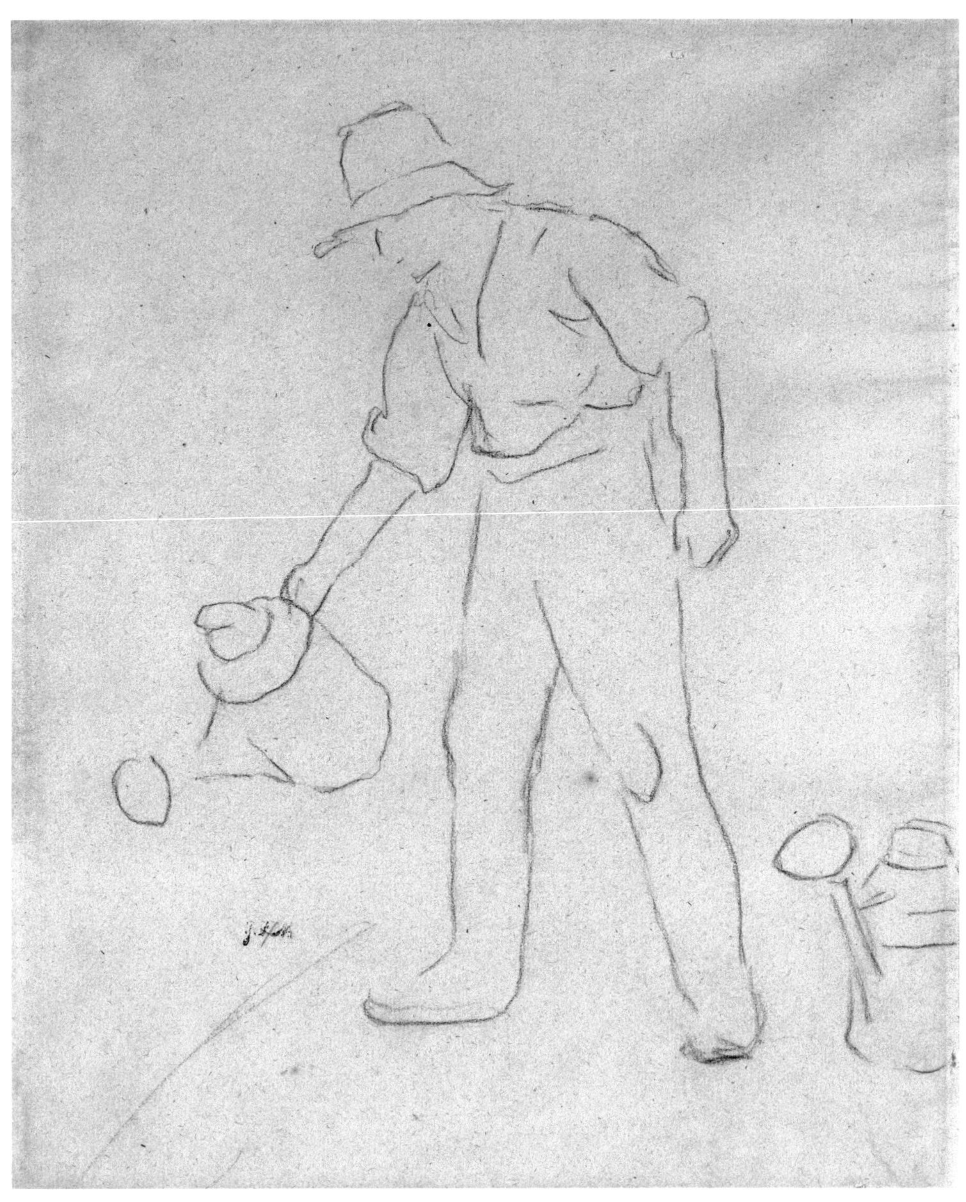

— 16 —

Jean-François Millet, Gardener with watering can, about 1860

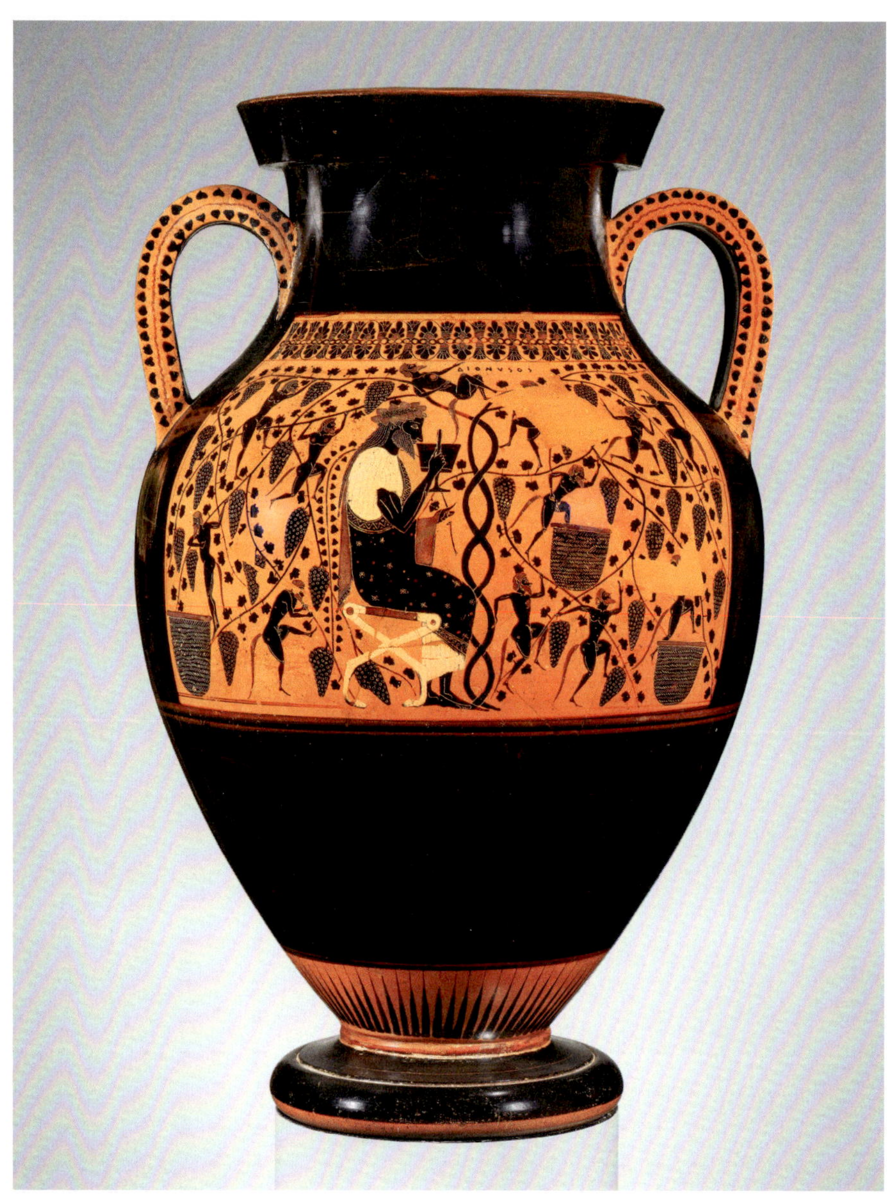

— 17 —

Amphora with Dionysos in a vineyard, Greek, 540–530 BCE

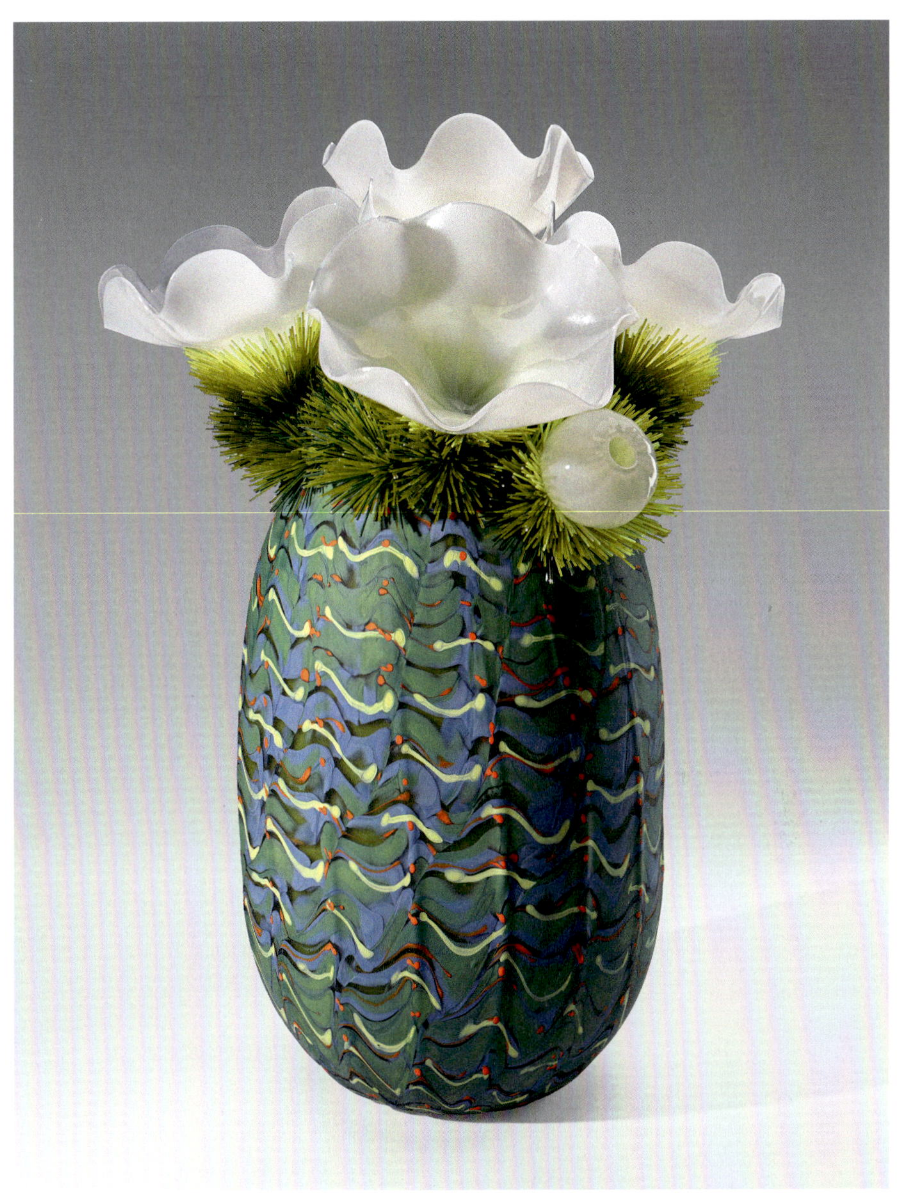

— 18 —

Flo Perkins, *87-Year-Old Cactus*, 2009

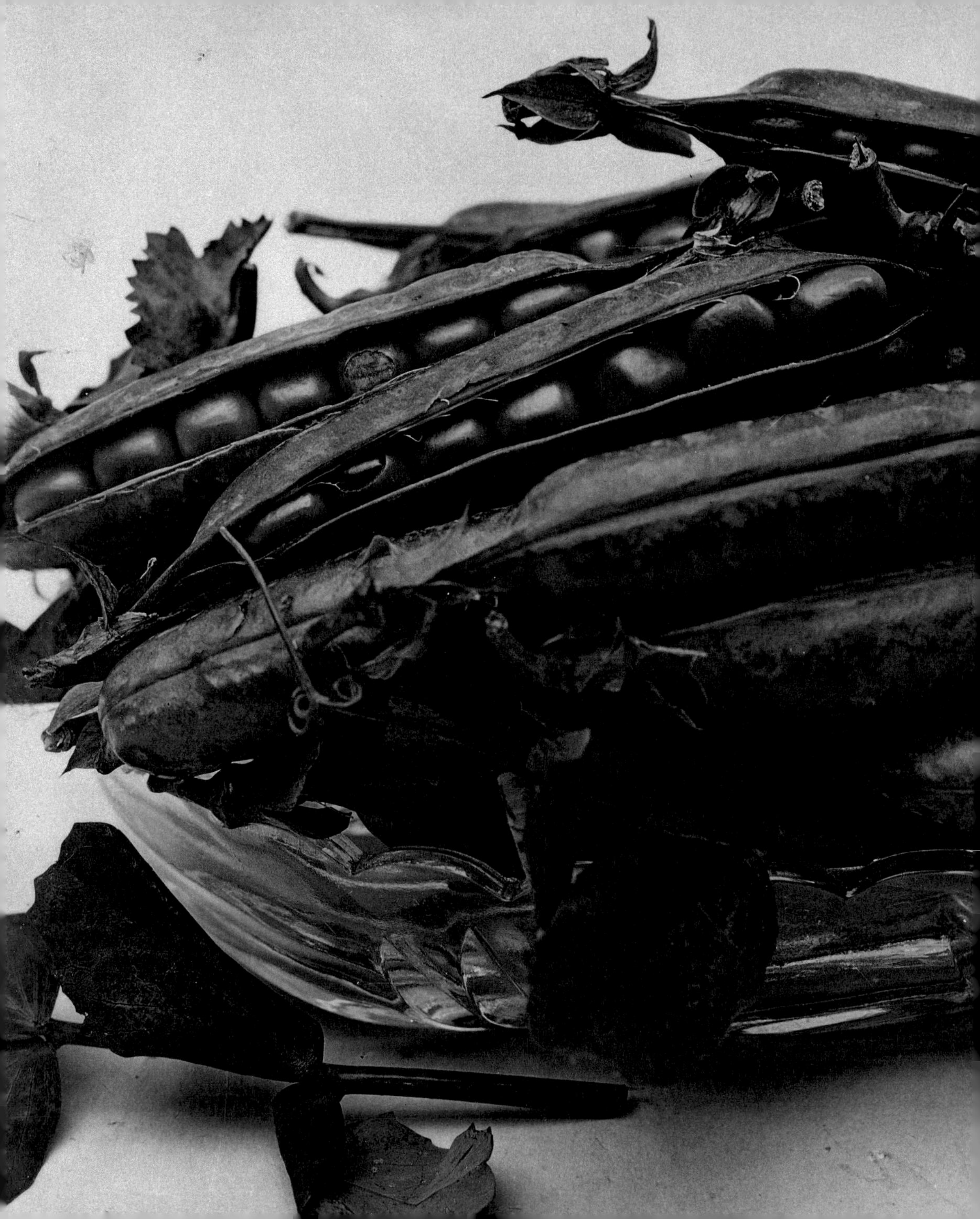

Gardens as Art

Representations of gardens pervade the artistic expressions of so many cultures and periods that it is easy to take garden imagery for granted. But dig deeper, and the resonances of gardens push into questions about human creativity itself, provoking new ways of thinking about gardens and art alike. This is because gardens are not merely places identifiable in art through the visual features of their flora, fauna, or architecture. Rather, gardens themselves are visually dynamic, emotionally evocative, and fully immersive experiences, all qualities that could just as easily be applied to encounters with the most powerful art. Taking this idea further, gardens might even be understood as places that transform features of the natural world into raw materials for art making. Plants, rocks, water features, and architecture all serve as media for gardeners to fashion, coax, and shape to produce new effects. Thus gardens might be seen as art forms in their own right, on par with creative forms like painting, sculpture, music, dance, or poetry. In this way, gardens not only inspire art, gardens are art.

It is remarkable how artists, makers, and writers across cultures and time similarly turn to the artistic possibilities of gardens to grapple with these conceptual concerns. Take, for example, the imaginary garden depicted in a series of eighteenth-century Chinese scrolls by Yuan Yao (21). Walls enclose a highly mannered space rendered in exquisite detail and placed in conversation with the rugged mountain landscape beyond it. No detail of this garden is incidental, but rather all its features reflect the aesthetic and formal standards of Chinese gardens rooted in centuries of literary and philosophical discussion. Comprehensive manuals, for example, describe the importance of mastering specific features that were seen to reflect owners' artistic appreciation, intellectual refinement, and scholarly achievements. The artist of the scrolls, steeped in these traditions, takes pains to convey exactly such associations of learnedness: at left, an entourage of servants and scholars observes a man in a red garment practicing the art of calligraphy directly on a rock. In this way, the fictive garden of the scrolls conveys all the potential of a real garden to serve as a place for human creativity, imagination, and skill.

In a parallel manner, architects and scholars in eighteenth-century Europe similarly considered the standards of gardening practice and the potential for gardens to serve as places for artistic expression and artistry alike. Eighteenth-century European texts, for example, explicitly describe gardening as an art form, part of broader Enlightenment philosophical reckonings about aesthetics. As an example, concerns about gardens' formal qualities appear throughout the writings and visuals of eighteenth-century drawings, prints, and books, such as Jacques Rigaud's *View*

of the Orangerie of Versailles or Salomon Kleiner's views of
Austrian and German palaces and gardens (22, 23, & 34).
Their visual and textual descriptions convey detailed information about garden vistas and plans, topiary and hedge
designs, fountains and water features, all in an effort not
only to describe existing gardens but also to define objective
standards for European garden arts. And even more, such
elite parks and gardens were often intended as backdrops
for other artistic forms such as musical and theatrical
performances, melding different artistic forms together
into a fully immersive framework. In this way, the designs
of real gardens rendered in practical terms the abstract
philosophical debates current in their time.

Almost two centuries later, Jean-Eugène Atget would
visit the allées and sculptures of Versailles as he experi-
mented in his own practice, turning his lens on the aesthetic forms of the past in the development of new artistic
expressions rooted in modernity (26). For Atget, the once
monumental forms of eighteenth-century gardens, now
in a state of slow decay, offered the opportunity to reflect
on and record the passage of time through art. It is little
wonder that so many early photographers saw gardens as
places for visual and technical experimentation, since the
garden's ever-changing features and ephemerality provided
ideal subjects for the photographer's eye.

Strains of contemporary artistic practice gesture
to similar aesthetic and material resonances, particularly
among artists who count themselves also as gardeners.
Elizabeth Talford Scott's *Flower Garden*, a quilt incorporat-
ing synthetic knits, cotton thread, glass beads, and other
media, demonstrates an effort to translate the multimedia
experience of her own garden into fiber form (35). With its
brightly colored elements, the work commemorates the
fleeting encounter of colorful flowers in a home garden,
preserving them for posterity through the memory making
inherent in the artistic process. The contemporary artist
and printmaker Andrew Raftery also riffs on ideas of real and
imagined gardens through a similarly layered, multimedia
encounter in his *Autobiography of a Garden* (32 & 33). Raftery
treats his mother's garden as a portrait, rooting it in place
through its practice of indigenous New England planting
traditions. Garden scenes become inspiration for his drawings, which then in turn are translated onto plates and
installed against handmade wallpaper to evoke the seasons
of the garden through art. Thus in these and many other
examples across the collection, we can trace how gardens
serve not only as inspiration for art, but as artistic forms
ripe for experimentation, creativity, and memory. — EDW

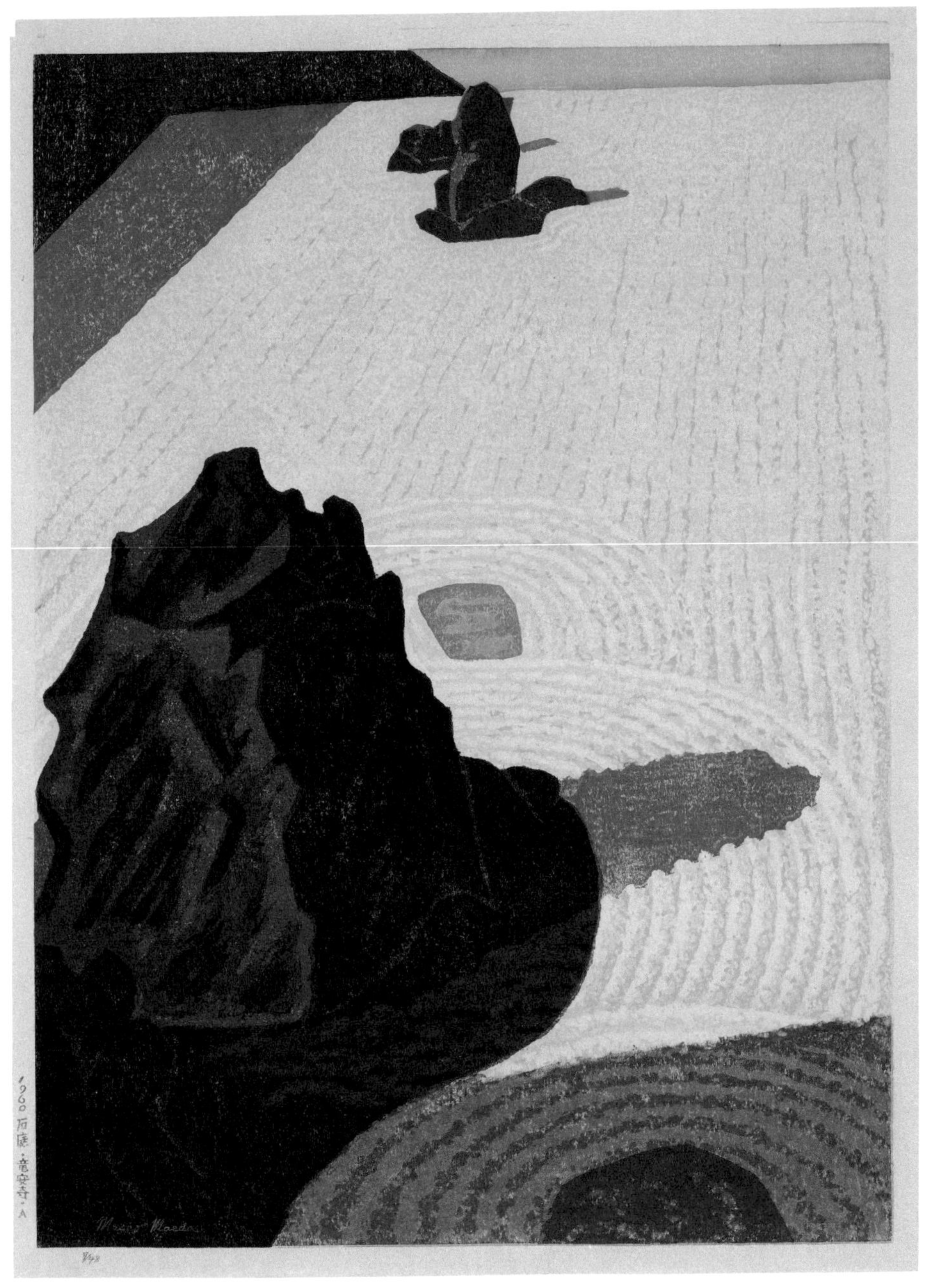

Maeda Masao, *Sand Garden*, 1960

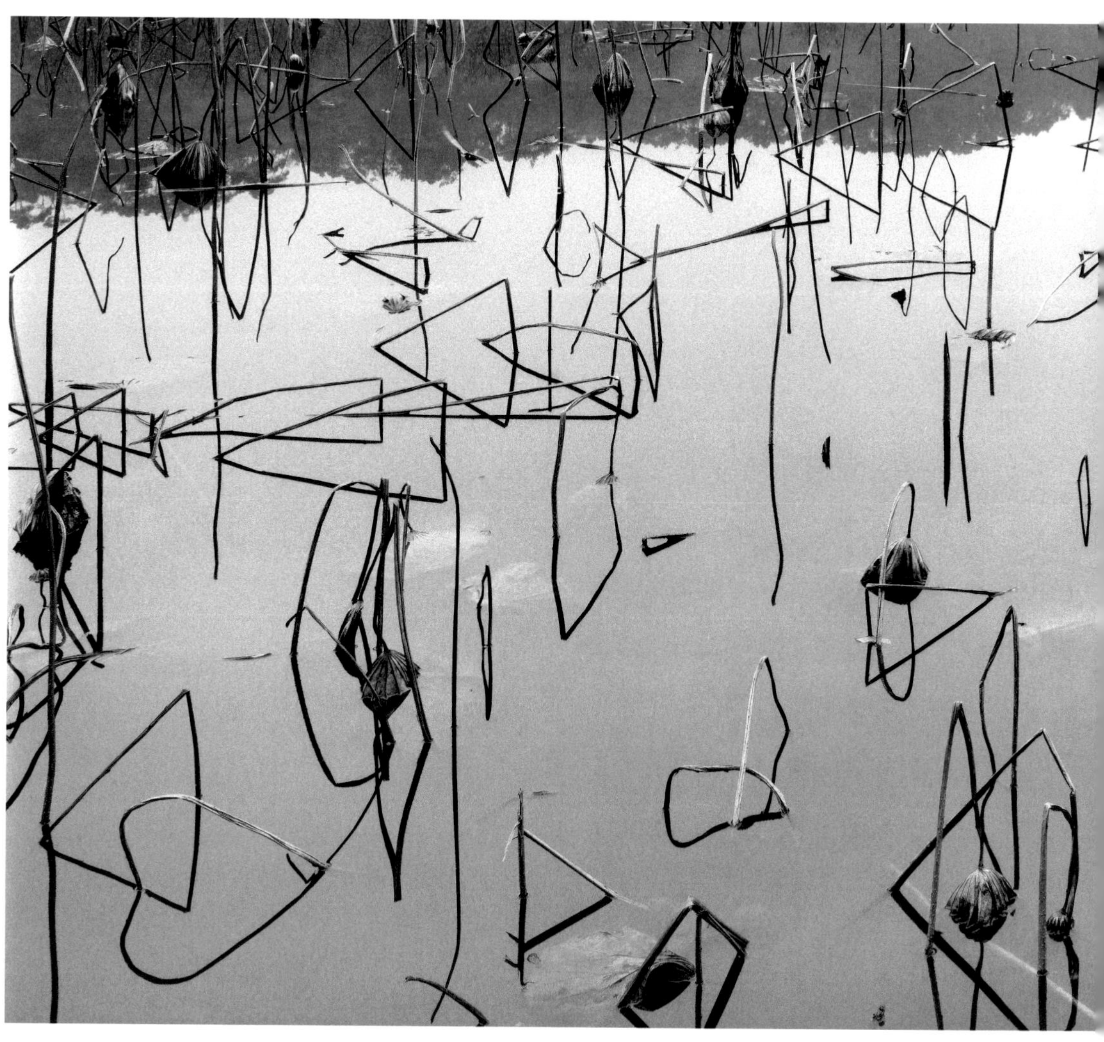

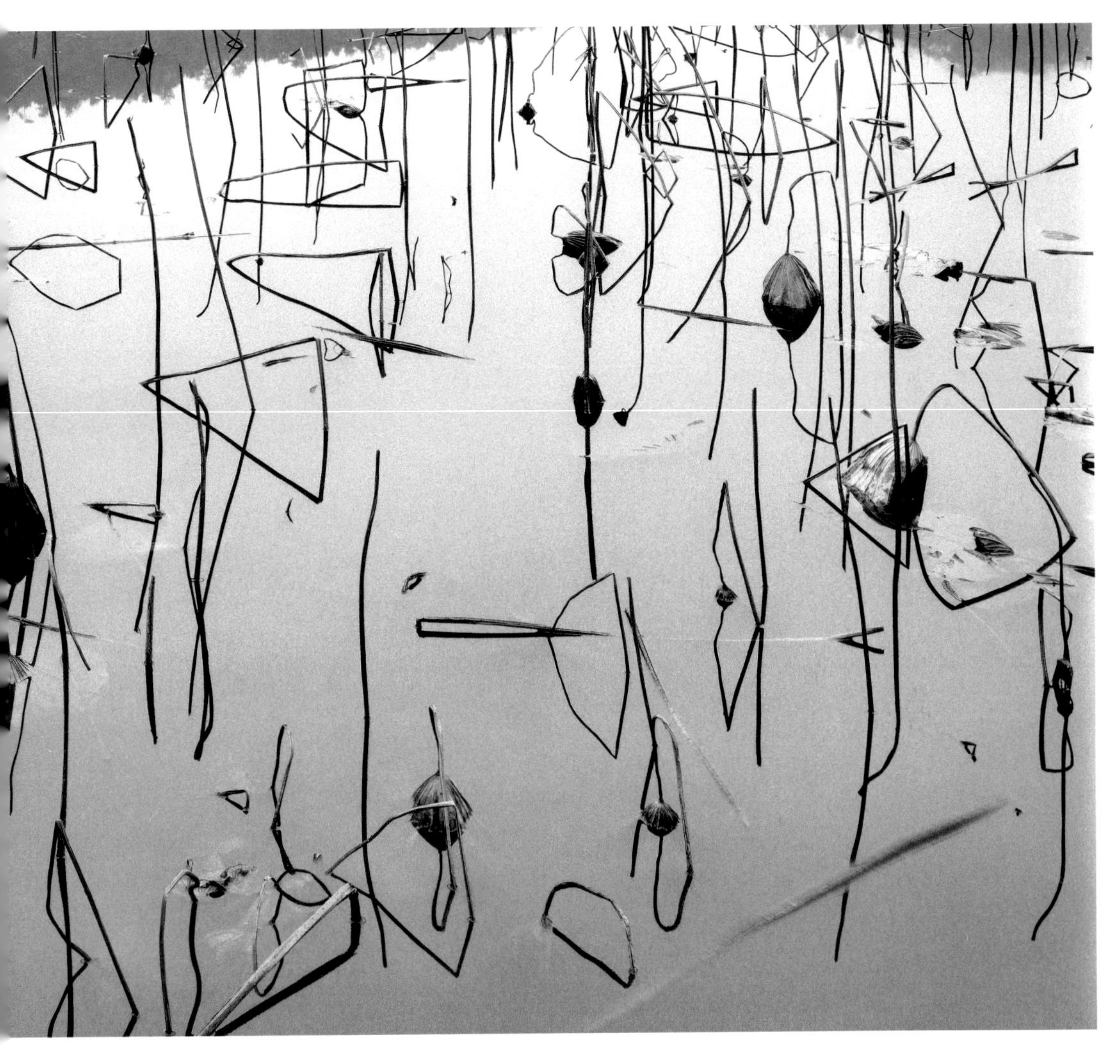

Lois Conner, *Xi Hu, Hangzhou, Zhejiang, China*, 1998

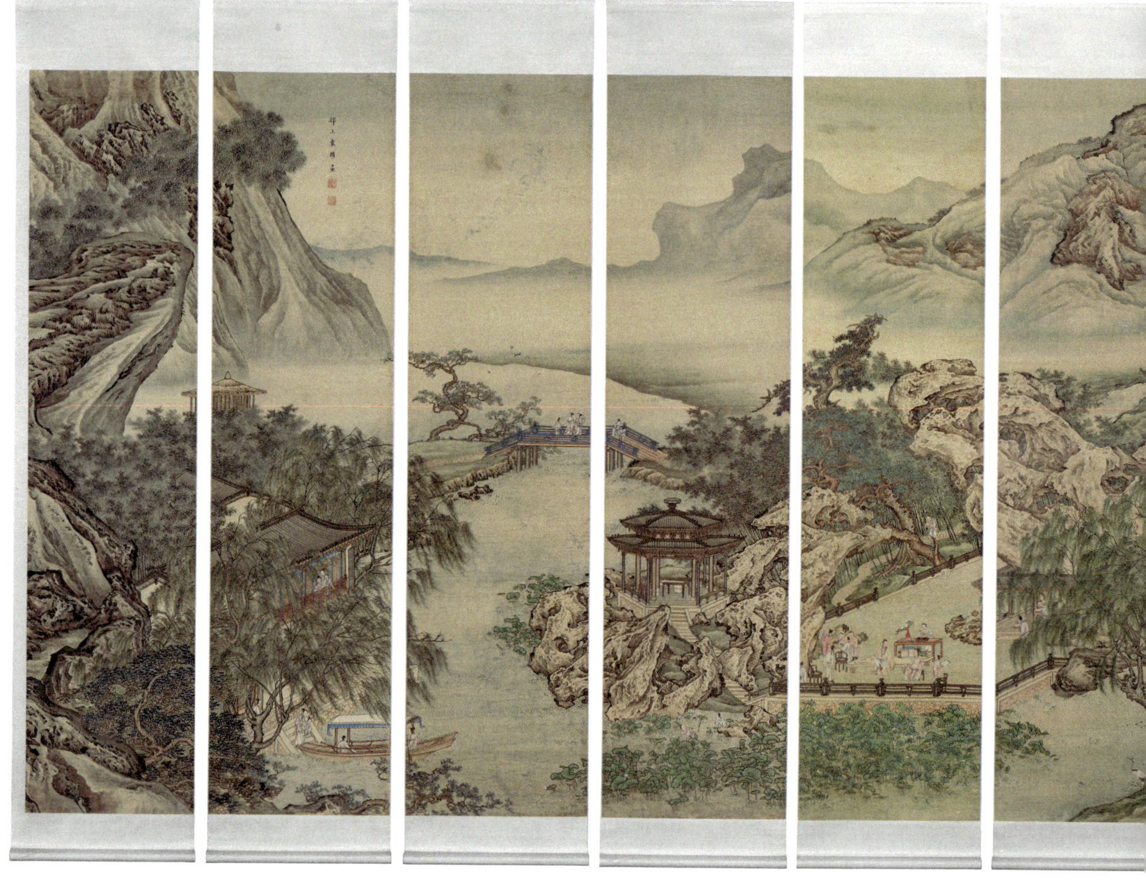

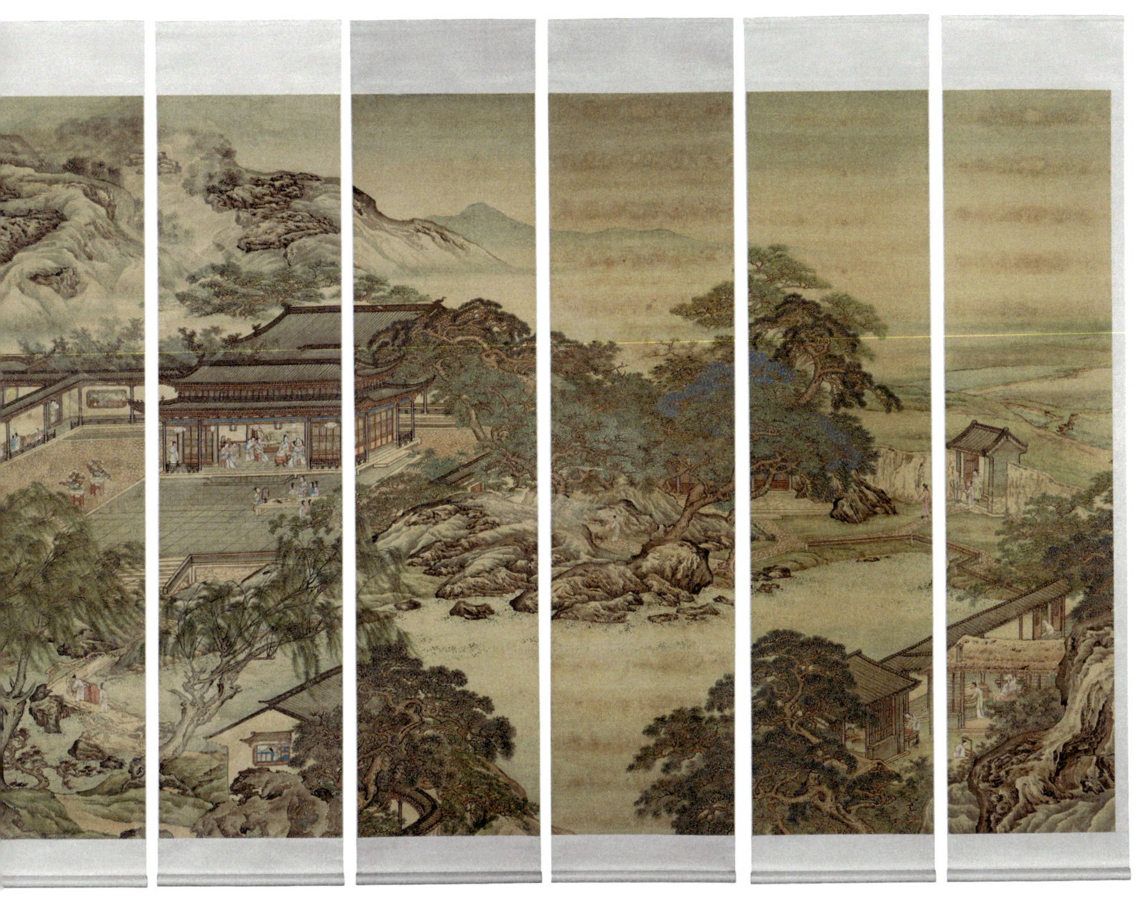

Yuan Yao, Elegant gathering in a secluded garden, mid-18th century

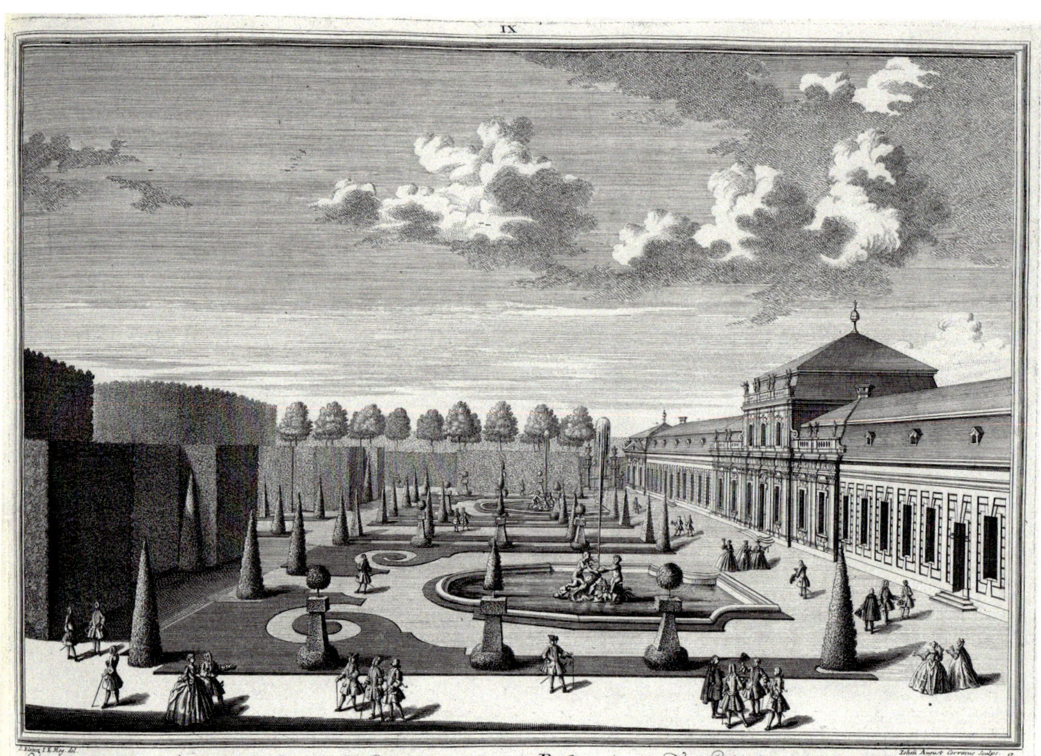

Johann August Corvinus after Salomon Kleiner,
View of the gardens at the Lower Belvedere, Vienna, 1731–38

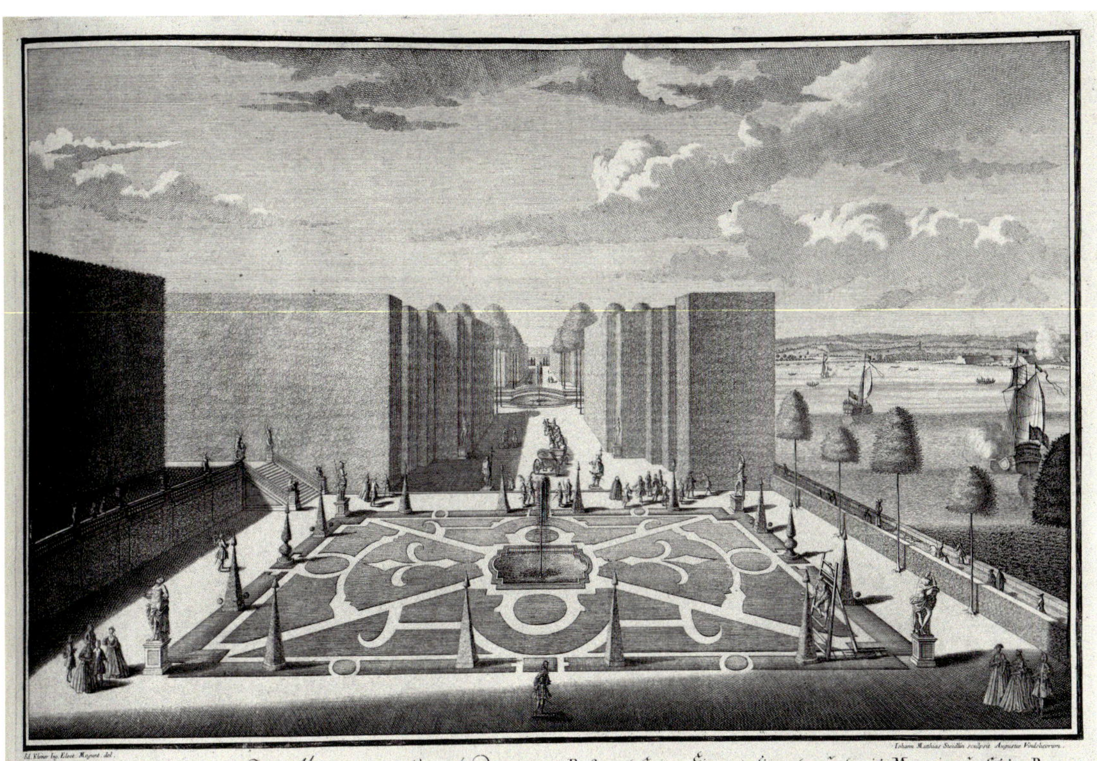

Johann Matthias Steidlin after Salomon Kleiner,
View of the gardens at Favorite Palace, Mainz, 1731–38

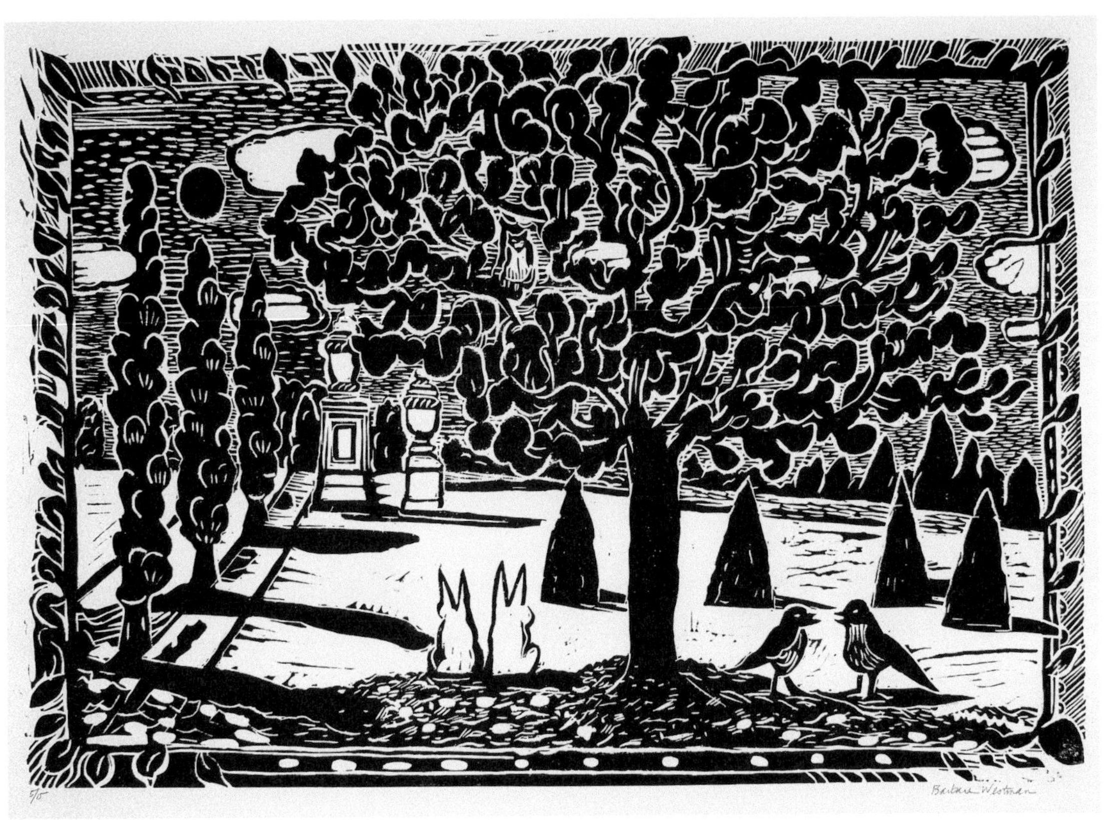

— 24 —

Barbara Westman, *Night Garden (Nymphenburg Palace)*, 1994–95

49

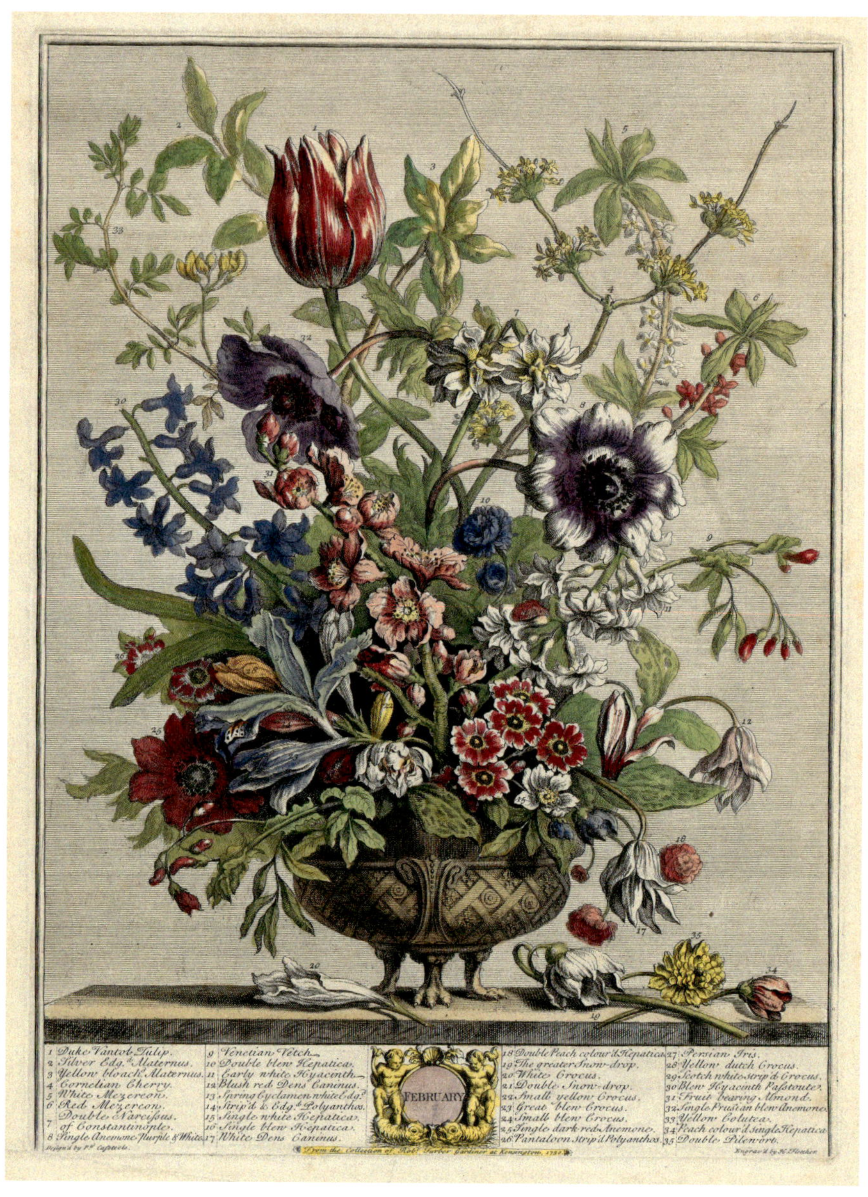

Henry Fletcher after Peter Casteels, *Flower Chart of February*, 1730

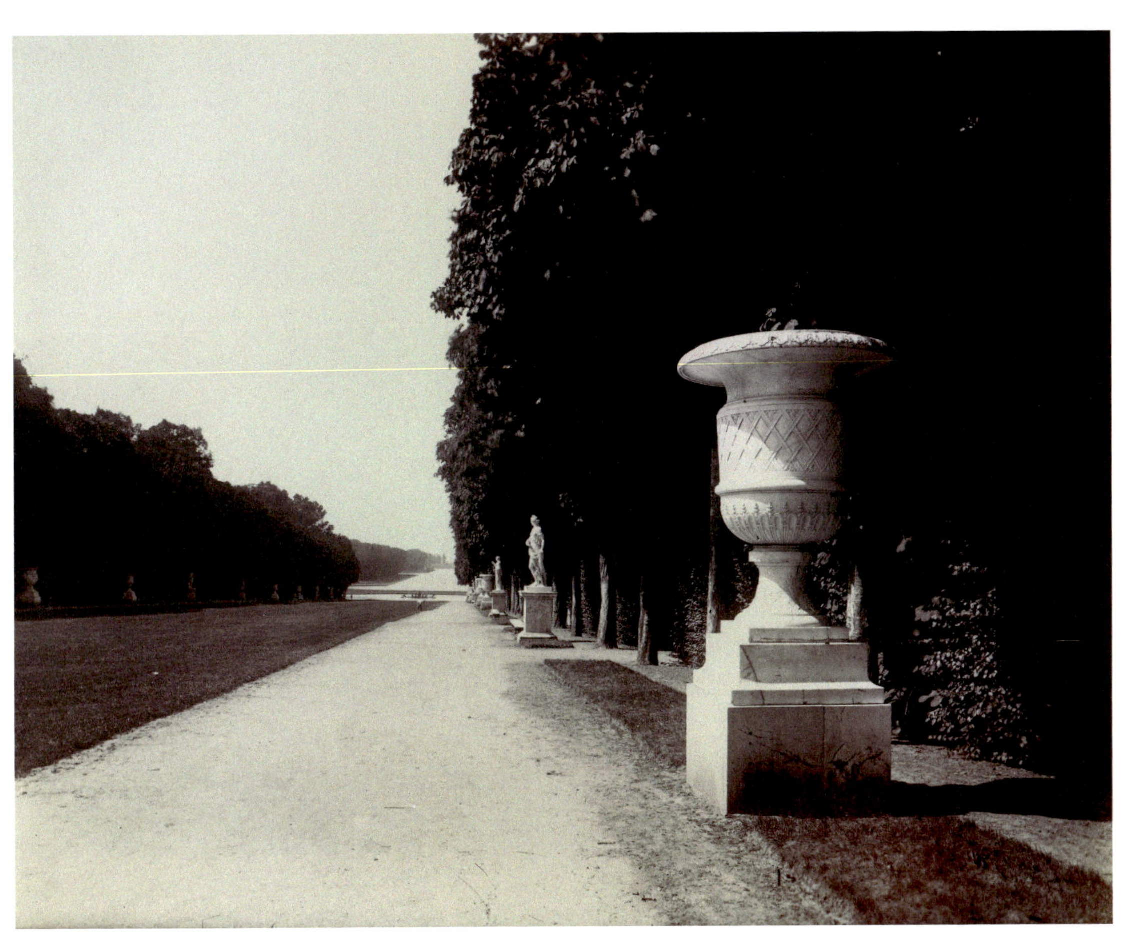

Jean-Eugène Auguste Atget, *Versailles*, 1902

Nancy Crasco, *Lauren's Rainbow Garden Quilt*, 1979

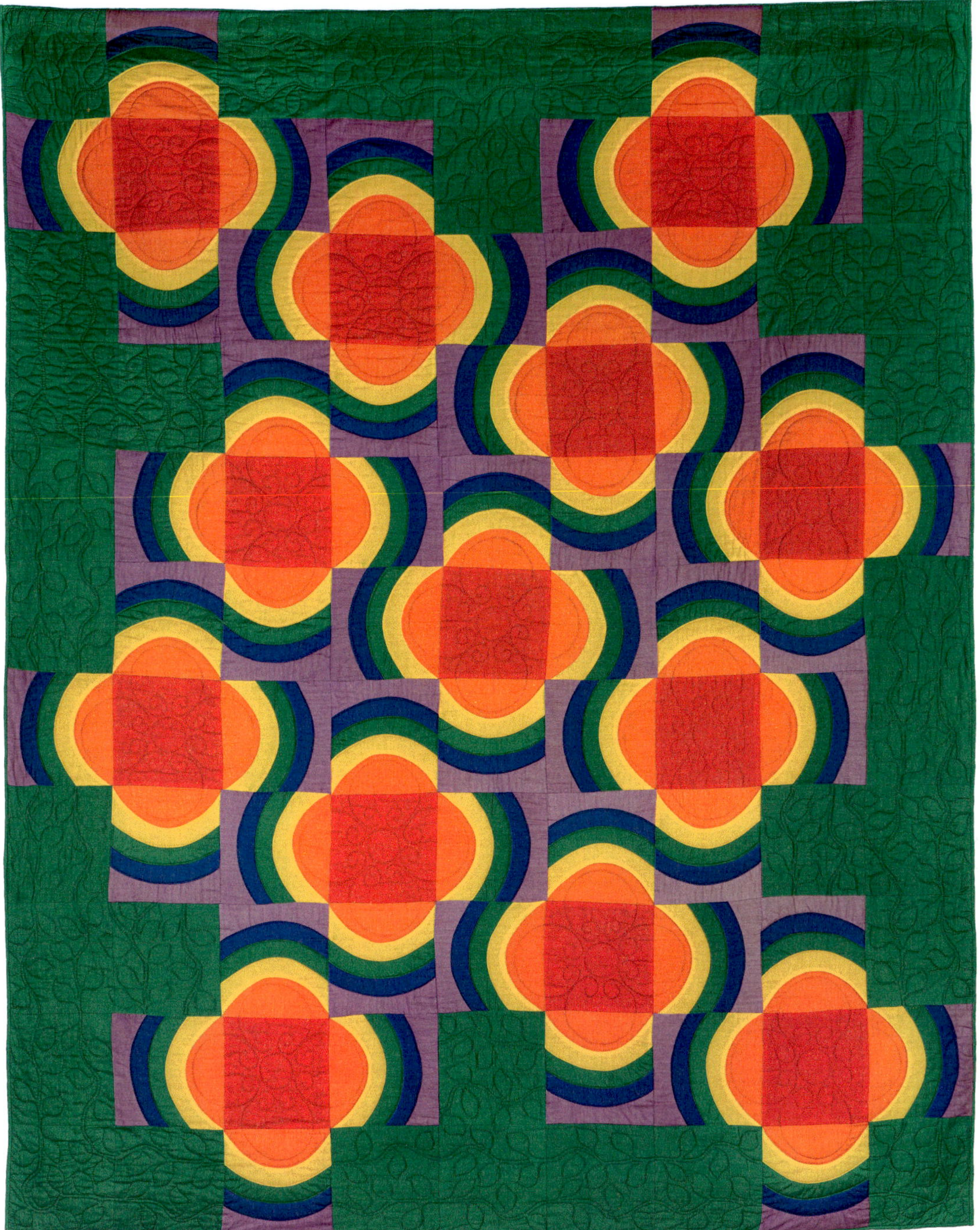

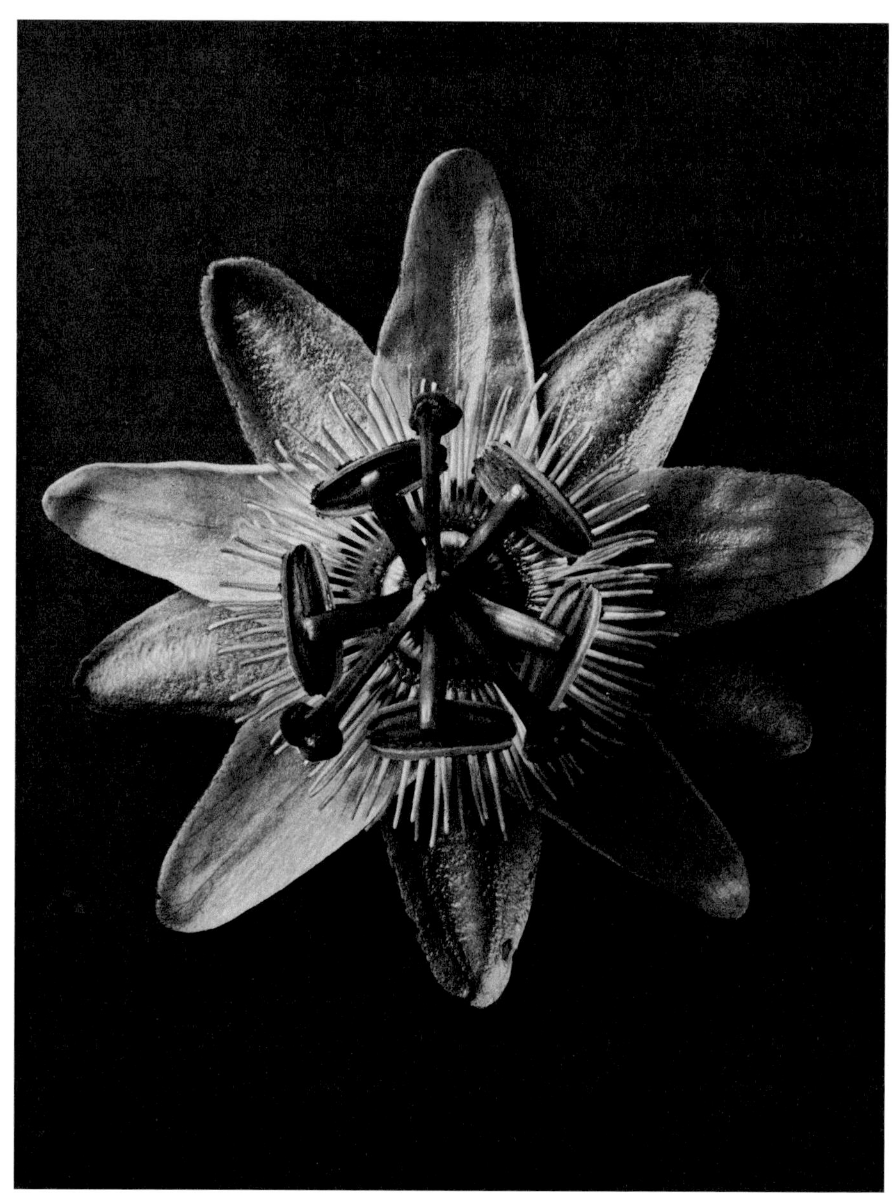

— 28 —

Karl Blossfeldt, *Wundergarten der Natur*, 1932

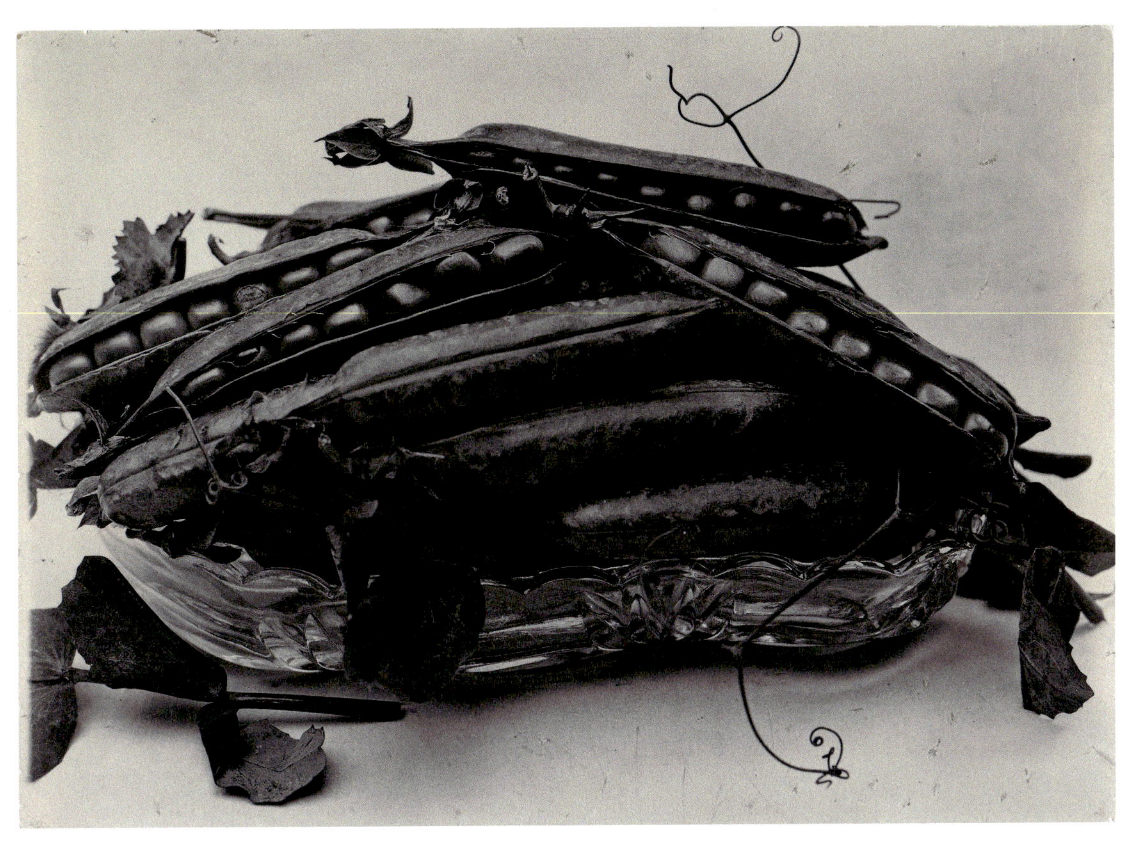

Charles Jones, *Pea, English Wonder*, about 1900

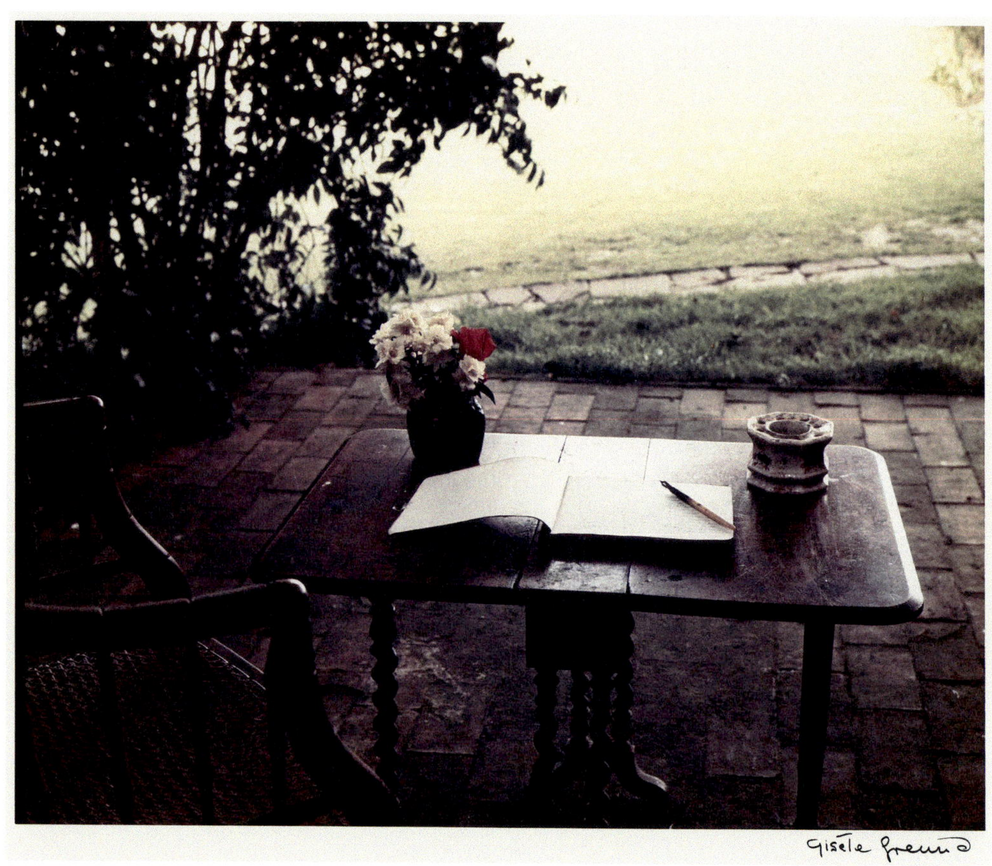

— 30 —
 Gisèle Freund, *Virginia Woolf's Writing Table*, 1939

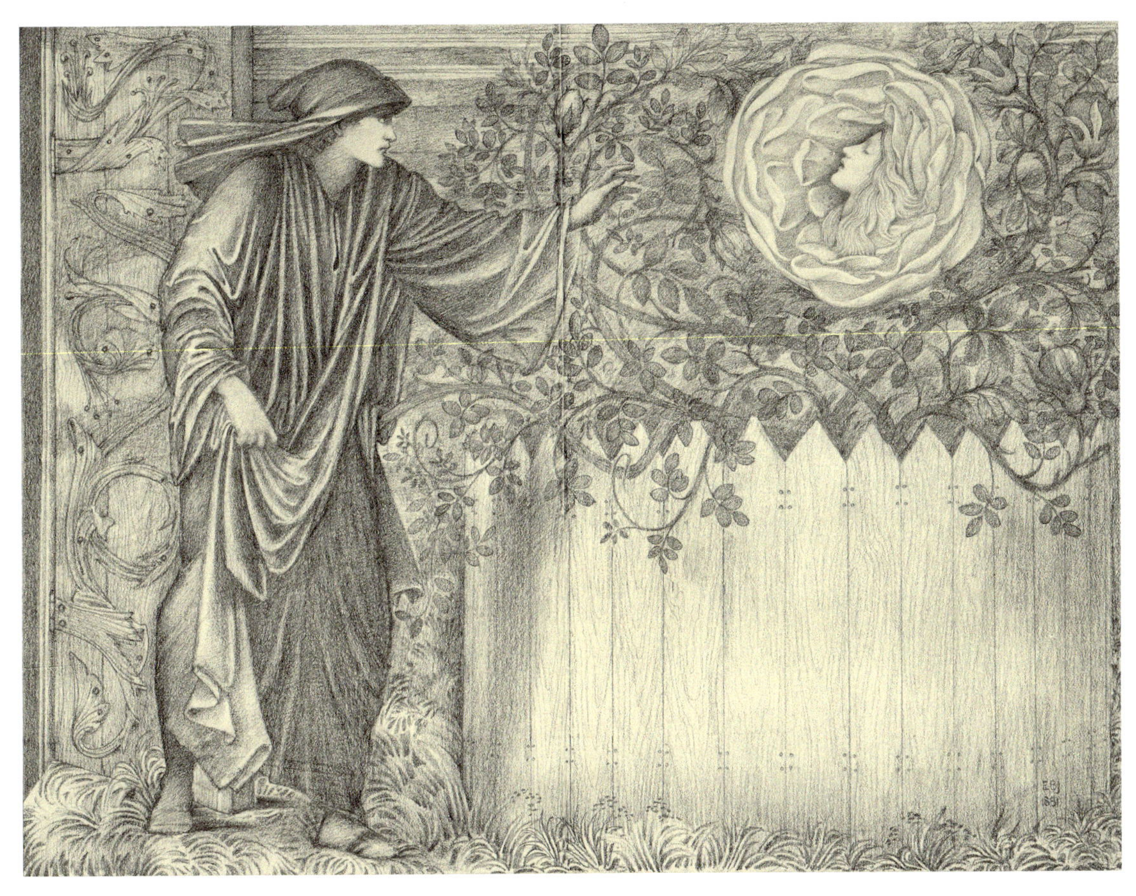

Sir Edward Coley Burne-Jones, *Pilgrim in the Garden*, 1881

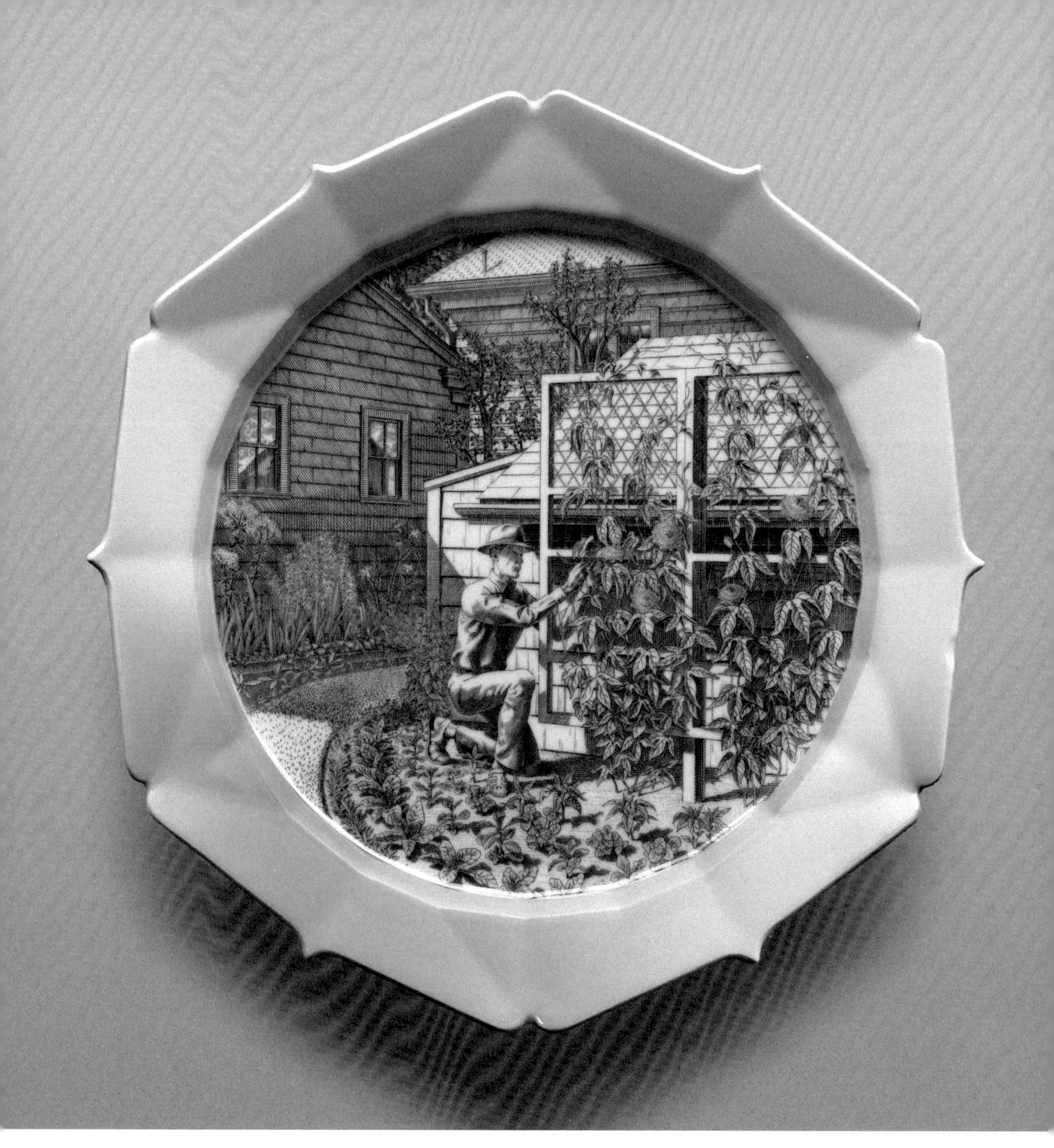

58   Andrew Raftery, *June, Training a Passion Vine*, 2009–16

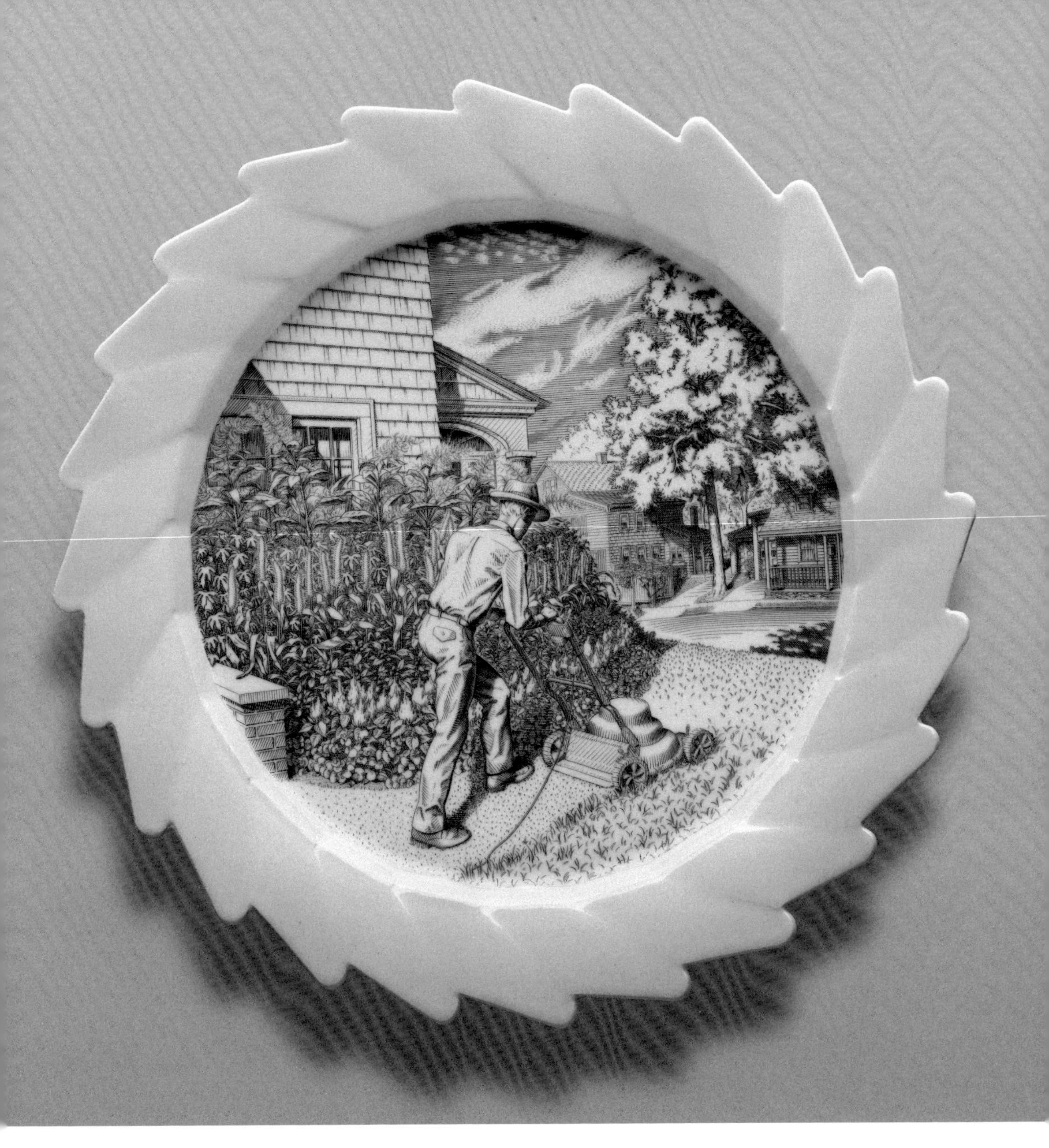

Andrew Raftery, *September, Mowing*, 2009–16

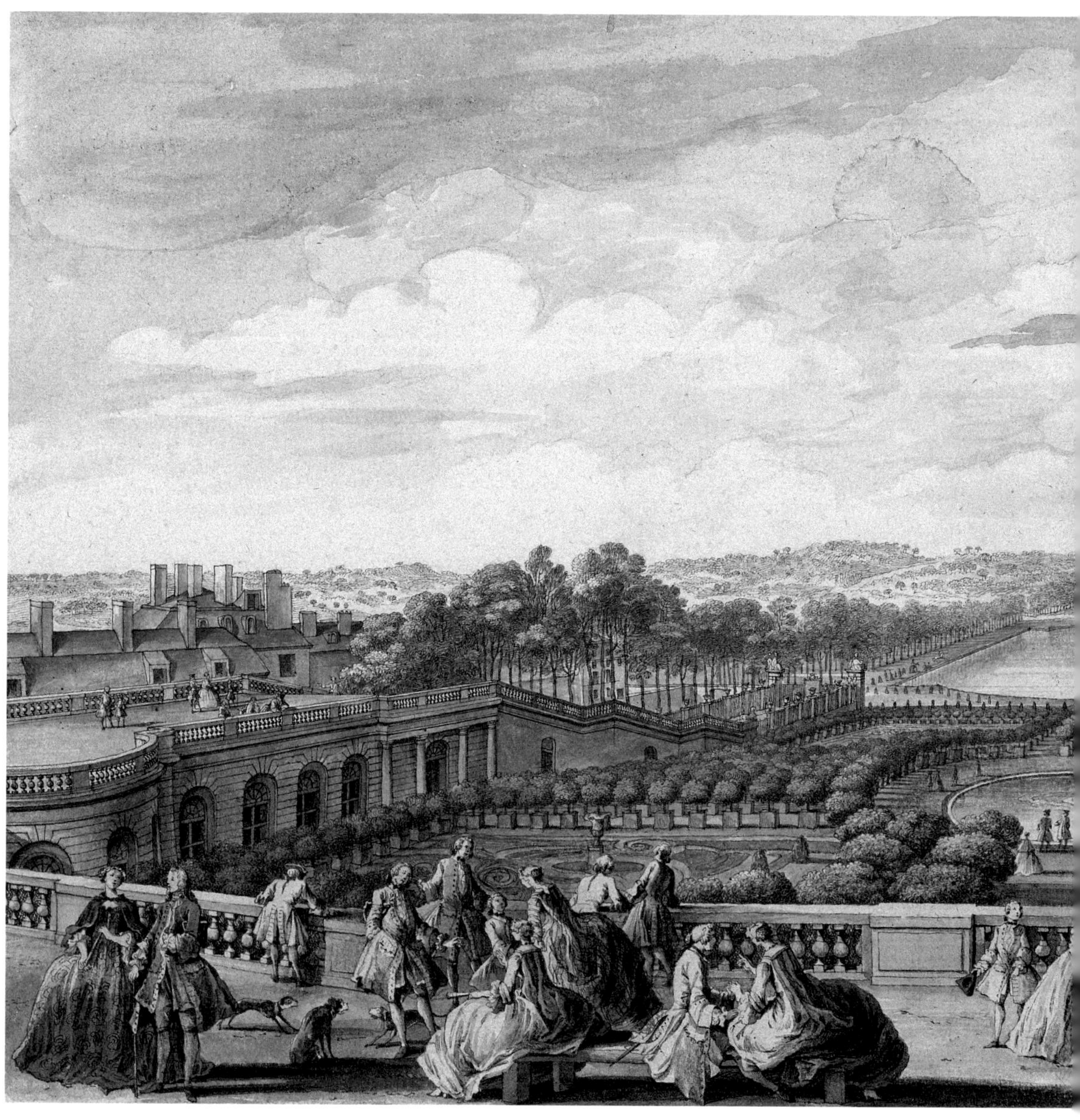

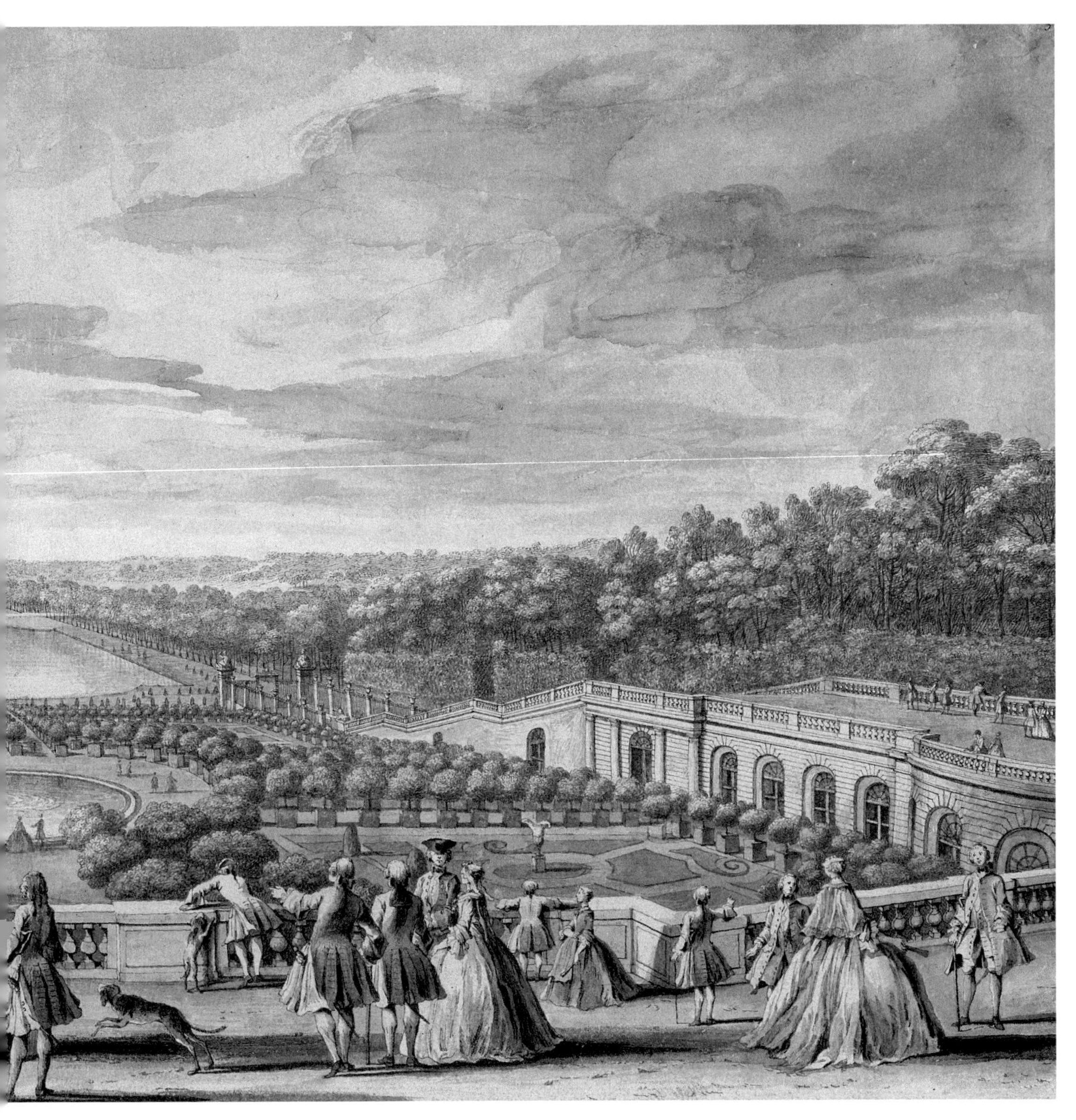

— 34 —

Jacques Rigaud, *Vue de l'Orangerie de Versailles*, 1720s

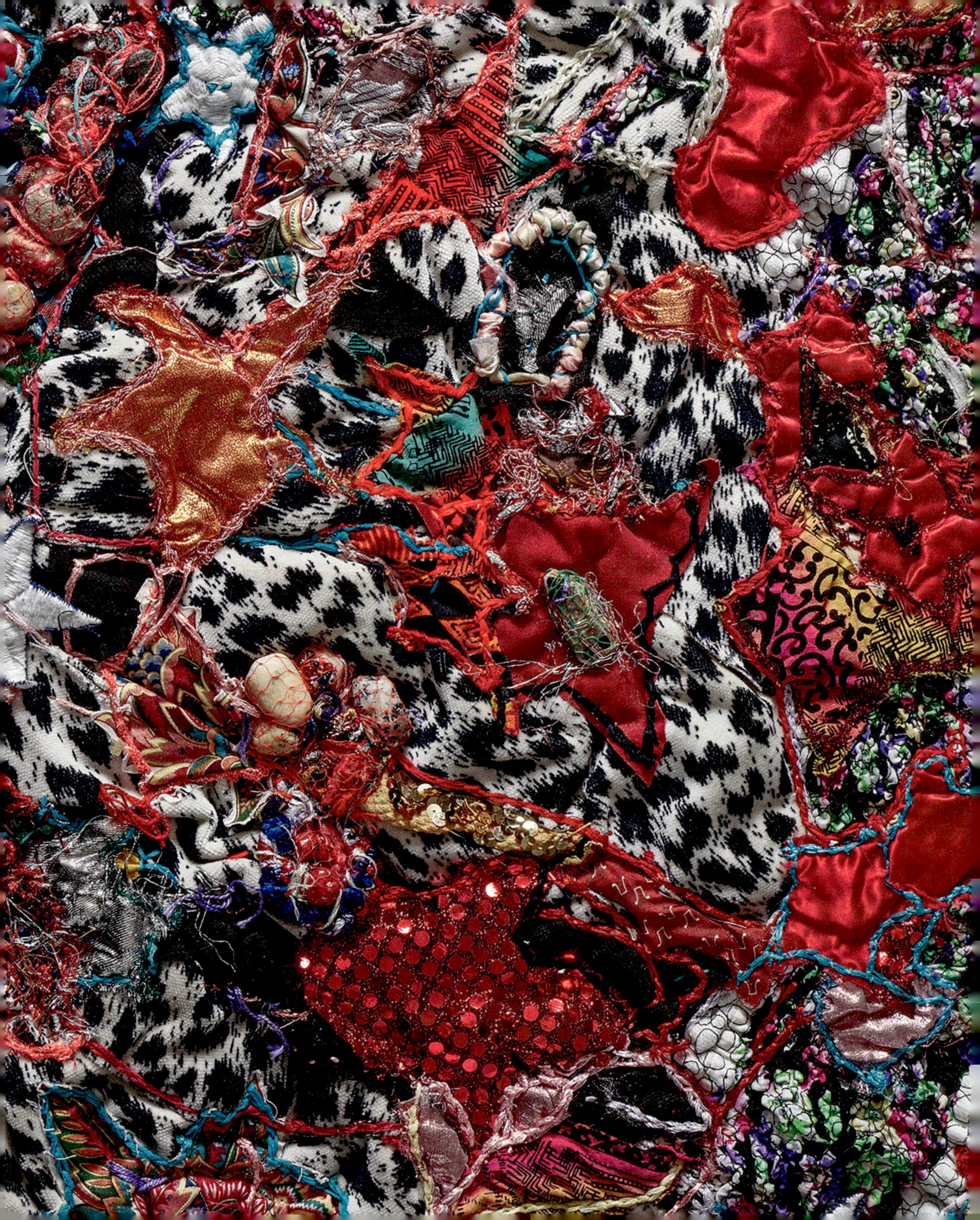

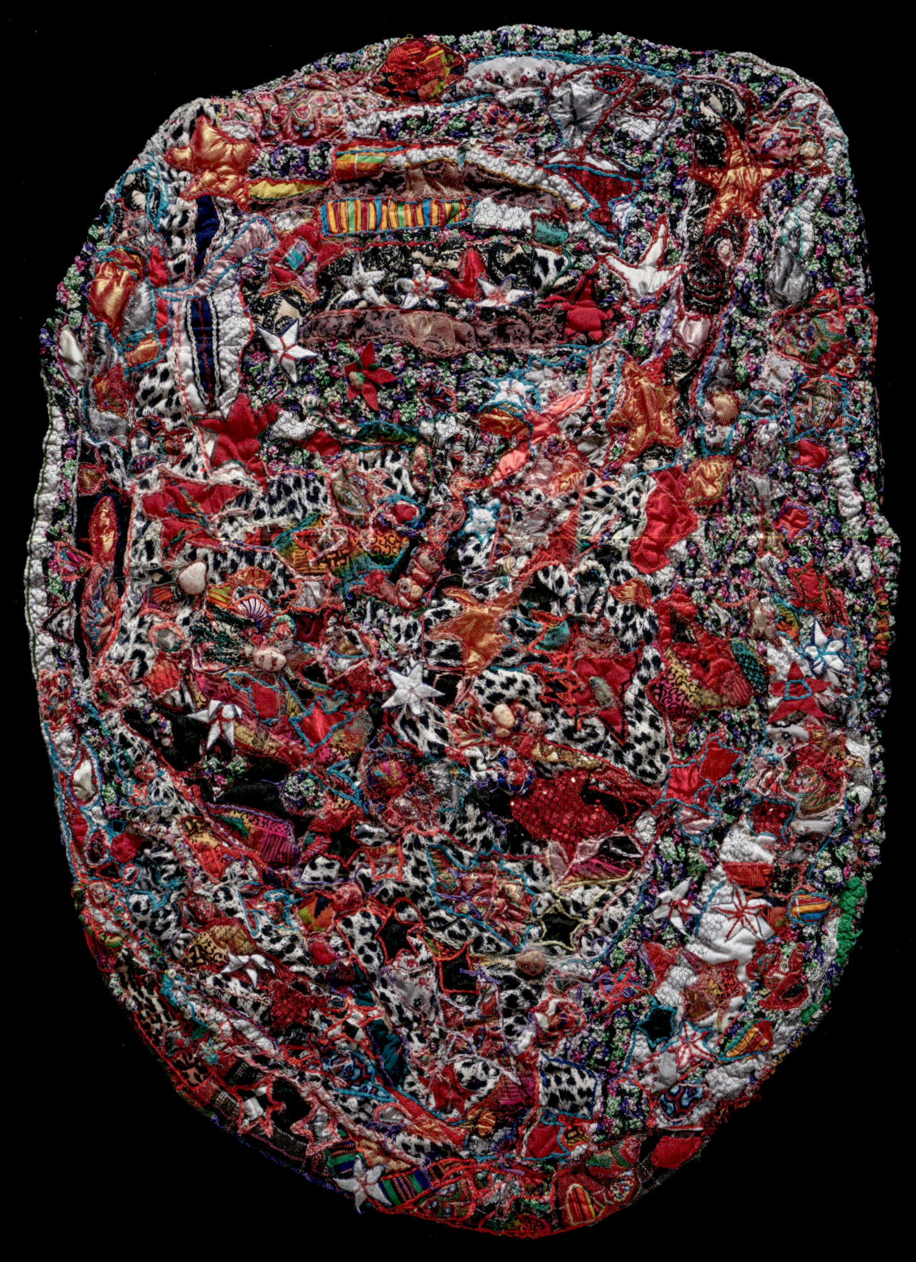

Elizabeth Talford Scott, *Flower Garden*, 1989

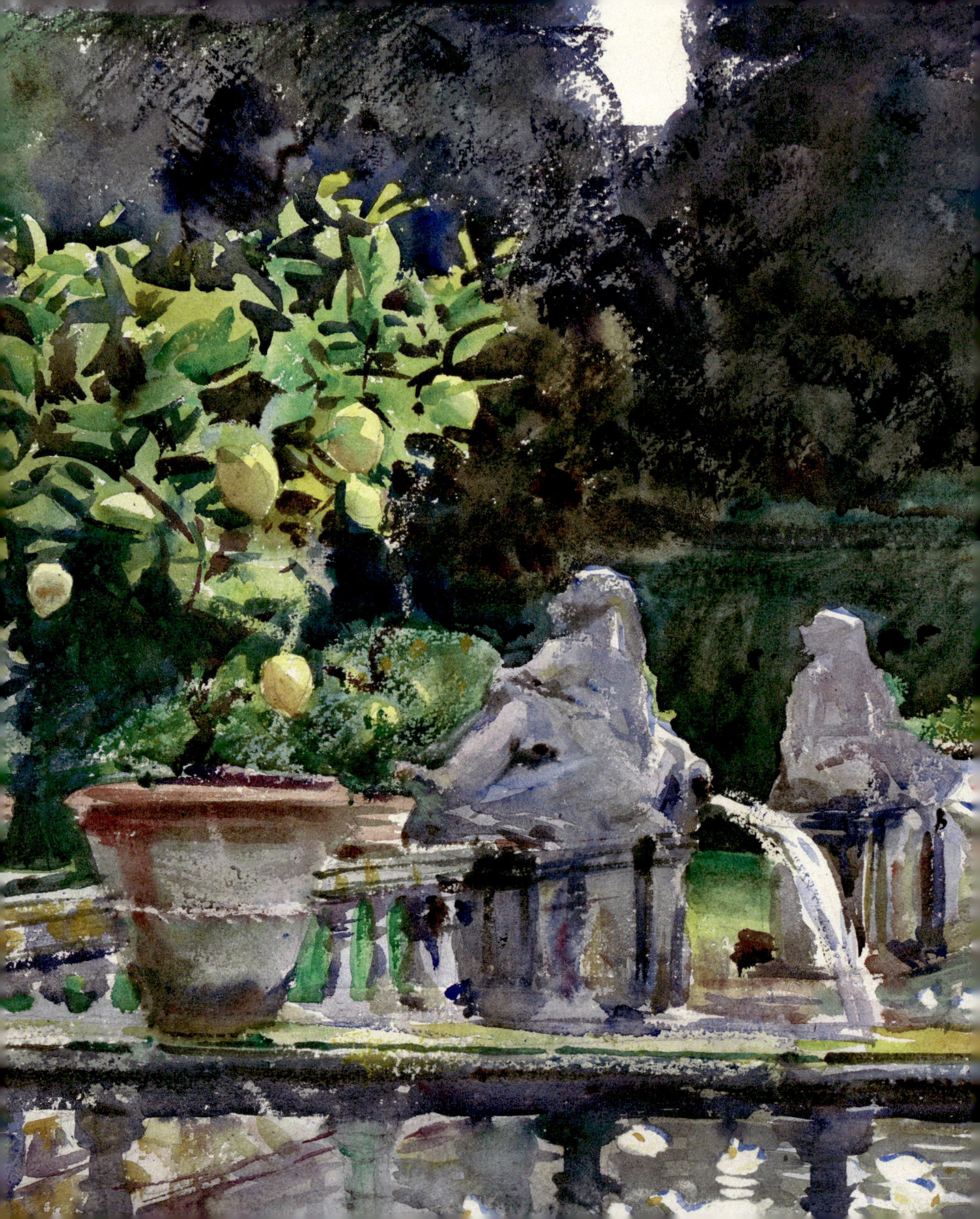

Gardens through Time

For all of the change gardens embody, aspects of contemporary gardening practice and landscape design can be traced back millennia, their origins sometimes rooted in simple universal practicality. A lemon tree thriving in a terracotta pot, captured in deft strokes of watercolor by John Singer Sargent in the nineteenth century, reflects documented ancient planting practices that continue to this day (50). The nearby reclining fountain sculptures represent the rivers Arno and Serchio and were installed in the seventeenth century. They continue an ancient Roman garden aesthetic that itself originated with the palace garden traditions of Persia. They also illustrate how over time the fundamental importance of water became increasingly elevated within garden design, shifting from essential irrigation to the development of elaborate water features. Garden ornaments, such as a Roman fountain honoring the Nile River in the form of a river god, would add an element of visual and auditory interest to a garden (43).

Gardens nearly always have a discernable perimeter, typically defined by plantings or architectural elements. During the Roman Empire, the walls of peristyle gardens (private domestic interior green spaces) were enhanced by frescoed panels, inserting an element of optical diversion in the flow between interior and exterior (42).

In turn, the structure of the Roman peristyle garden influenced the development of the medieval cloisters in Christian religious communities. Similarly characterized by a central garden open to the elements and surrounded by a walkway delineated by columns, such gardens allowed essential cultivation while undisturbed by worldly distractions.

Across cultures and origin stories, artistic visions of paradise often manifest as gardens. Recurring points of connection are found in these spaces—real or imagined—where nature flourishes in an ordered environment, a cultivated setting worthy of a divinity, dignitary, or mere mortals. Gardens are both expressions and reflections of humankind's desire to engage with the beauty and mystery of creation.

The earliest known references have been found in the Sumerian civilization, where the divided garden space was perceived as a home for the gods. *Pairidaēza*, ancient Persian walled gardens with cultivated fruit trees, influenced later Christian concepts of Paradise.

Judeo-Christian concepts of the *hortus conclusus*, an enclosed or walled garden, originate, in part, in the biblical poem Song of Solomon. Over time, one interpretation in the Catholic Christian tradition positions Mary, the mother of Jesus, as a living representation of a pristine enclosure, having conceived without sin. Depictions of the Virgin

Mary often place her within a walled garden to emphasize her unblemished physical being and the beauty of divinely inspired fecundity, as reflected in Giovanni di Paolo's presentation of the *Madonna of Humility* (36).

In contrast to the ordered environment of an enclosed orchard, the Garden of Eden is visualized more frequently as a place of abundant wilderness where humankind lives in harmony with the animal kingdom. Erastus Salisbury Field imagined a semi-cultivated paradise with a notable variety of flora and fauna (48). At center, Eve reaches to pluck the fateful apple that will result in Adam and Eve's expulsion. Joyce J. Scott presents a provocative alternate vision of this age-old creation story. The protagonists of her beadwork *Adam and Eve Being Cast from the Garden of Eden* project strength and determination as they stride through the foliage, seemingly untroubled to the angel berating them (49). Something about their stance suggests that it might not be a punishment to leave the sacred garden behind. This tension between human cultivation and wilderness, a recurring cross-temporal theme across cultures, is reflected in the composition of a Mughal carpet with scenes of court life and hunting in garden spaces delineated in the upper register (37).

A secular variant of the Christian hortus conclusus envisions the garden as a place for entertainment, pleasure, or rejuvenation. In contrast to chaste Marian imagery, *The Small Garden of Love* depicts a paradise on earth where couples can freely engage in courtship (54). A nineteenth-century vision of earthly paradise took the form of the domestic garden with a white picket fence, an American social ideal that persists to this day. Tyler Mitchell's portrait of a woman posing at ease on a comforter, against a painted backdrop of just such an idealized garden space, questions this stereotype through his ongoing examination of Black quietude (55). The flowering bushes invite the viewer to draw on their memory of floral scent, to slow their pace, and to reflect more deeply on who can enjoy such simple, restorative havens. — MM

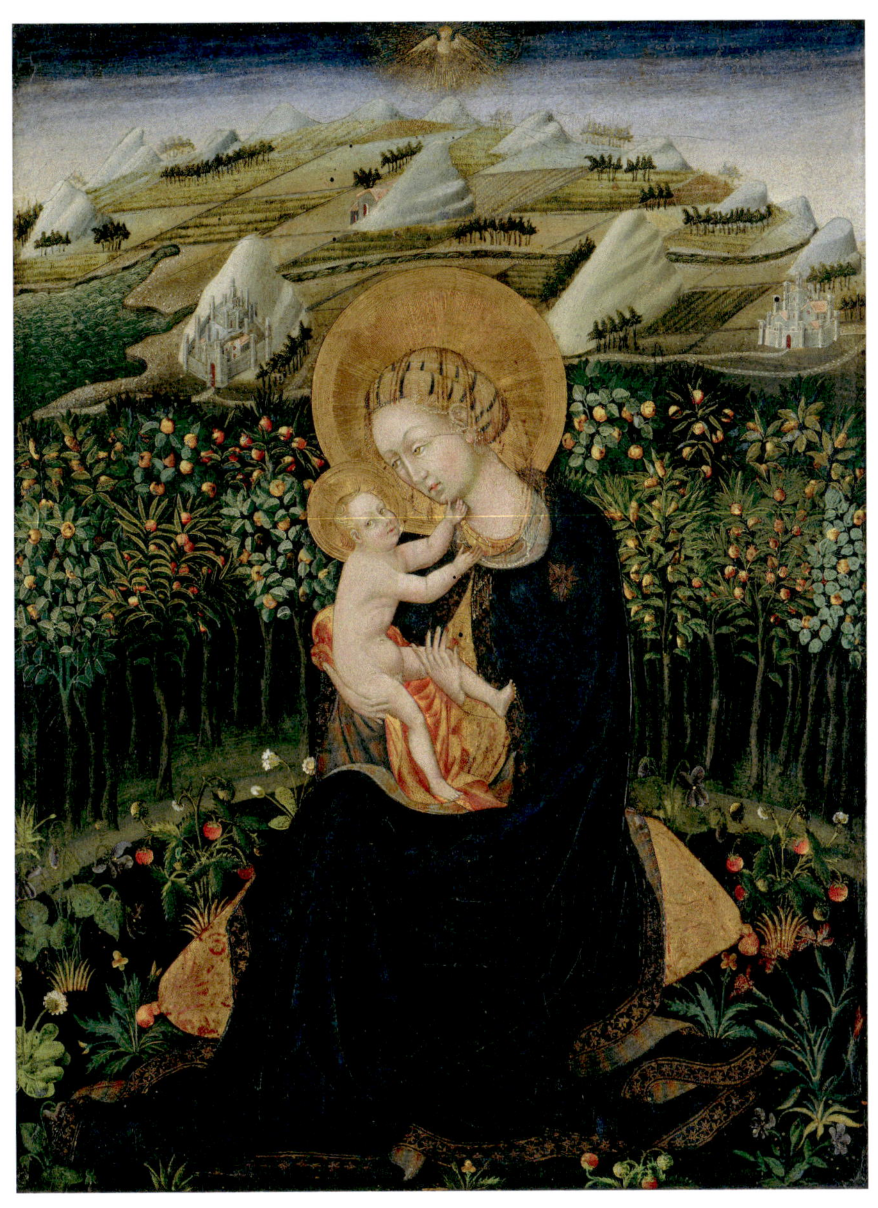

— 36 —

Giovanni di Paolo, *Madonna of Humility*, about 1442

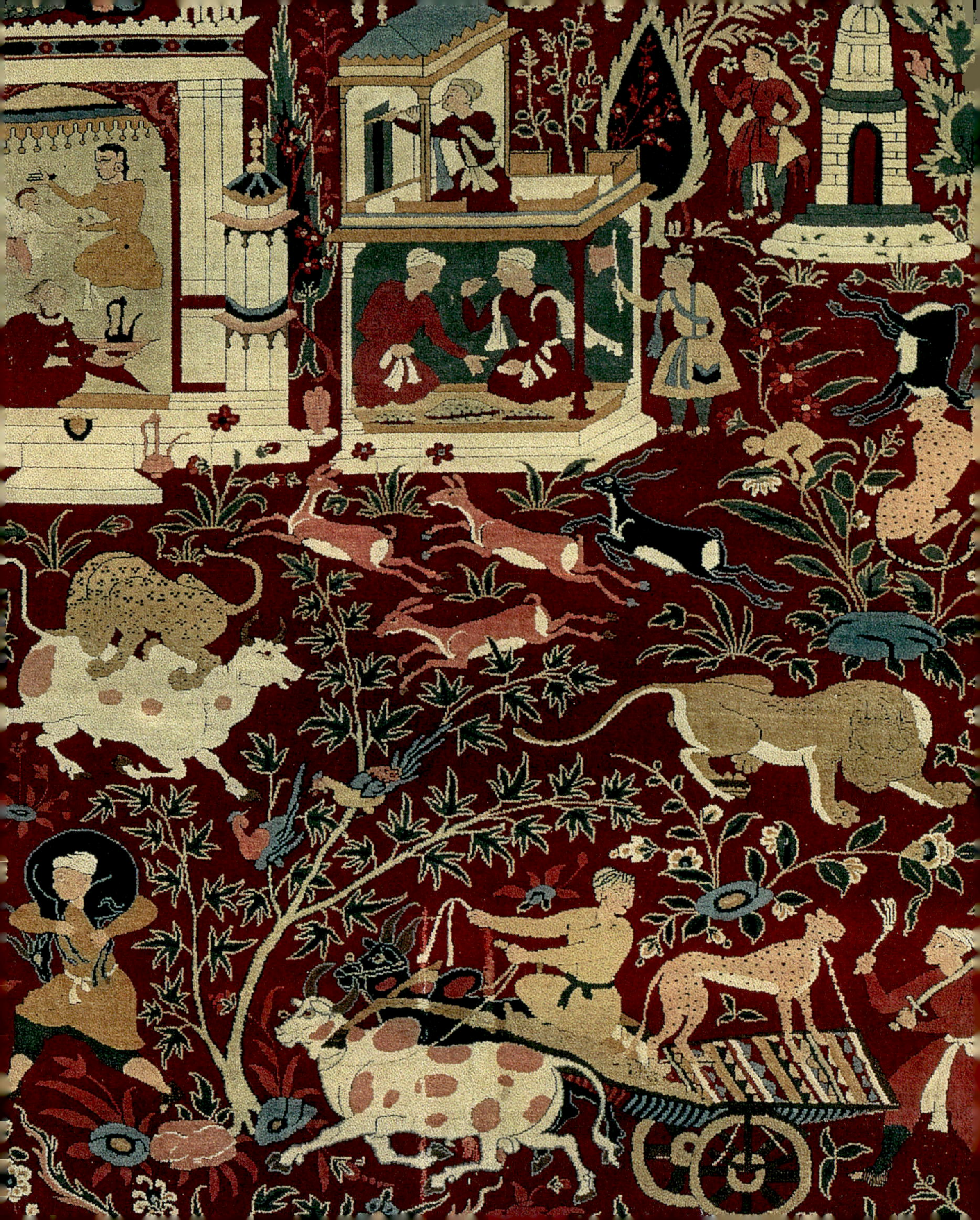

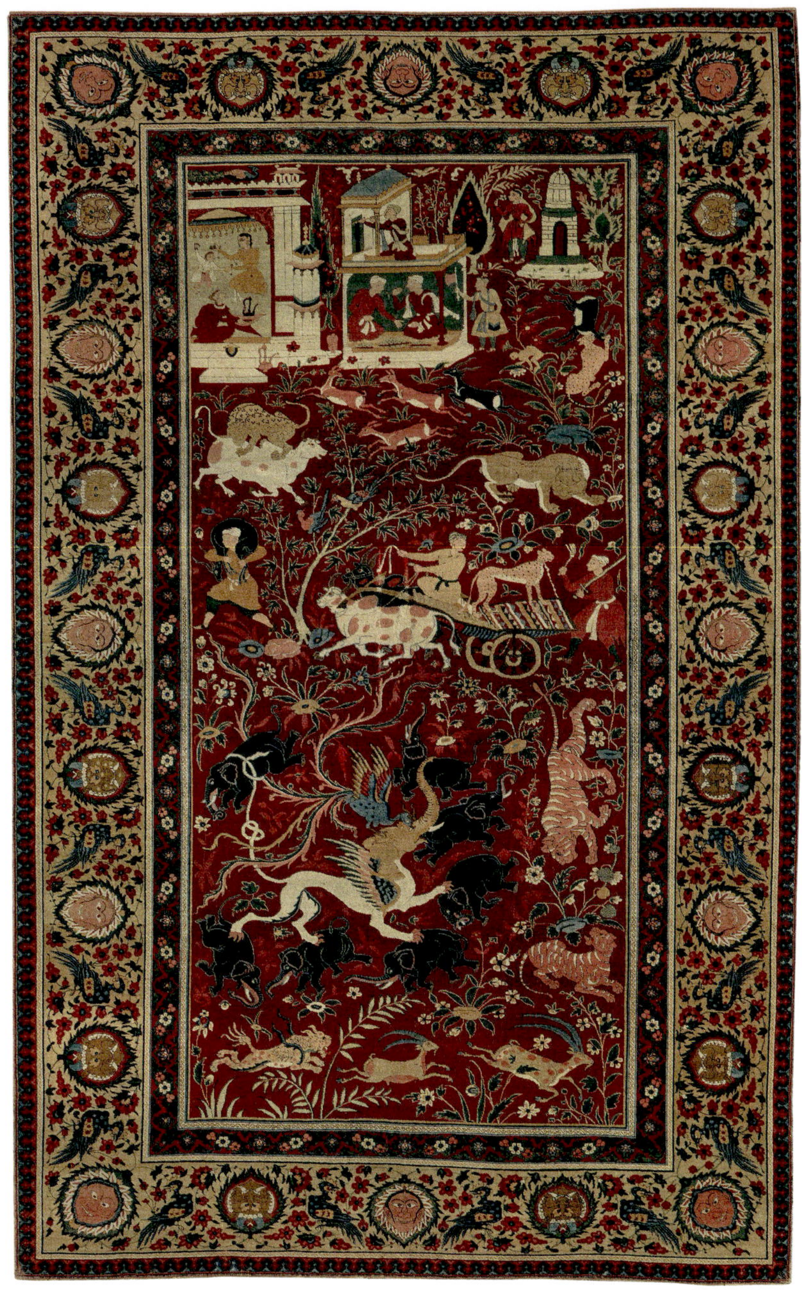

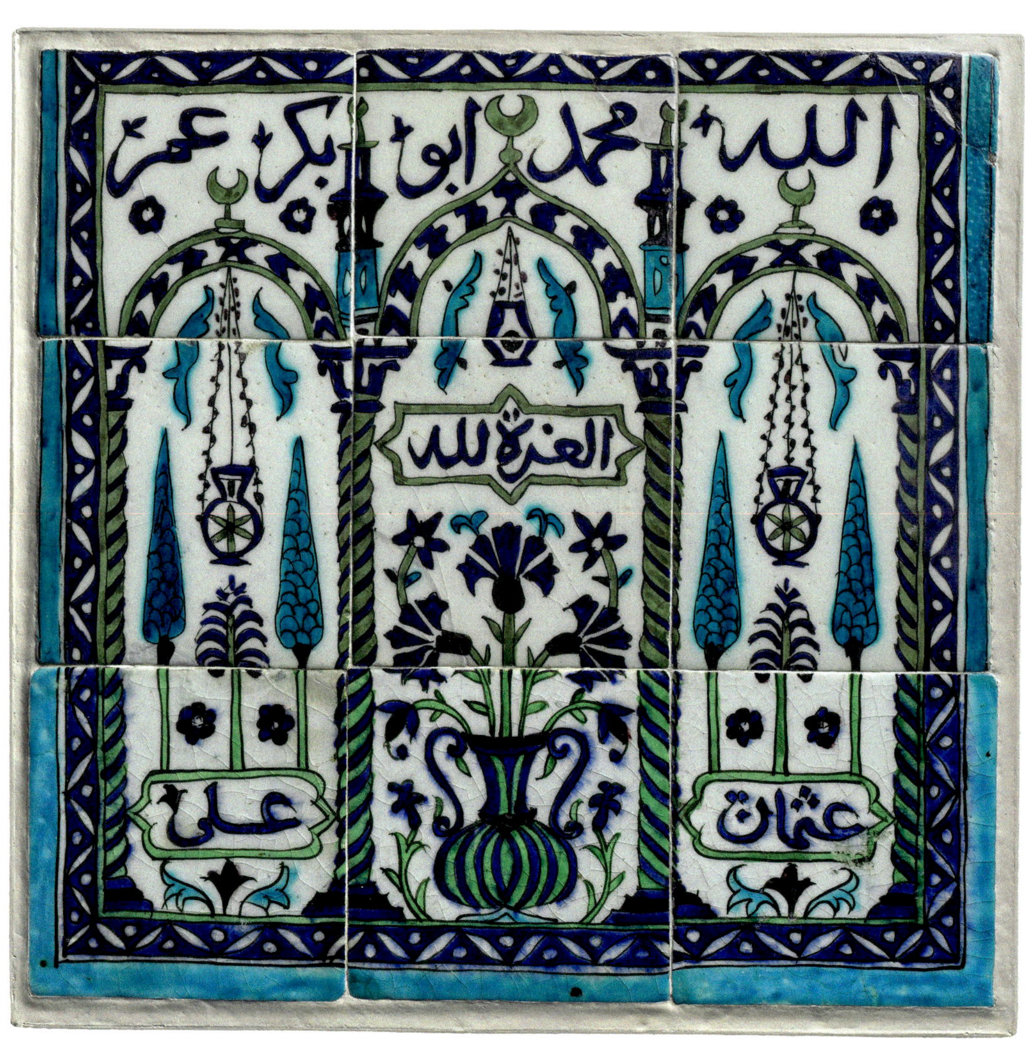

— 38 —
Tile depicting the gateway to Paradise,
Ottoman, about 1600

— 39 —
Elizabeth Courtis, Sampler, 1796

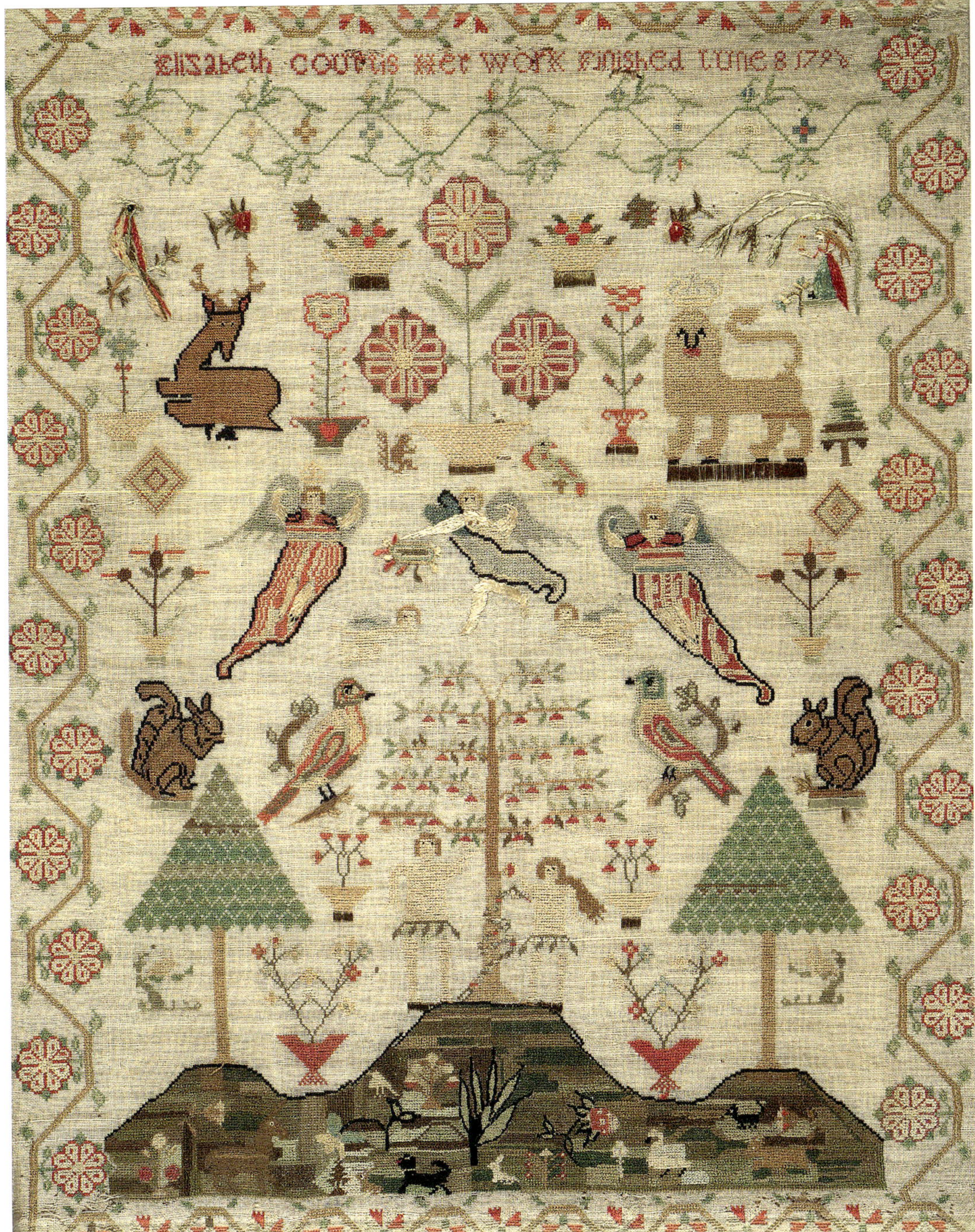
Elizabeth Coutts her work finished June 8 1795

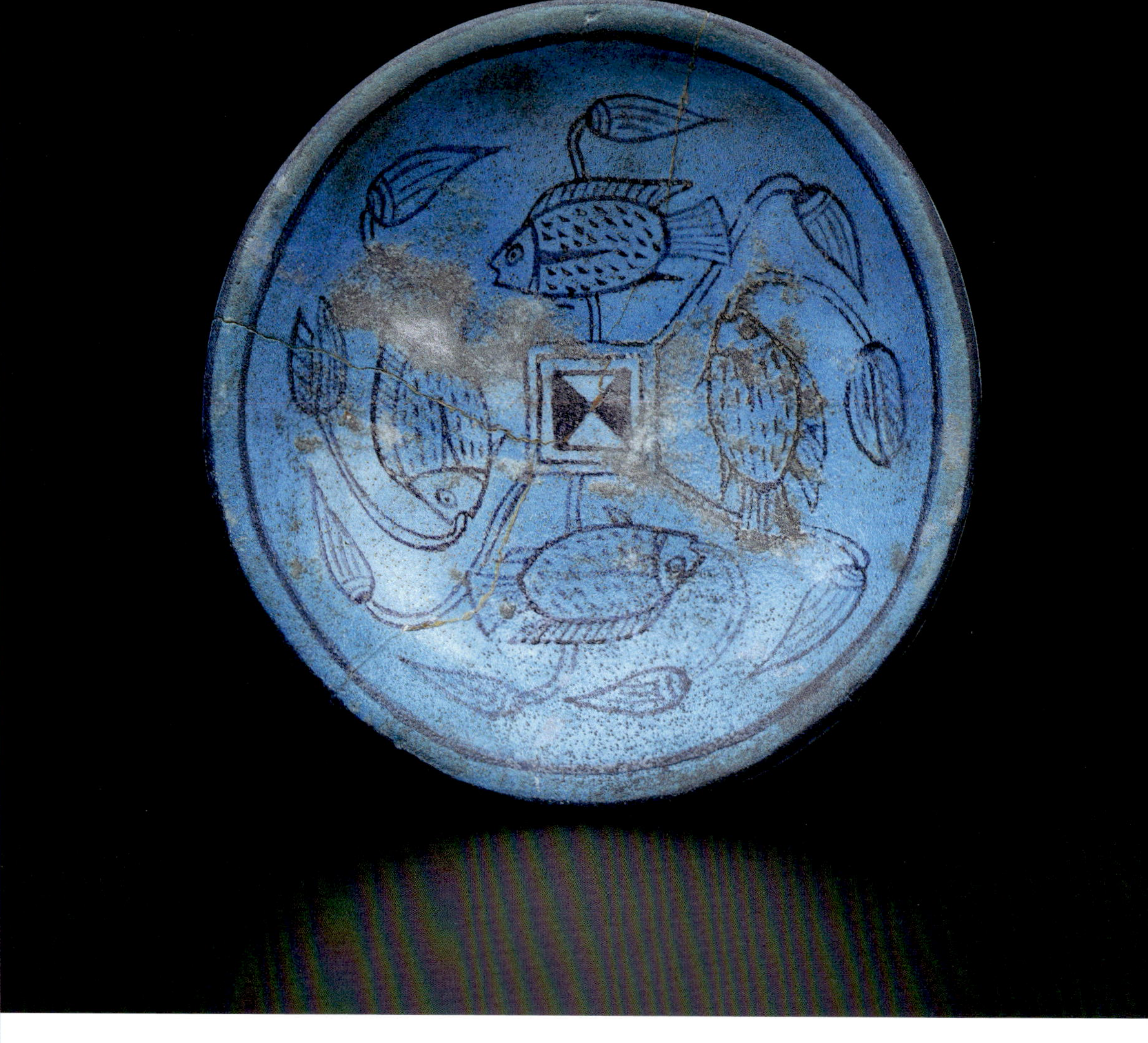

— 40 —
Bowl with fish and lotuses, Egyptian, 1550–1295 BCE

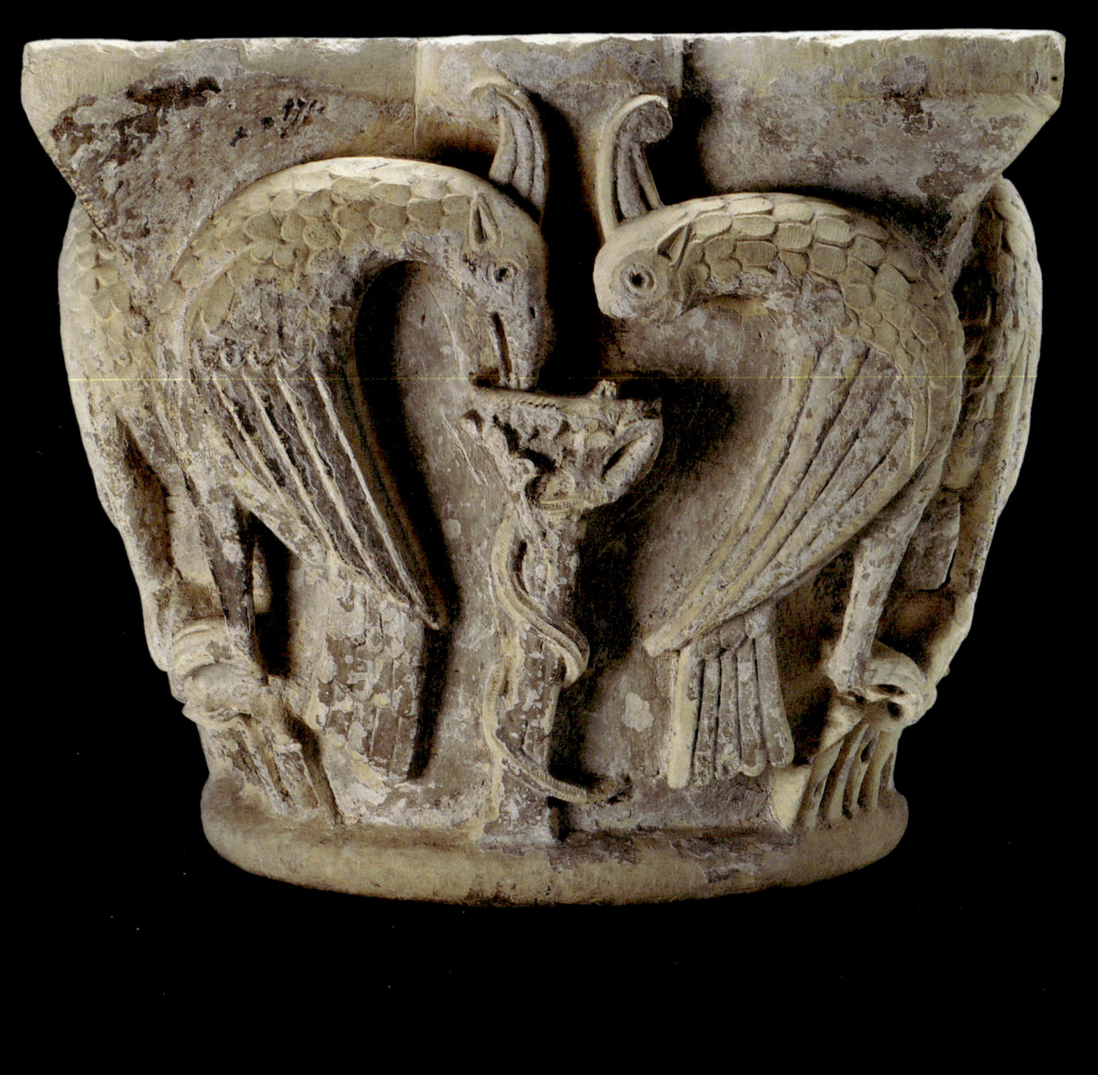

Capital from La Charité-sur-Loire, French, about 1100–25

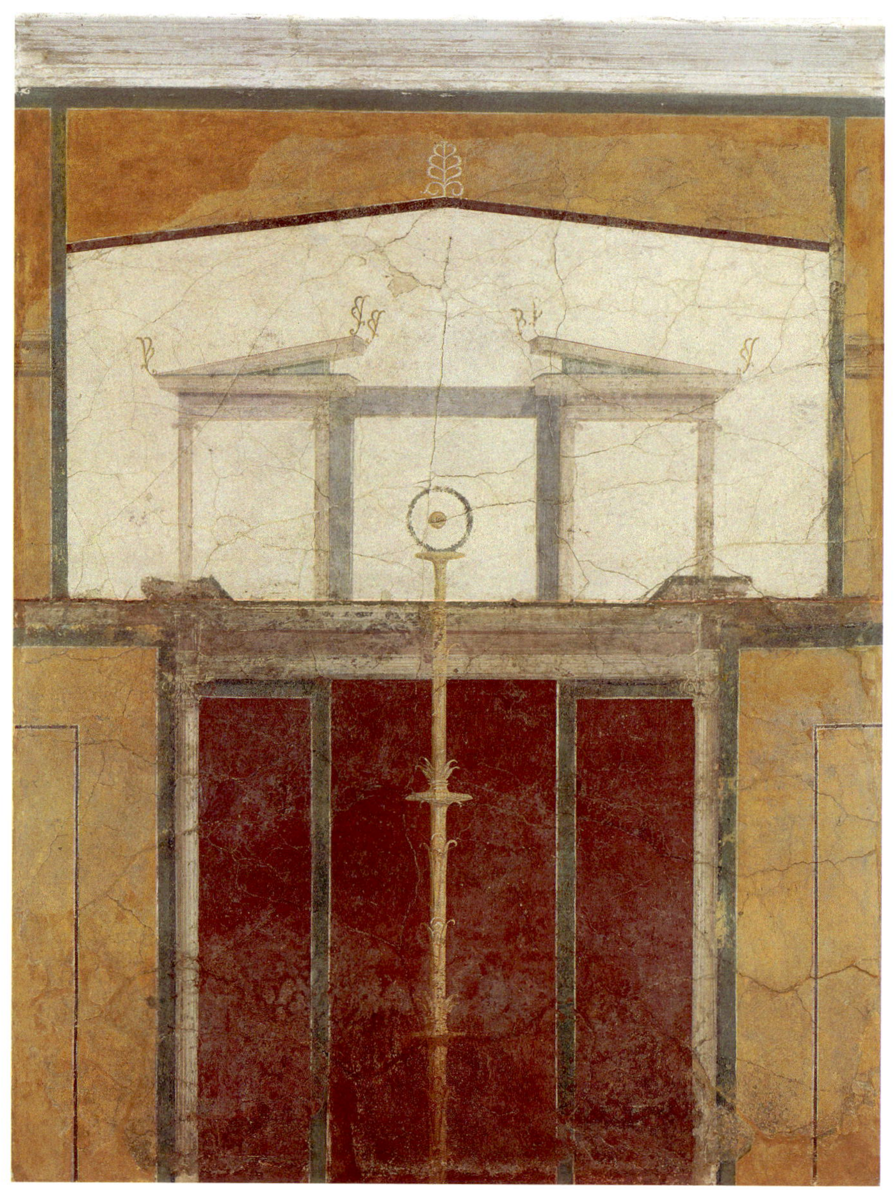

— 42 —
Fresco panel from Villa of the Contrada Bottaro, Pompeii, Roman, 14–62 CE

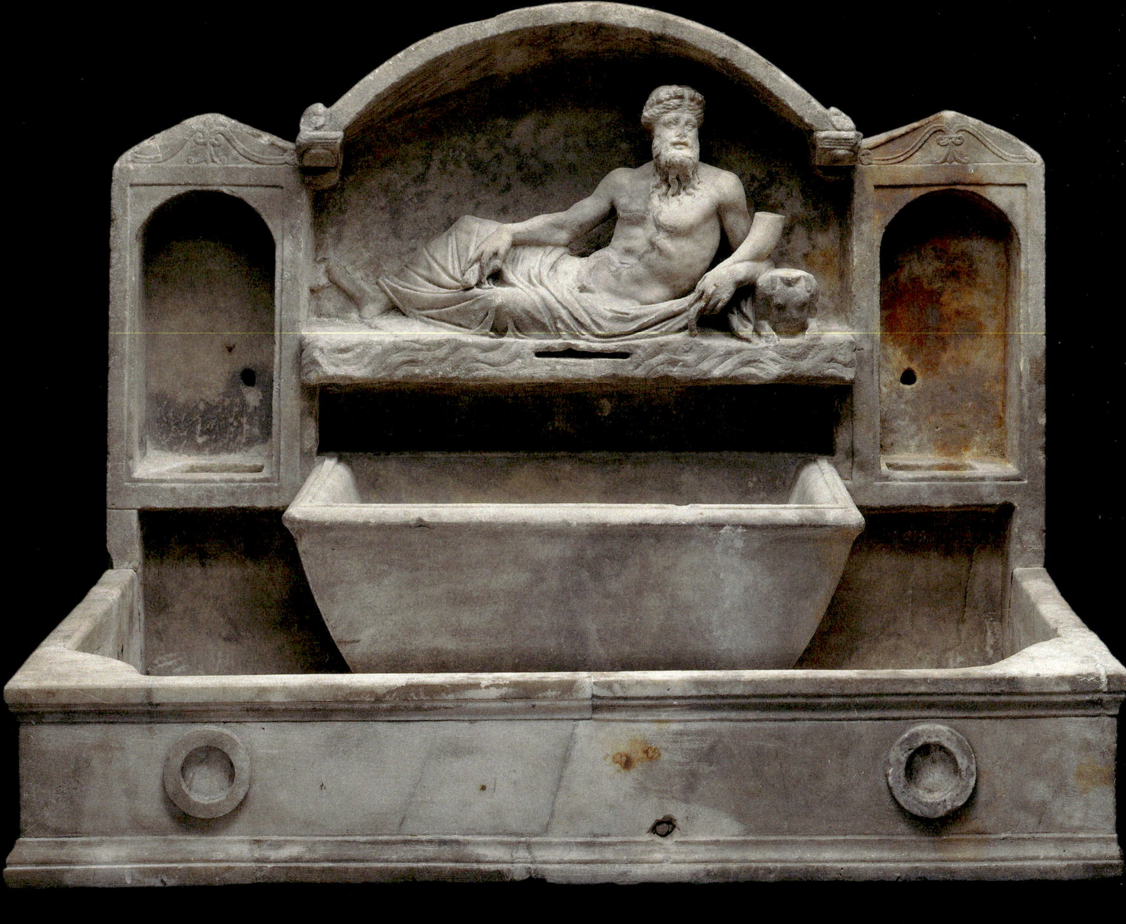

— 43 —

Fountain basin with a reclining river god, Roman, 98–138 CE

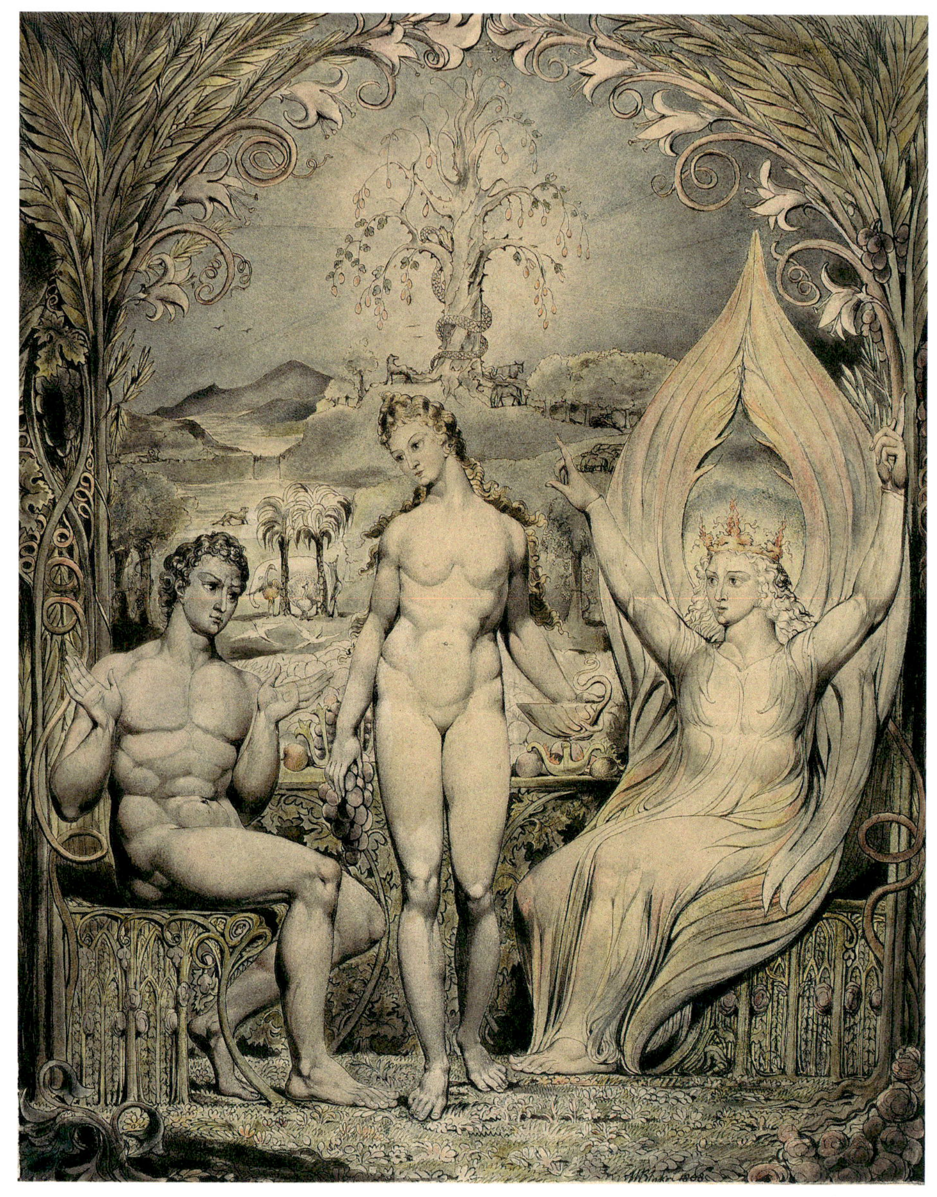

— 44 —

William Blake, *The Archangel Raphael with Adam and Eve*, 1808

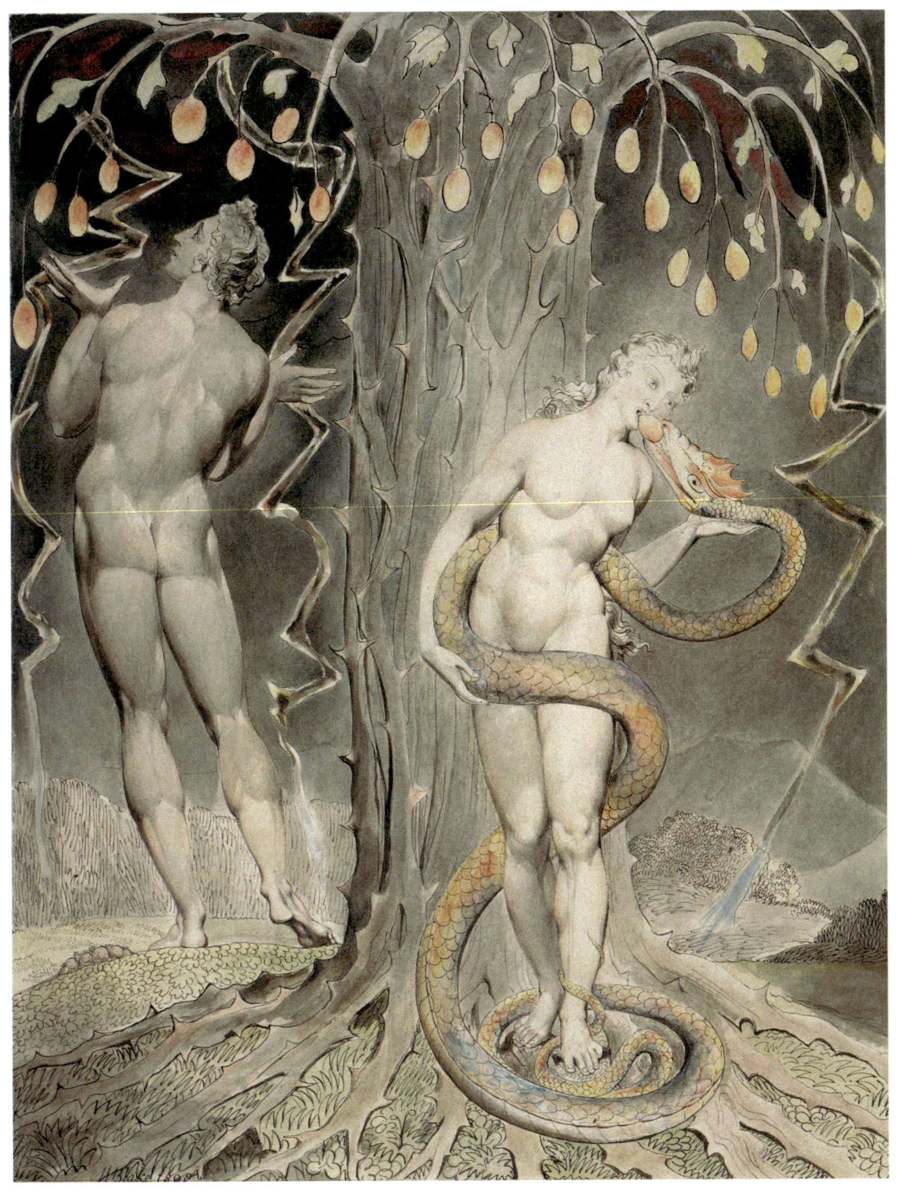

— 45 —

William Blake, *The Temptation and Fall of Eve*, 1808

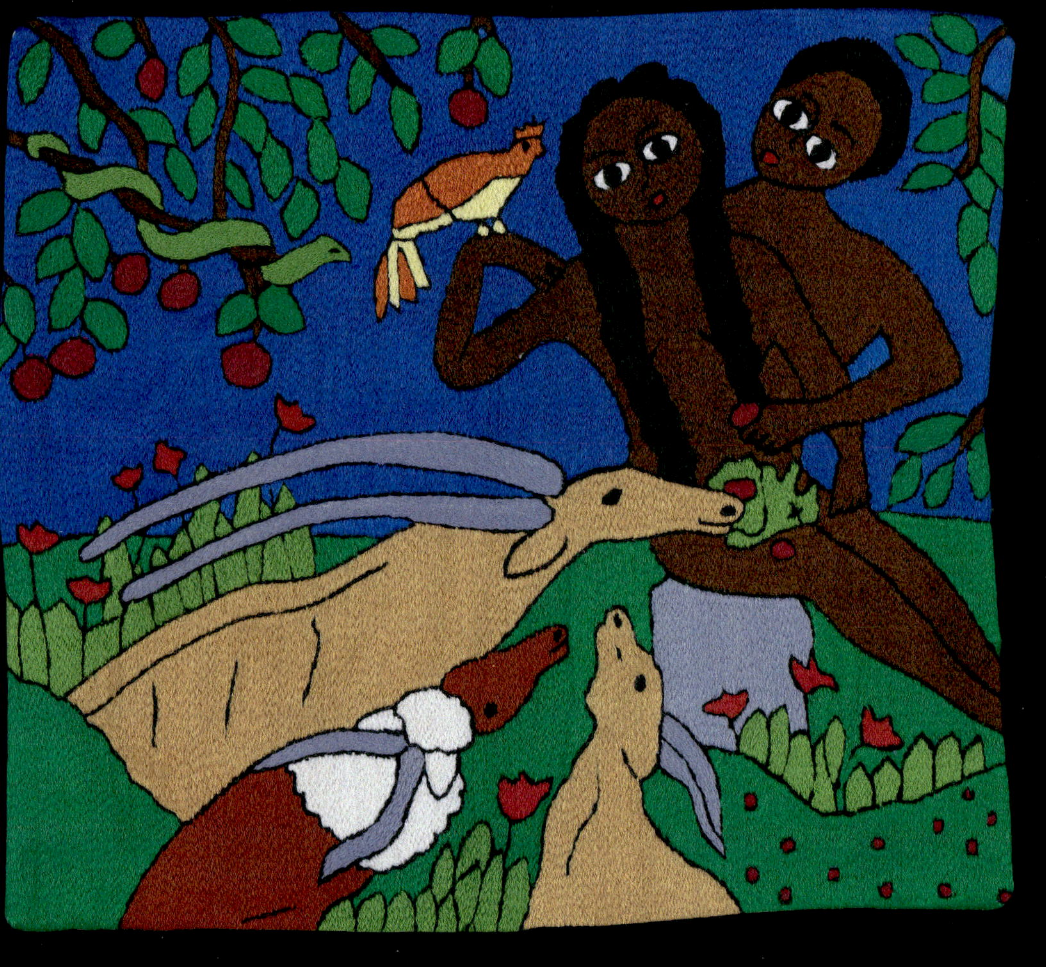

Attributed to Asnaku Melese, Pillow sham, 1990–2012

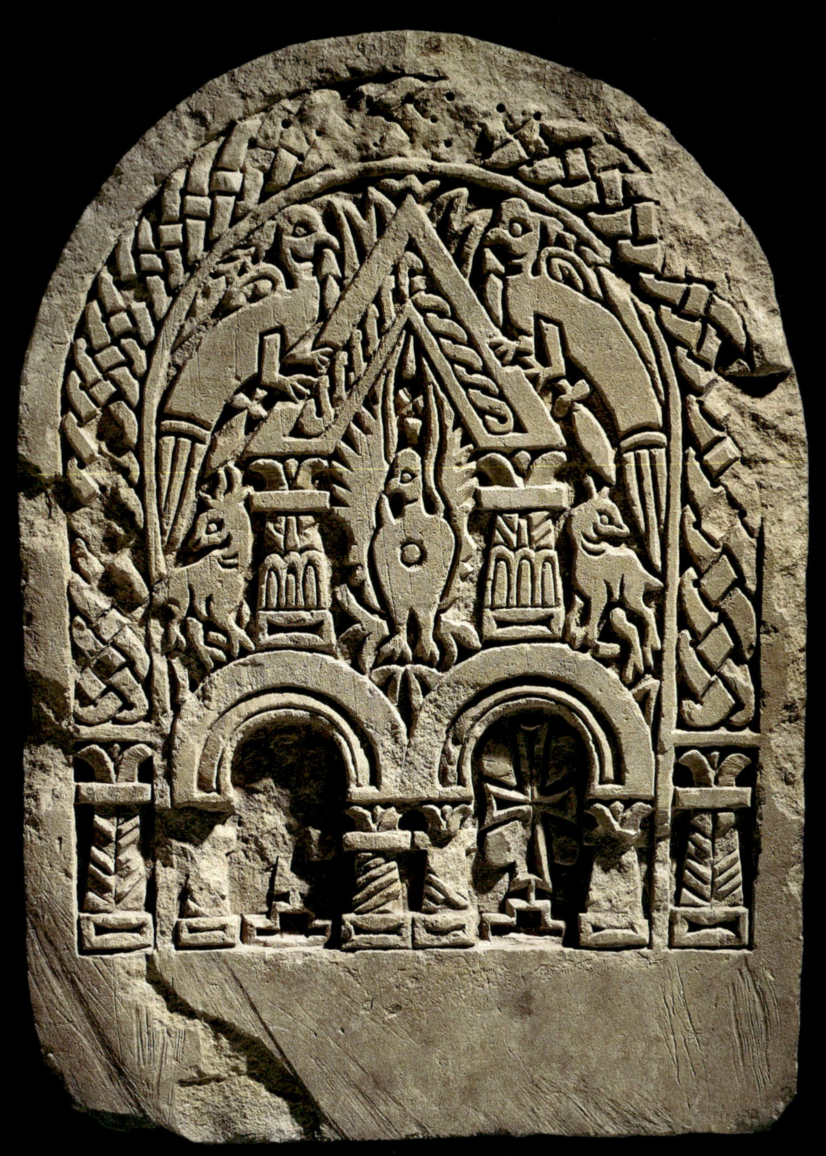

Funerary stele with paradisiacal motifs, Coptic, 6th–7th century CE

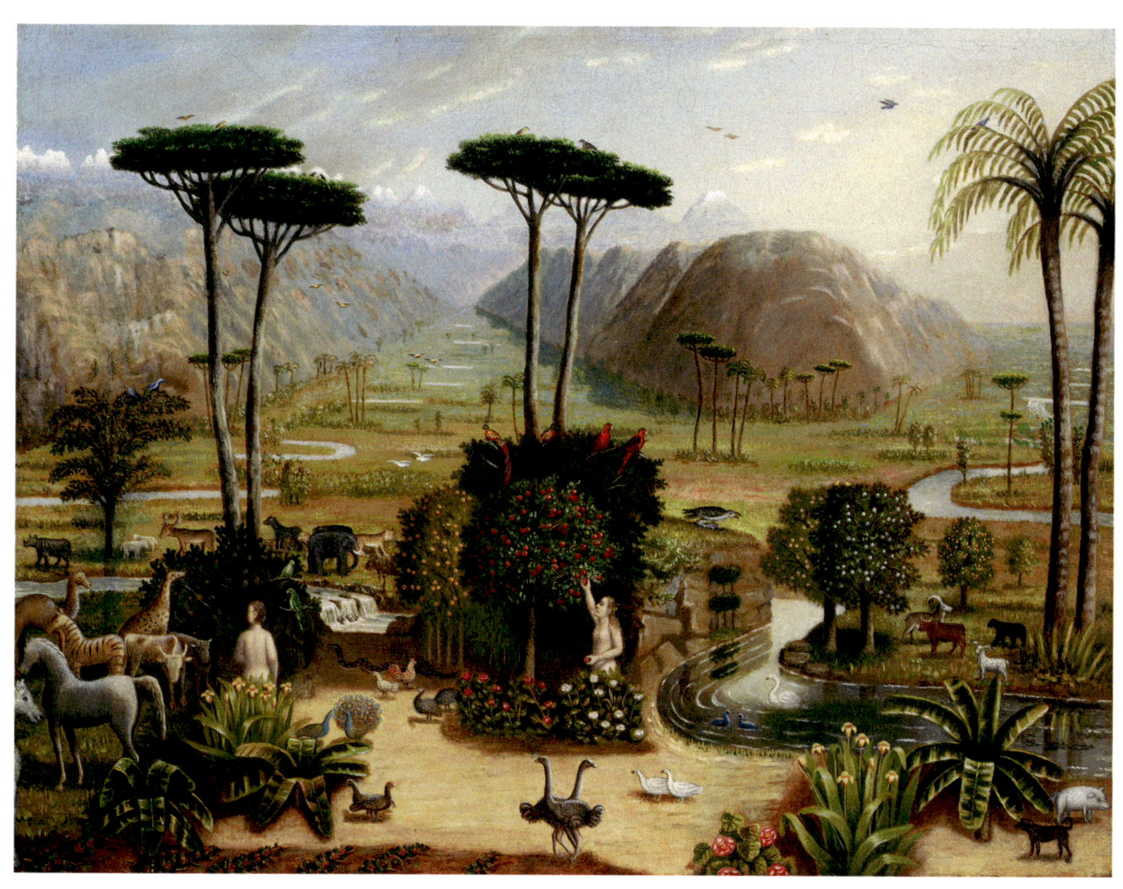

— 48 —

  Erastus Salisbury Field, *The Garden of Eden*, about 1860

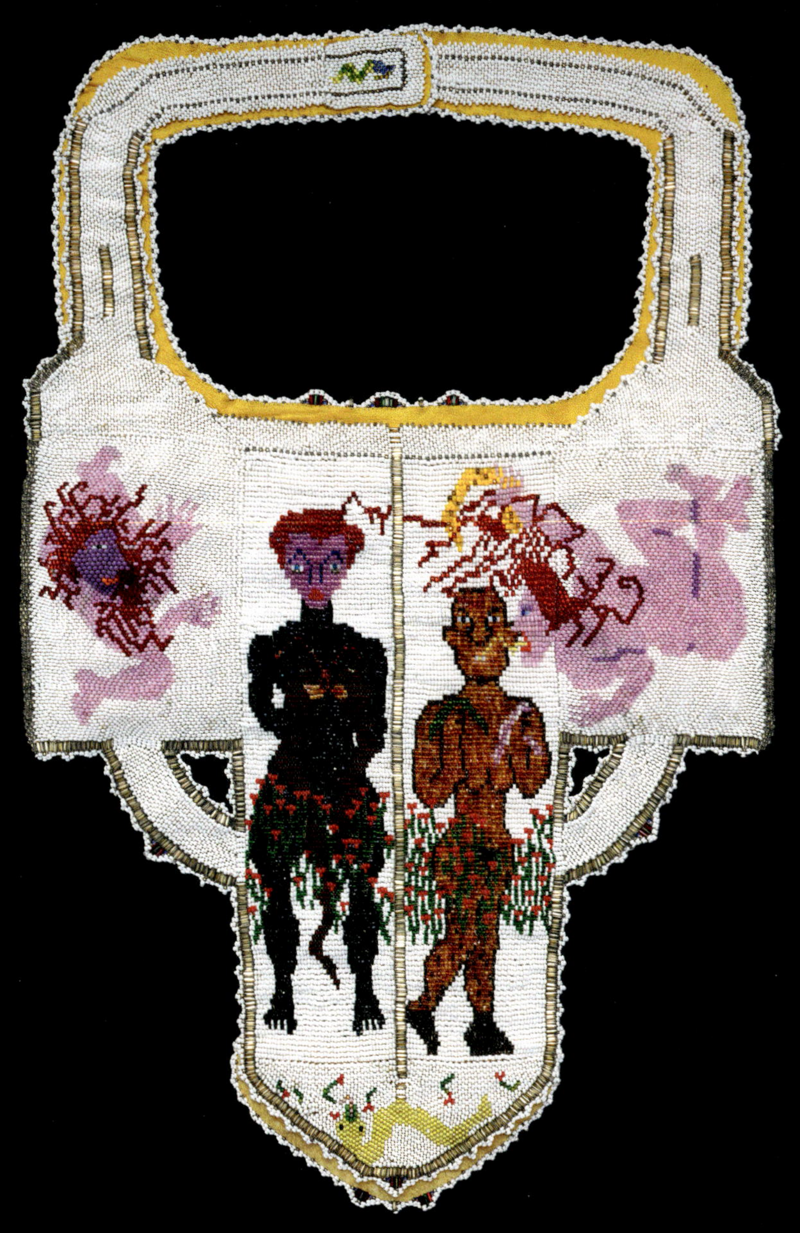

Joyce J. Scott, *Adam and Eve Being Cast from the Garden of Eden*, 1981–82

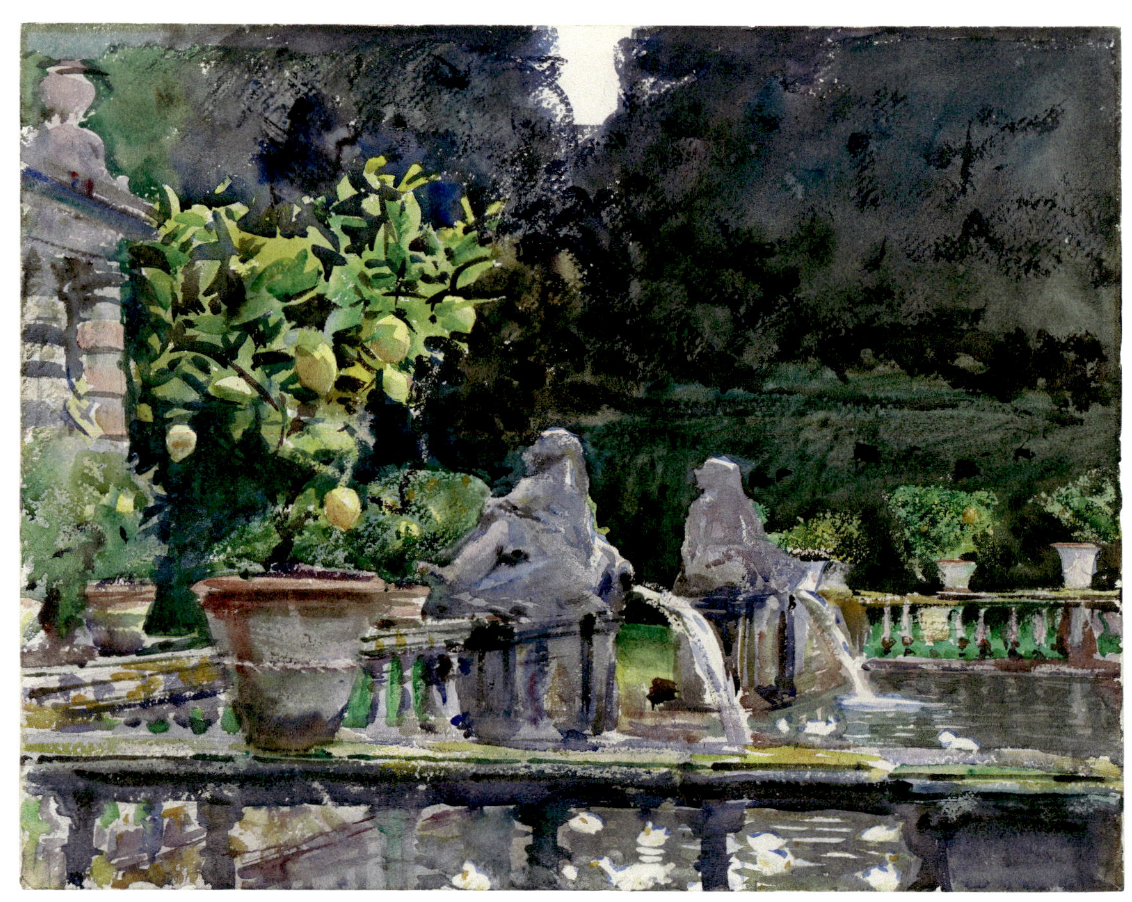

— 50 —

John Singer Sargent, *Villa di Marlia, Lucca: A Fountain*, 1910

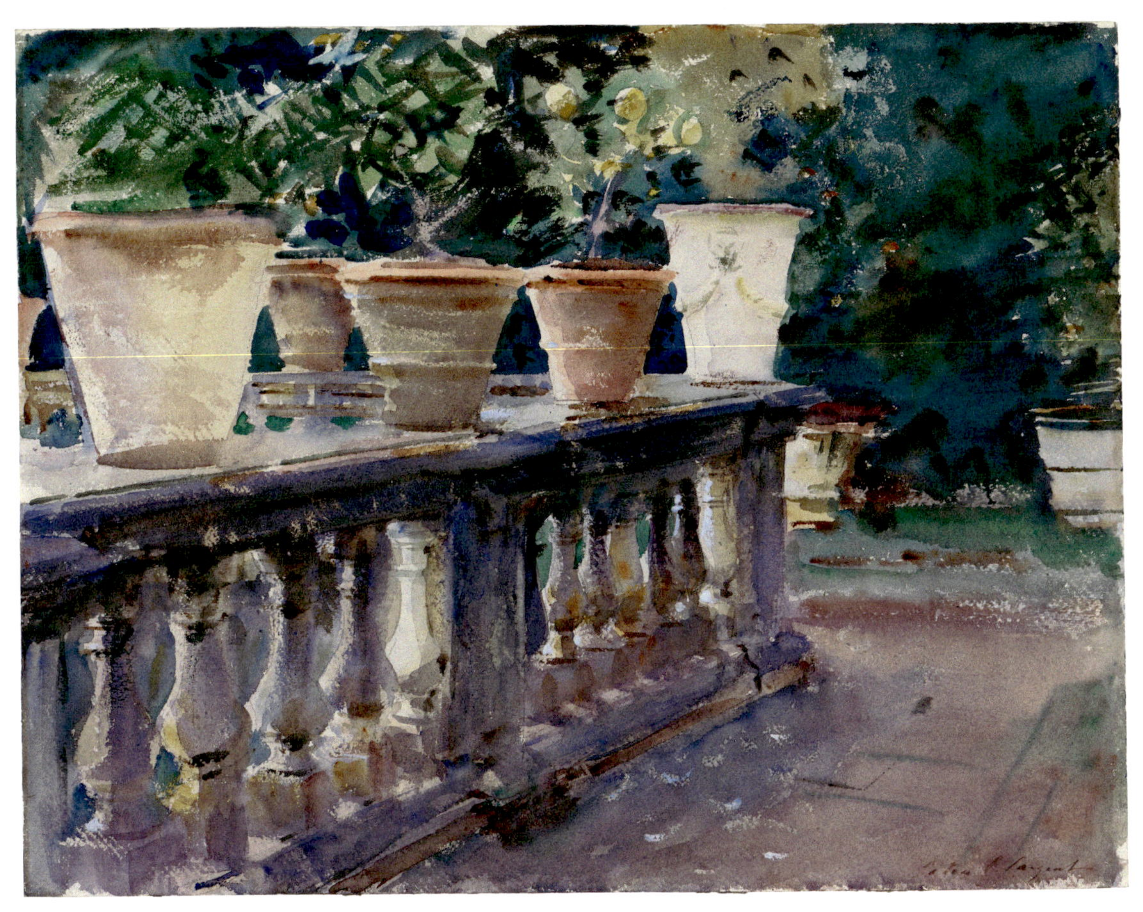

John Singer Sargent, *Villa di Marlia, Lucca: The Balustrade*, 1910

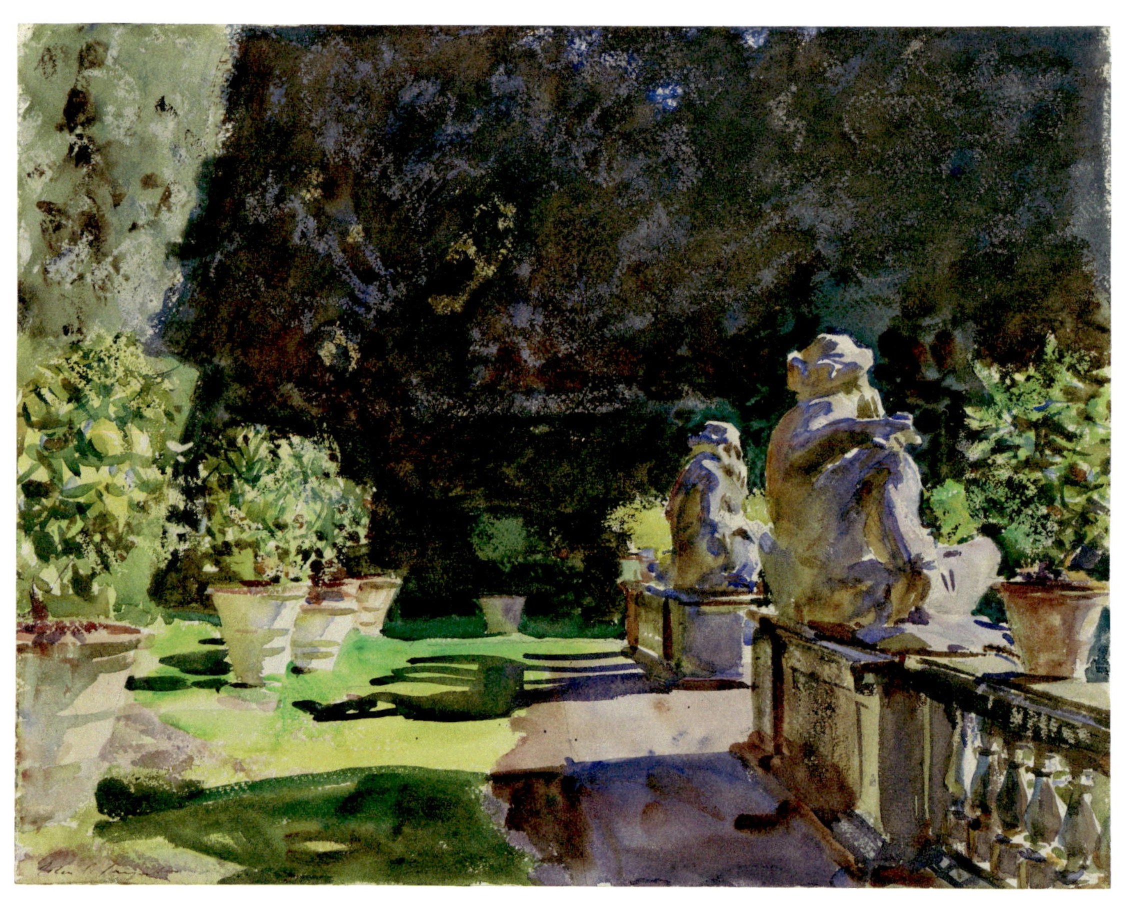

— 52 —
John Singer Sargent, *Villa di Marlia, Lucca*, 1910

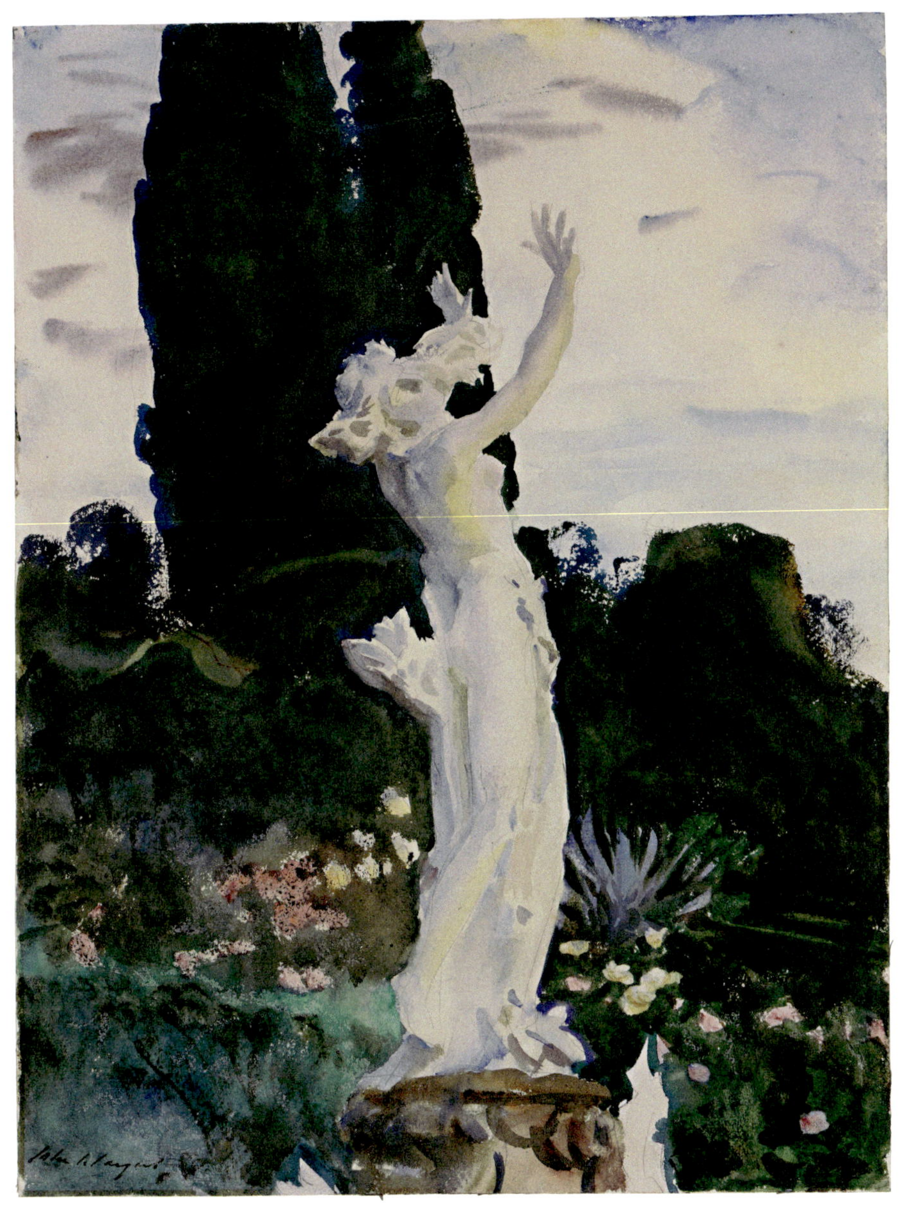

— 53 —

John Singer Sargent, *Daphne*, 1910

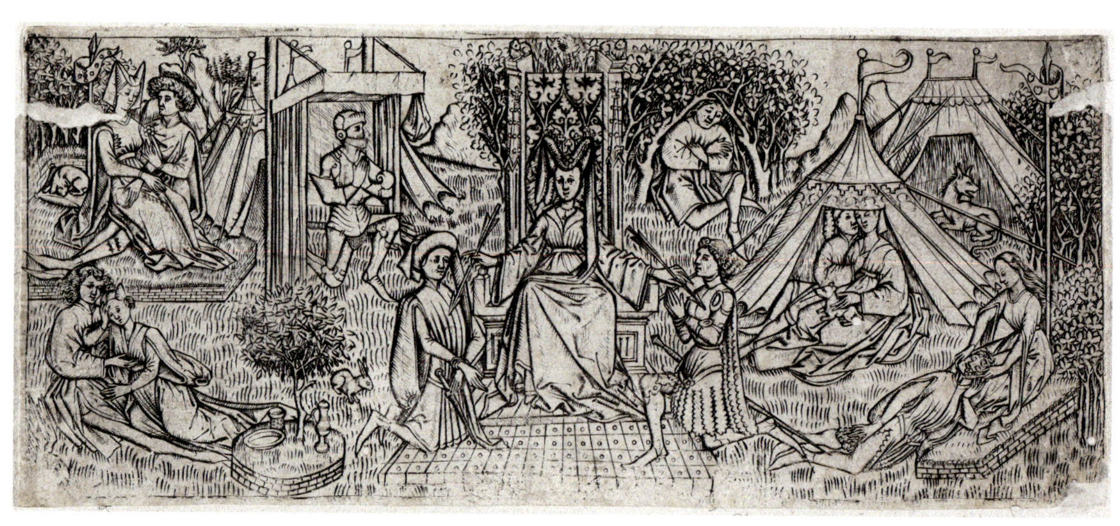

— 54 —
Master of the Gardens of Love,
The Small Garden of Love, 1440–50

— 55 —
Tyler Mitchell, *Cage*, 2022

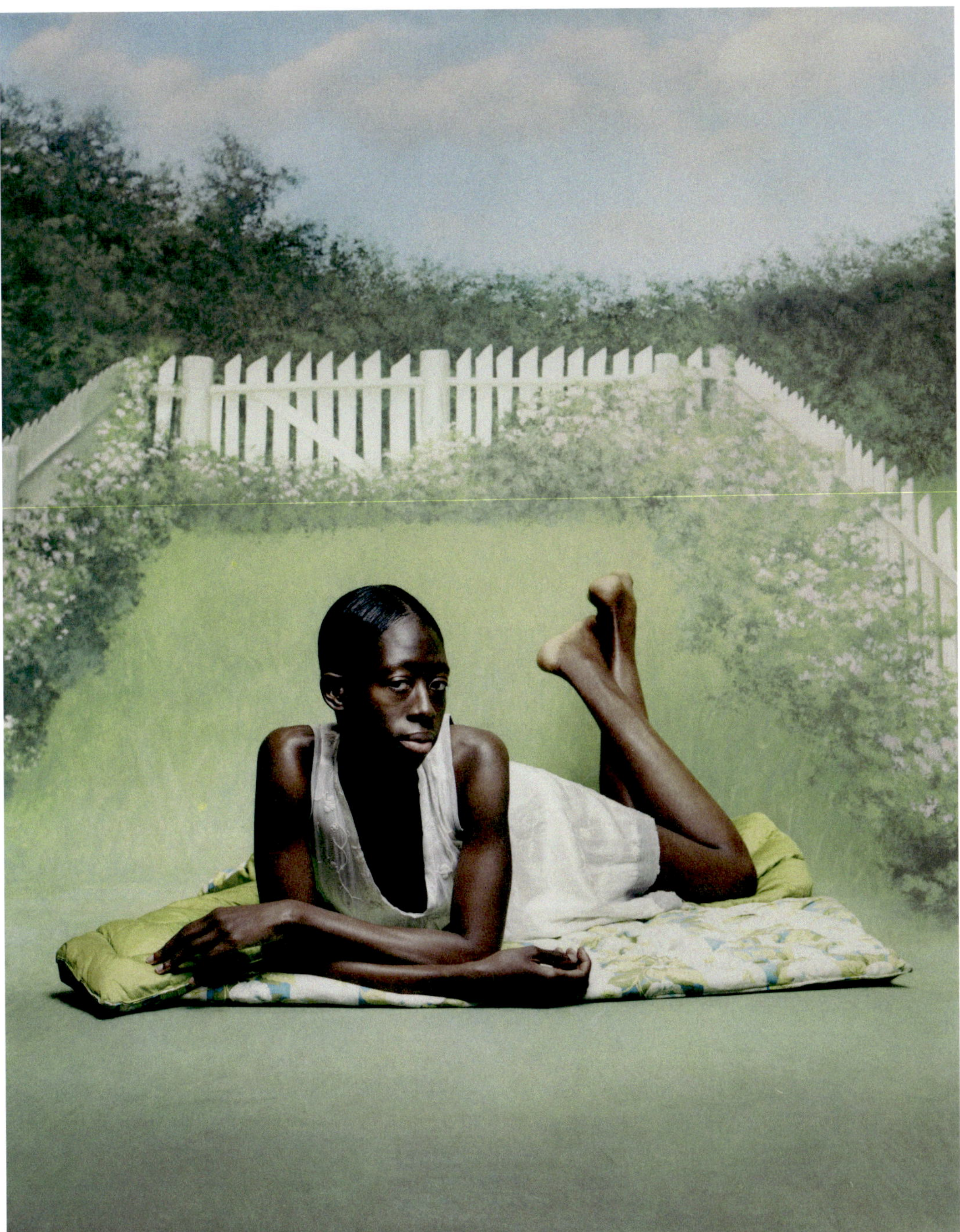

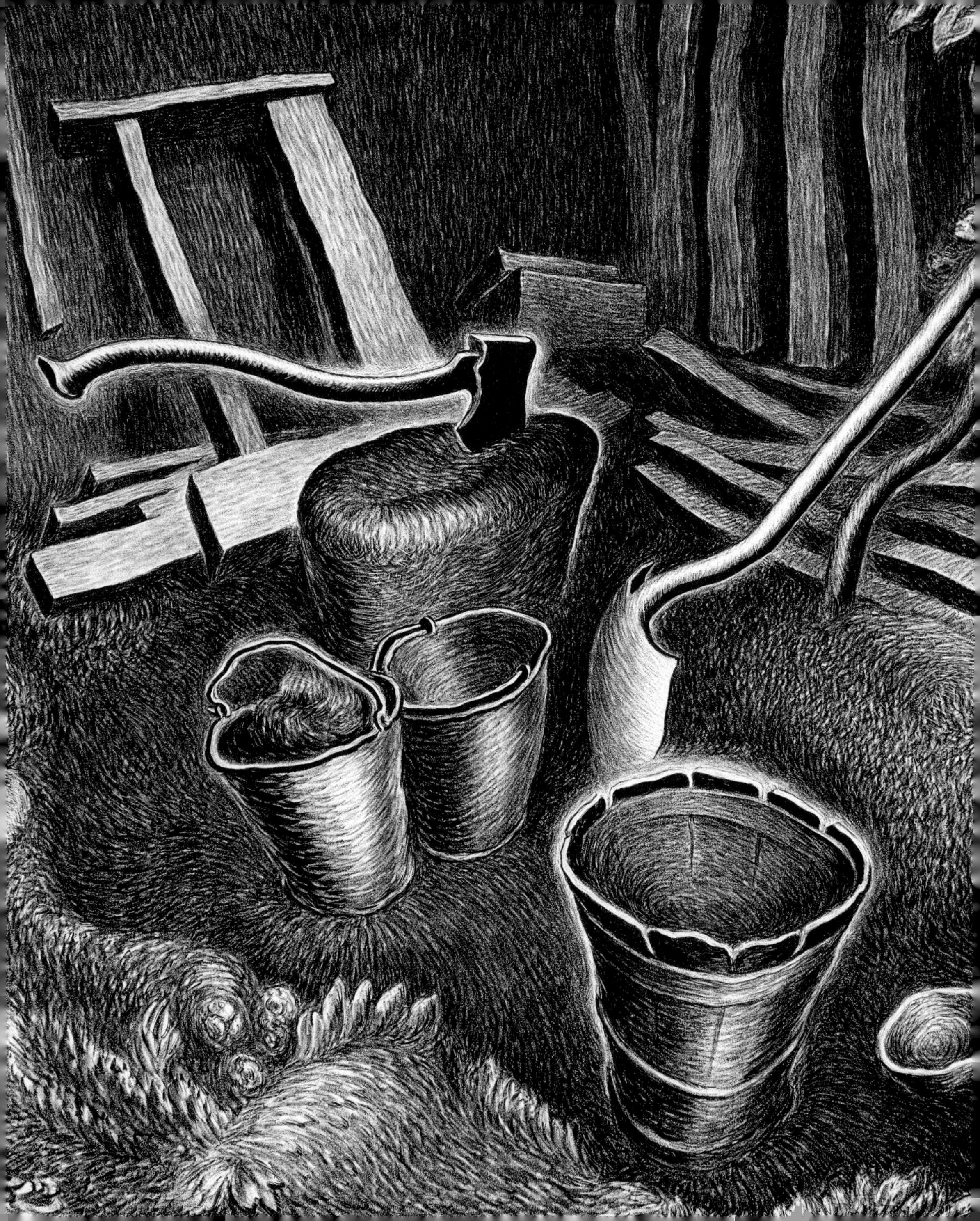

Gardeners

Every garden has a gardener, sometimes many, to cultivate and care for the land through the changing of the seasons. Gardens require great effort to create and maintain them, but the individuals who perform this labor are oftentimes unsung, even invisible.

Ancient representations of gardens frequently feature mythological characters, rather than humans, performing tasks associated with horticulture, such as the sowing of seeds, tilling of soil, and gathering of harvests. A late second- to early third-century Roman mosaic, for example, features a vignette of tiny cupids collecting roses in baskets and stringing them into decorative garlands like those used in springtime rose festivals celebrating Venus, the goddess of love and mother of Cupid, as well as in funerary rites, where the fragility of flowers symbolized the brevity of life (68).

From centuries later, a Flemish tapestry depicts one of a series of scenes from the courtship of Vertumnus, the Roman god of growth and the seasons, and Pomona, goddess of orchards and harvests, as recounted in Ovid's epic poem *Metamorphoses*. In a formal garden resplendent with fountains and verdant allées, and framed with a fruit-laden colonnade, Vertumnus appears partially disguised before Pomona in a valiant attempt to win her heart. Ovid recounts their harmonious union as the ideal marriage of nature's seasons and the abundance of lovingly tended gardens like that of Pomona depicted in the tapestry (67).

Taming and containing a natural landscape into a cultivated garden demand a variety of specialized skills and tools as well. Sixteenth-century Netherlandish printmaker Pieter van der Heyden's *Spring*, after Bruegel, represents the range of work typically undertaken by laborers in the garden during the months of March, April, and May—spreading seeds, watering flower beds, and turning the soil with shovels, rakes, and hoes (56). In addition, smaller figures in the distance are shown busying themselves with other springtime activities, such as sheep shearing, arbor construction, the migration of birds, dancing, and general merrymaking.

Agostino Gallo, also active in the sixteenth century, produced an illustrated garden journal that describes his experiences cultivating a large country estate outside of Brescia, Italy (61). His impulse to carefully document the seasonal work carried out on his land is one shared by many gardeners across time. The woodcuts, with their particular emphasis on tools like the scythes, sickles, and other implements he employed, would have been extremely rare in this early period.

In 1991, artist Michael Mazur started a lovingly detailed sketchbook centered on his own gardens and particularly his prized tulips outside his Cambridge, Massachusetts, studio (70). It is filled with delicate pen and ink renderings of carefully planned flower beds, some of them highlighted with watercolor to record their range of colors—from white, to pale pink, to a deep purple, almost black—and handwritten inscriptions noting their botanical names and the number of bulbs he had planted for each type.

During roughly the same moment, also in Cambridge, photographer Barbara "Bobbie" Norfleet set out to record the activities of a local garden club—founded in the 1880s and claiming to be the oldest in America—and its all-female membership at work and play. Norfleet's portrait of Anne Mazlish seen from below documents her perched in a tree, wearing a straw hat and floral-patterned dress and wielding a very large pair of clippers (60). Some of the work of the earliest garden clubs centered on food production, while others were responsible for the care and preservation of historic gardens, arboretums, and later the beautification of urban spaces. More recently, many have expanded their reach to include environmental issues such as the protection of endangered species and the promotion of native plants.

Gardens are sometimes the livelihood of a single person, but more often they are spaces of shared work and collaboration with others. Today, for example, luxurious gardens and private estates necessitate huge expenditures

of physical labor frequently carried out by crews of seasonal
workers who take on the back-breaking jobs of planting
and maintaining acres of land, laying sod, and pruning trees.
Los Angeles–based artist Jay Lynn Gomez is especially
aware of the challenges of this often-anonymous low-paid
labor force as both her parents were formerly undocumented
immigrants from Mexico, a group all too often exploited
for this type of precarious labor. Her painting *Resting*
captures a powerful double portrait of *literally* faceless
workers seated on the ground in front of a massive, closely
trimmed hedge, their brooms and trash barrel suggesting
that they have finished the work and are only now finding
a moment to relax (59). — KEH

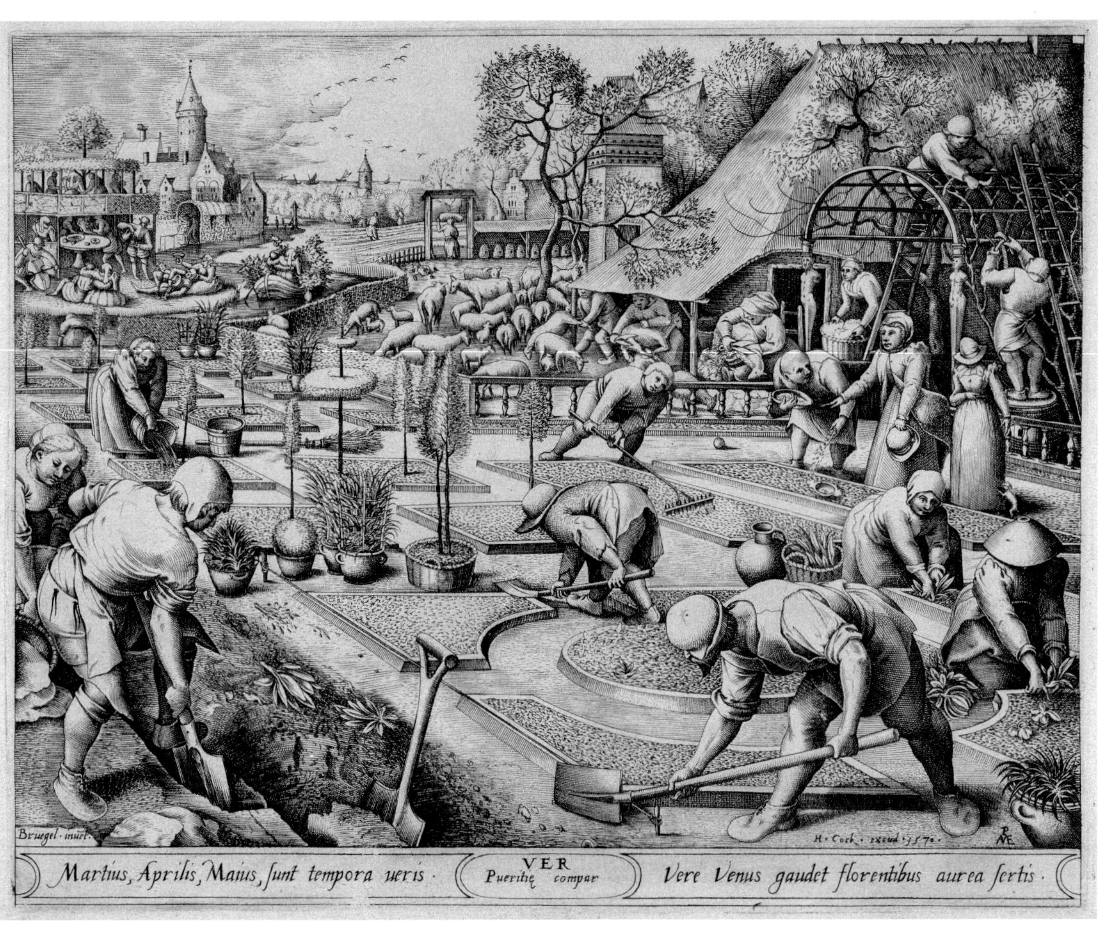

Pieter van der Heyden after Pieter Bruegel the Elder, *Spring*, 1570

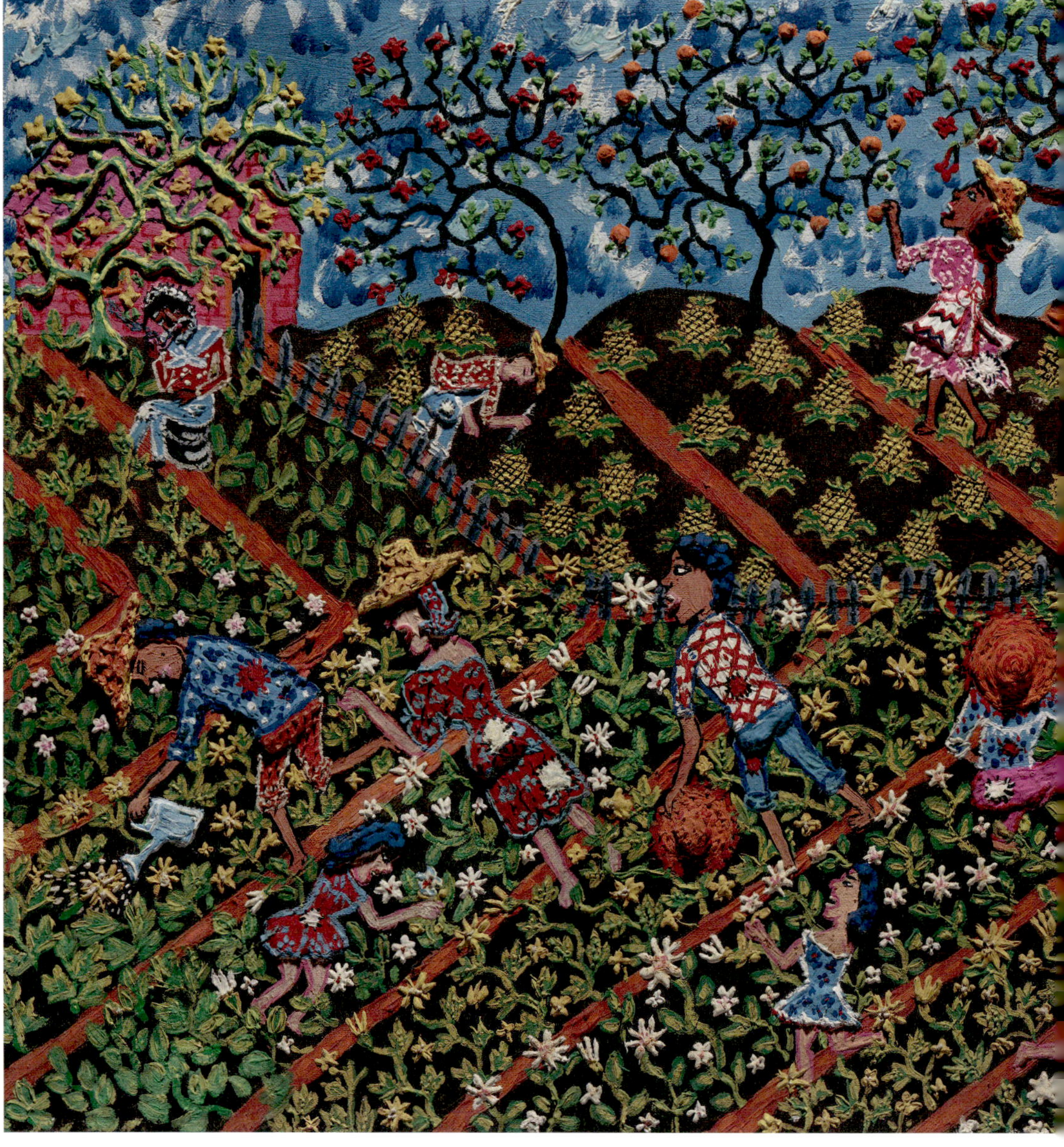

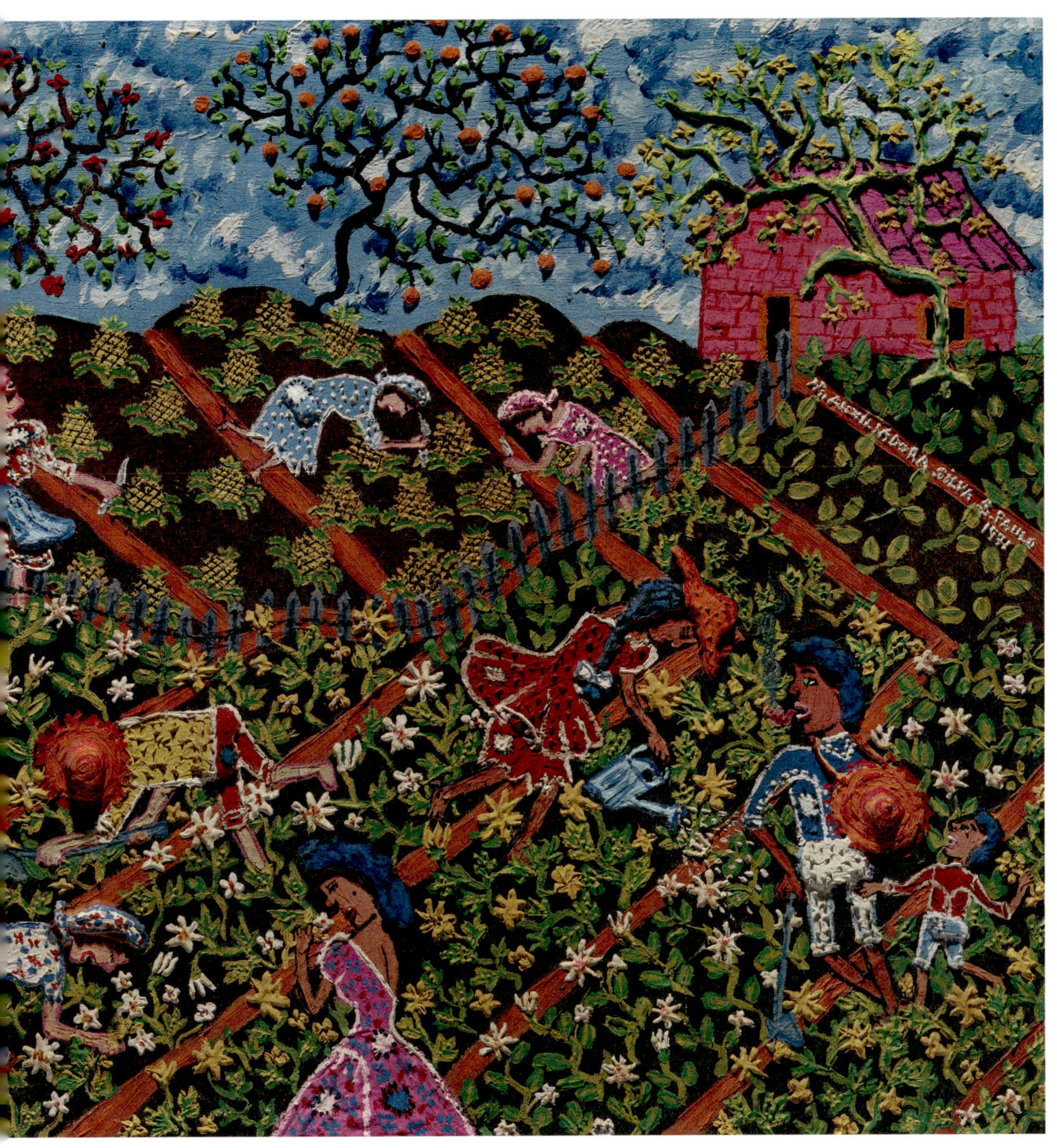

— 57 —
Maria Auxiliadora da Silva, *Plantação*, 1971

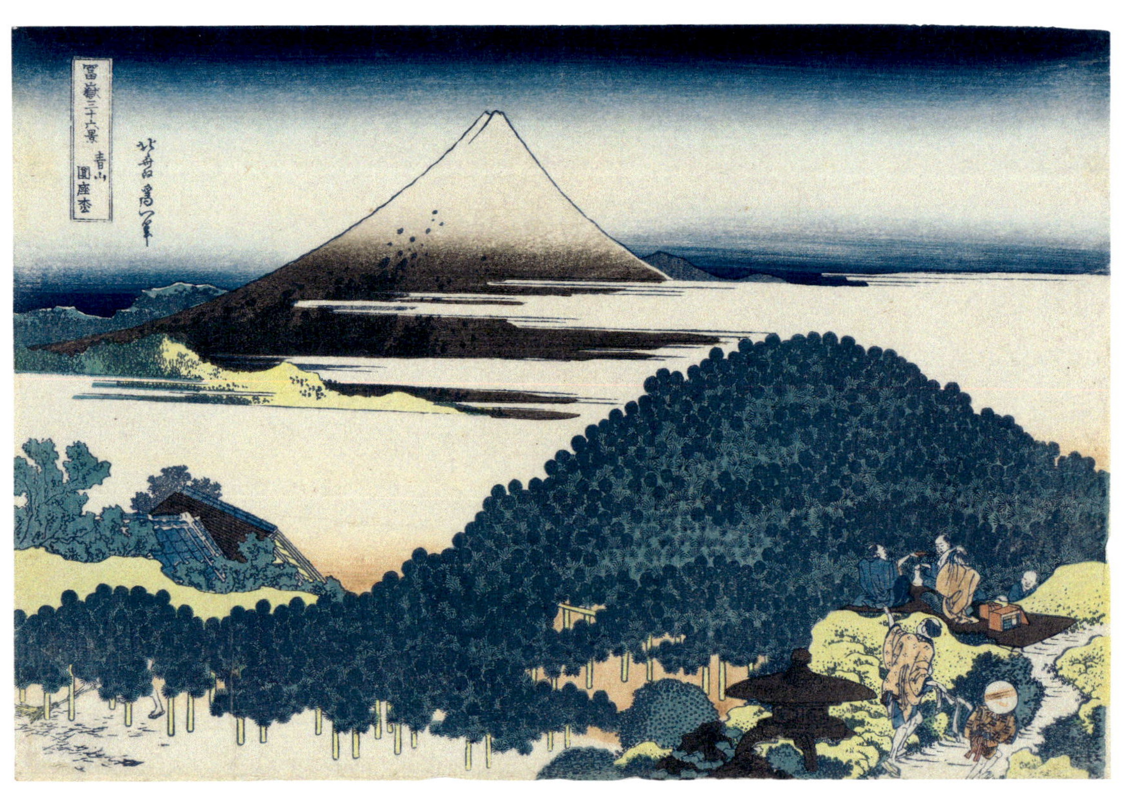

102   Katsushika Hokusai, *The Cushion Pine at Aoyama*, about 1830–31

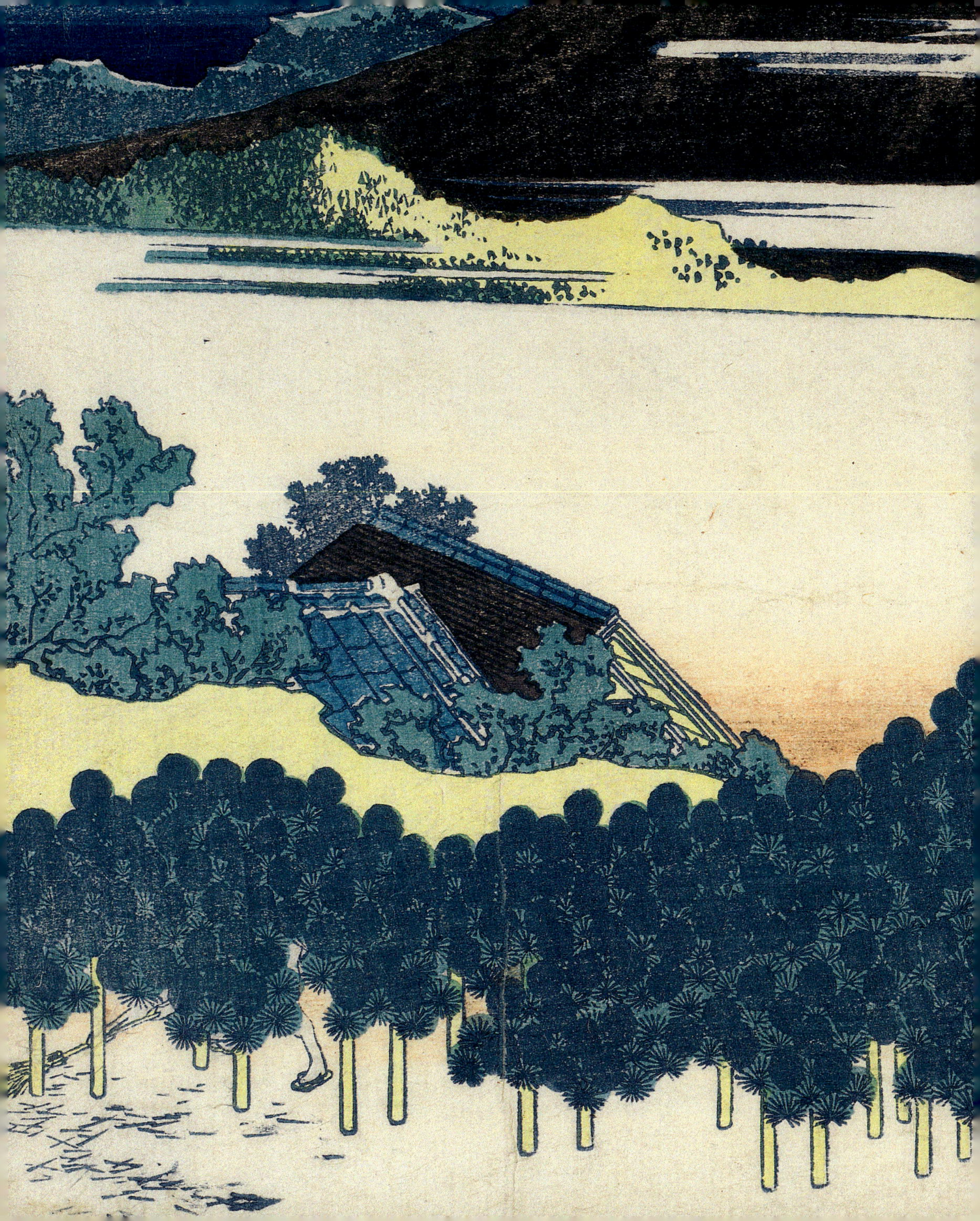

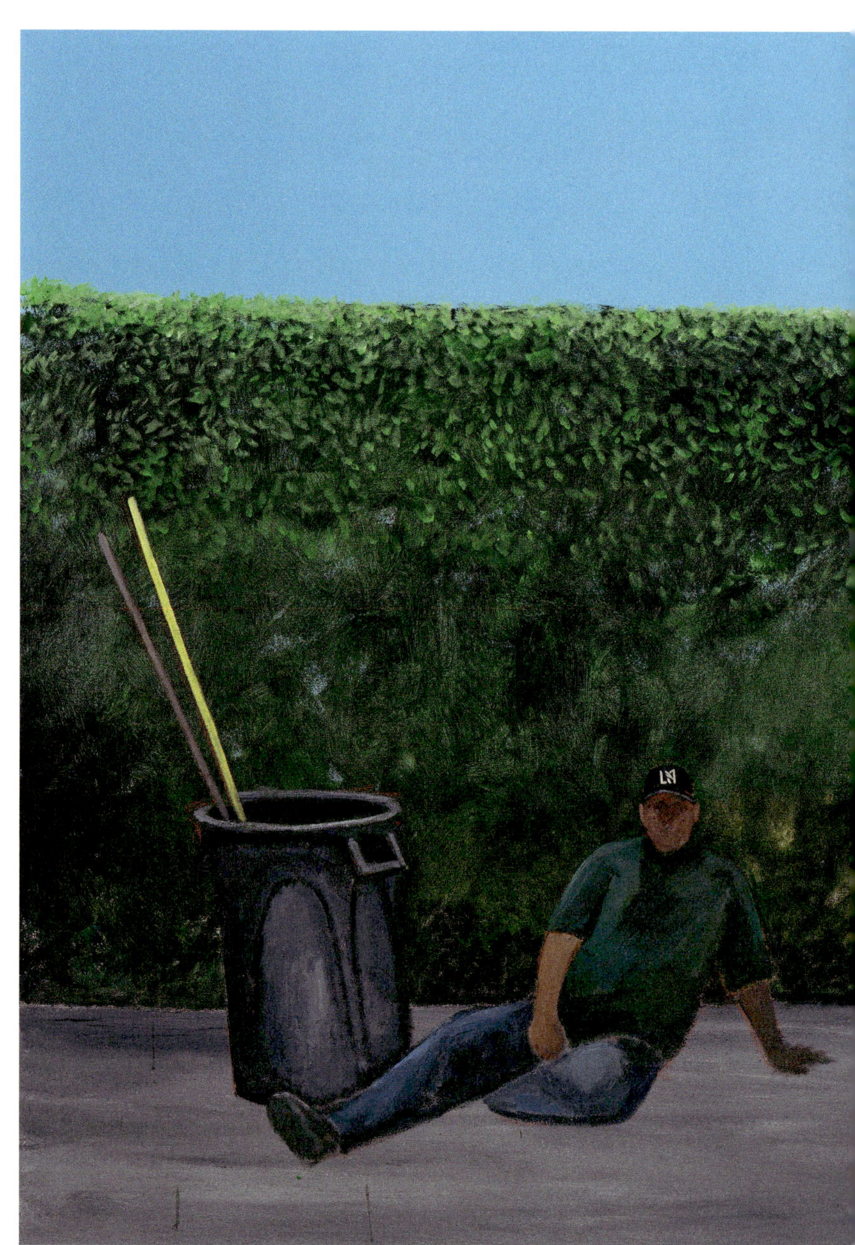

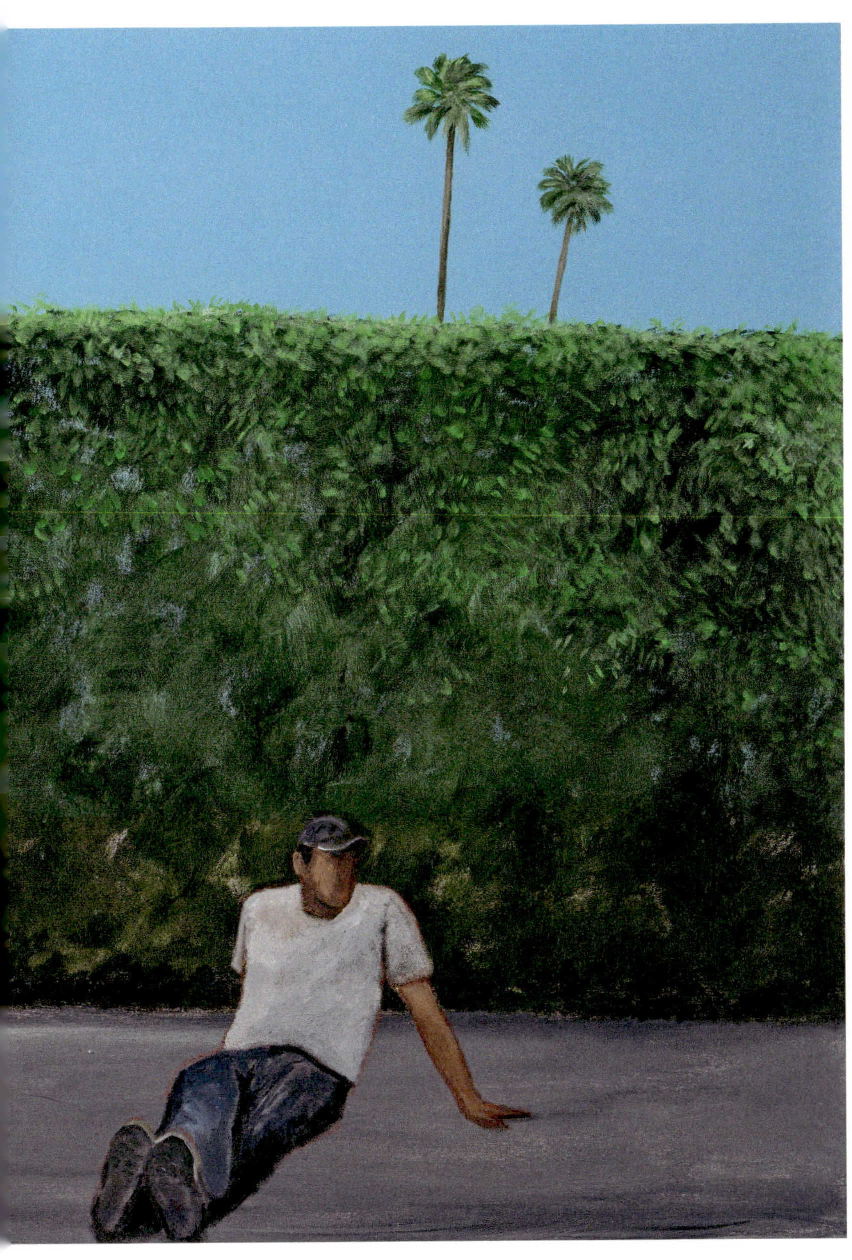

Jay Lynn Gomez, *Resting*, 2019

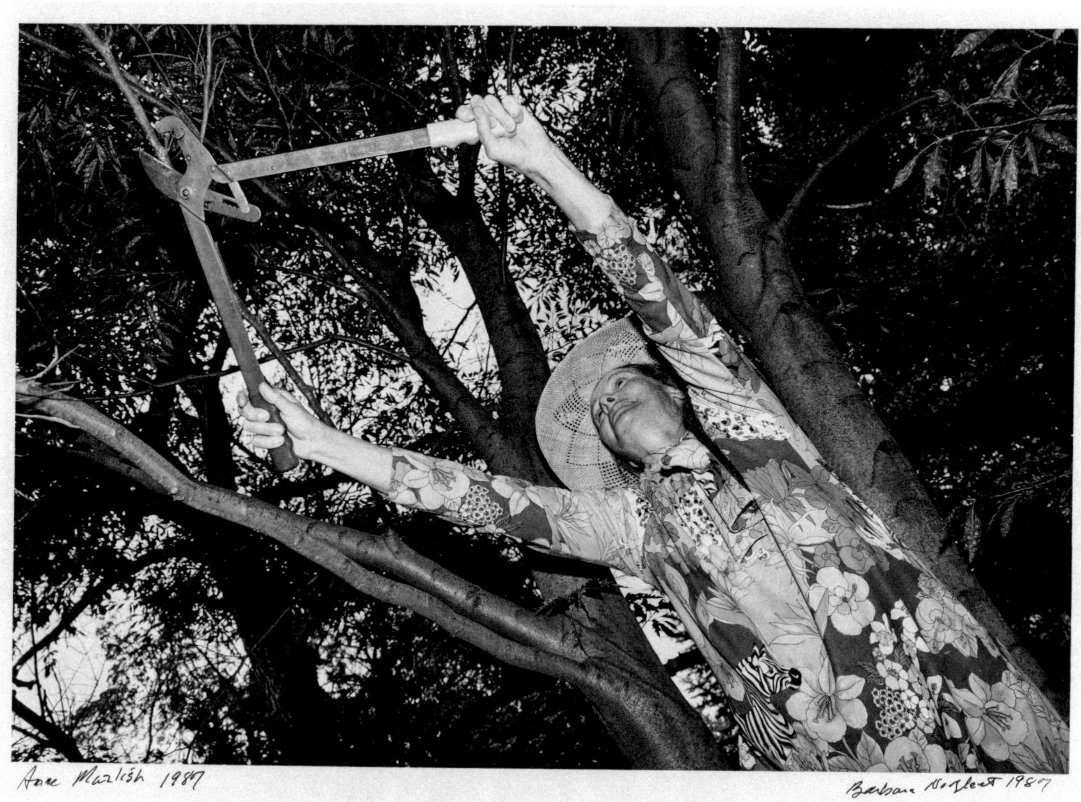

Barbara P. Norfleet, *Anne Mazlish*, 1987

Baili

Baili

Vanga d'hortolano

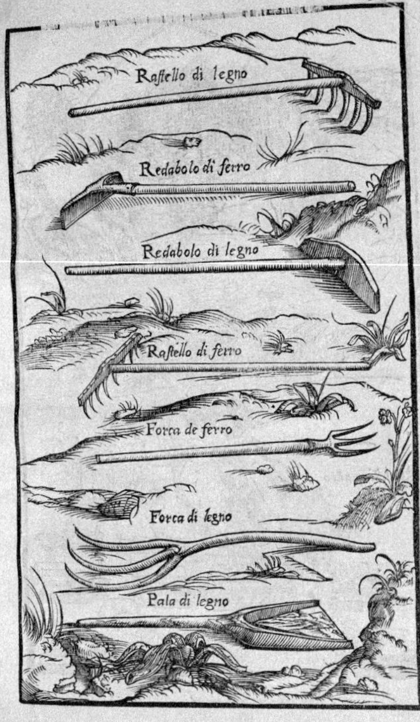

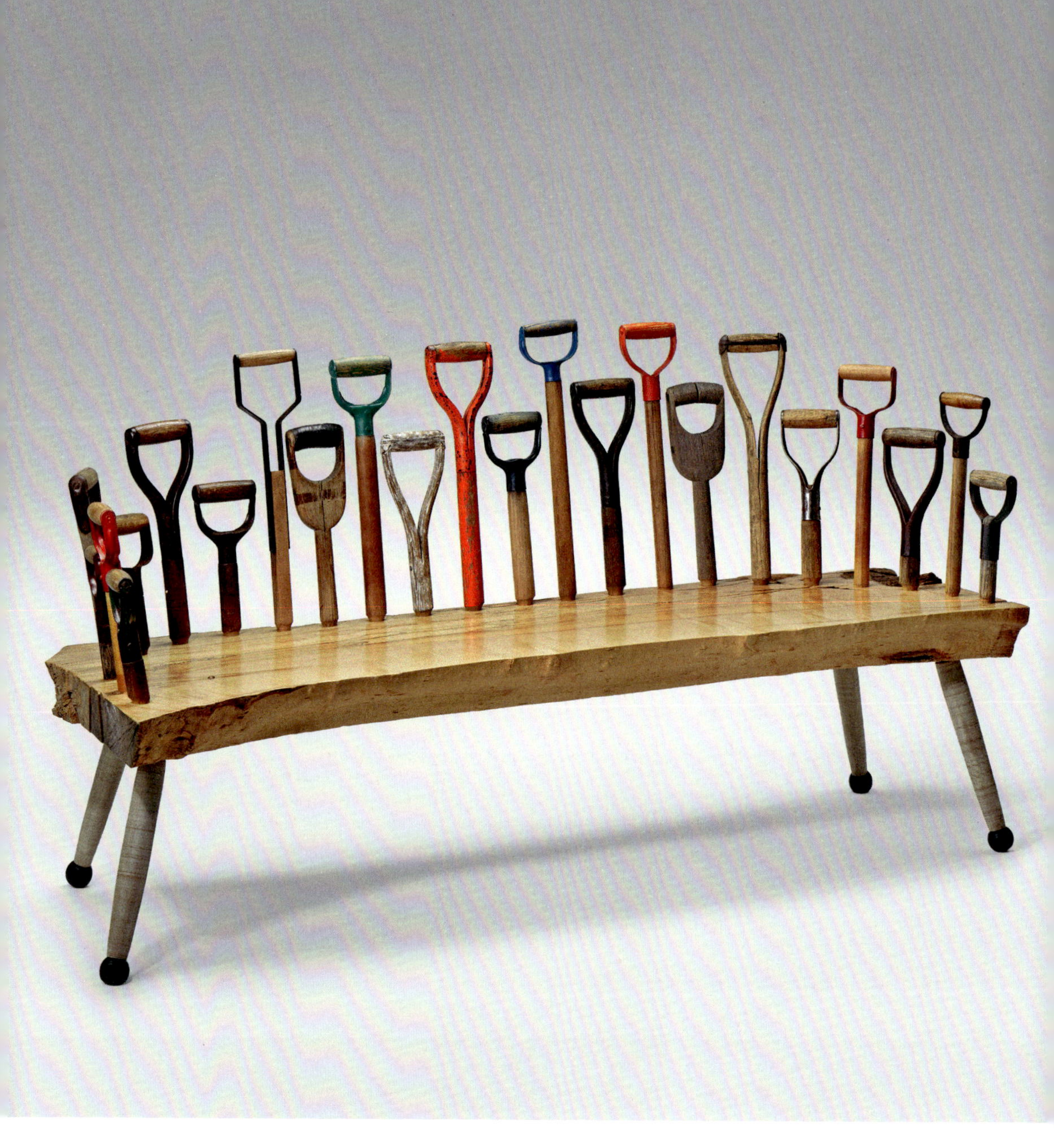

— 62 —

Tom Loeser, *Dig 23*, 2015

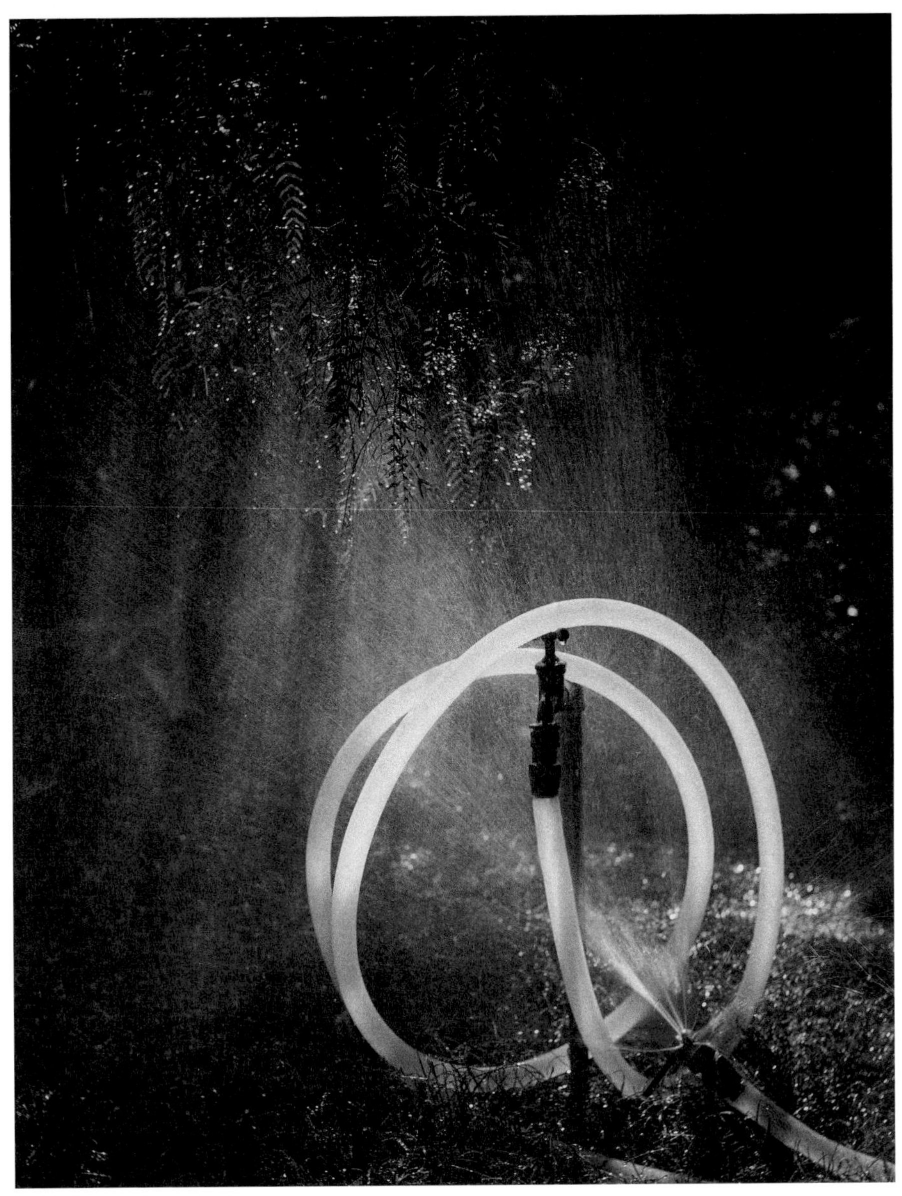

— 63 —

Ruth Bernhard, *Garden Hose*, 1969

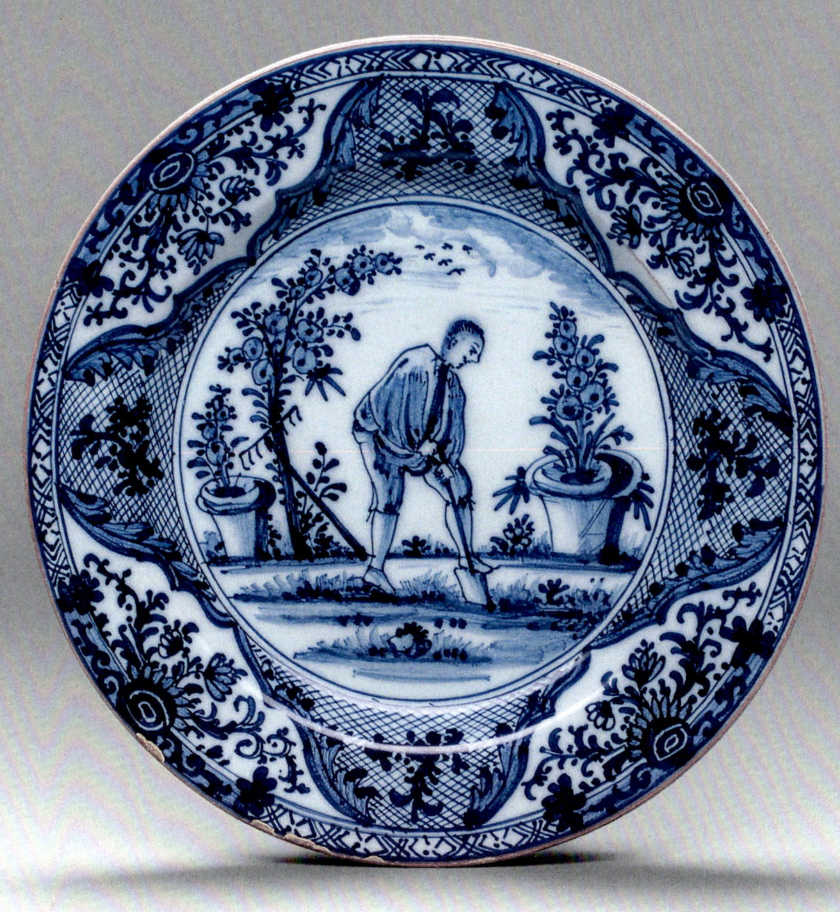

— 64 —

Plate, English, 1774

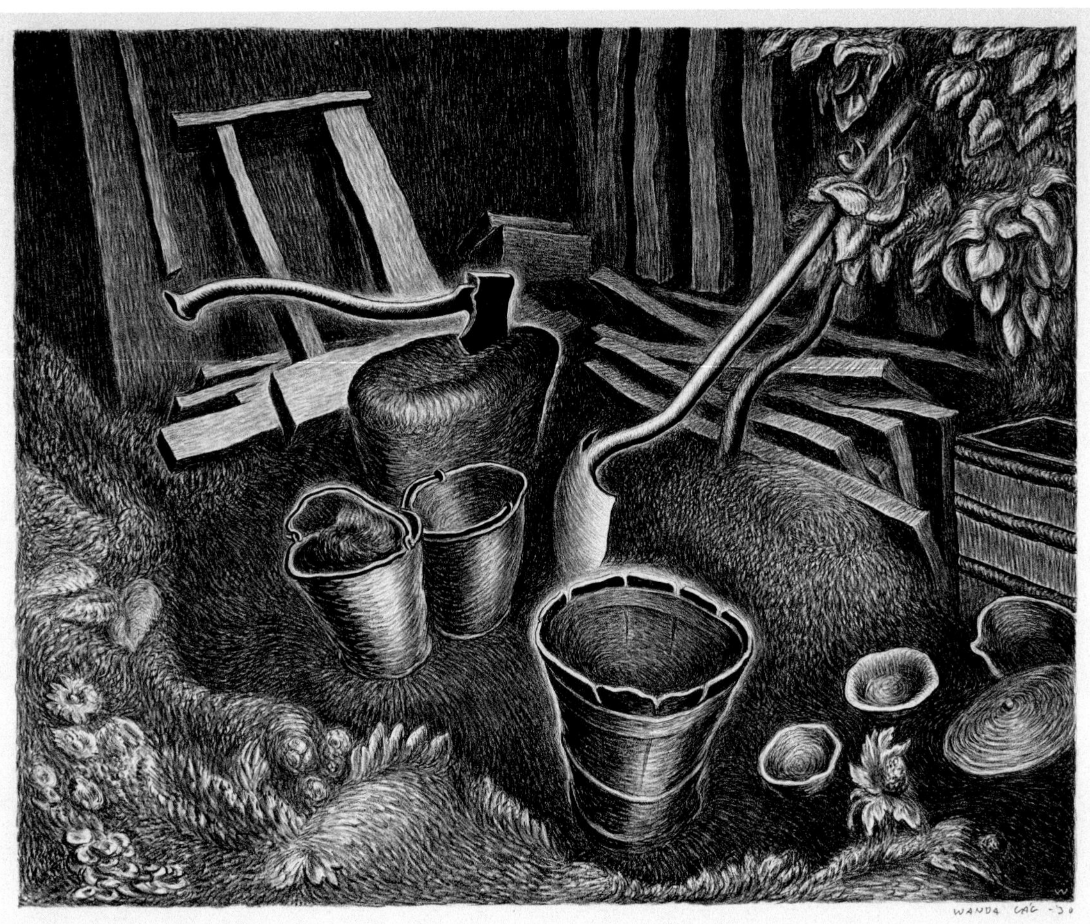

— 65 —

Wanda Gág, *Backyard Corner*, 1930

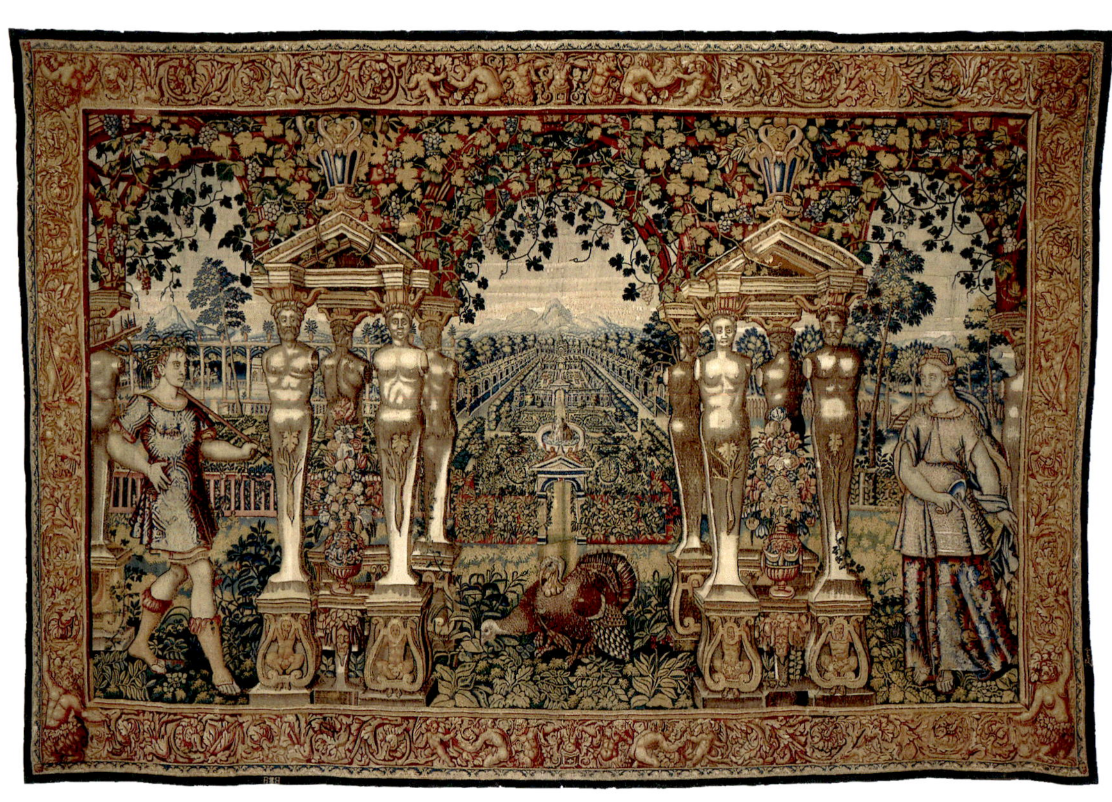

112   Attributed to Jan Cornelisz., *Vertumnus as a Haymaker*, first half of the 17th century

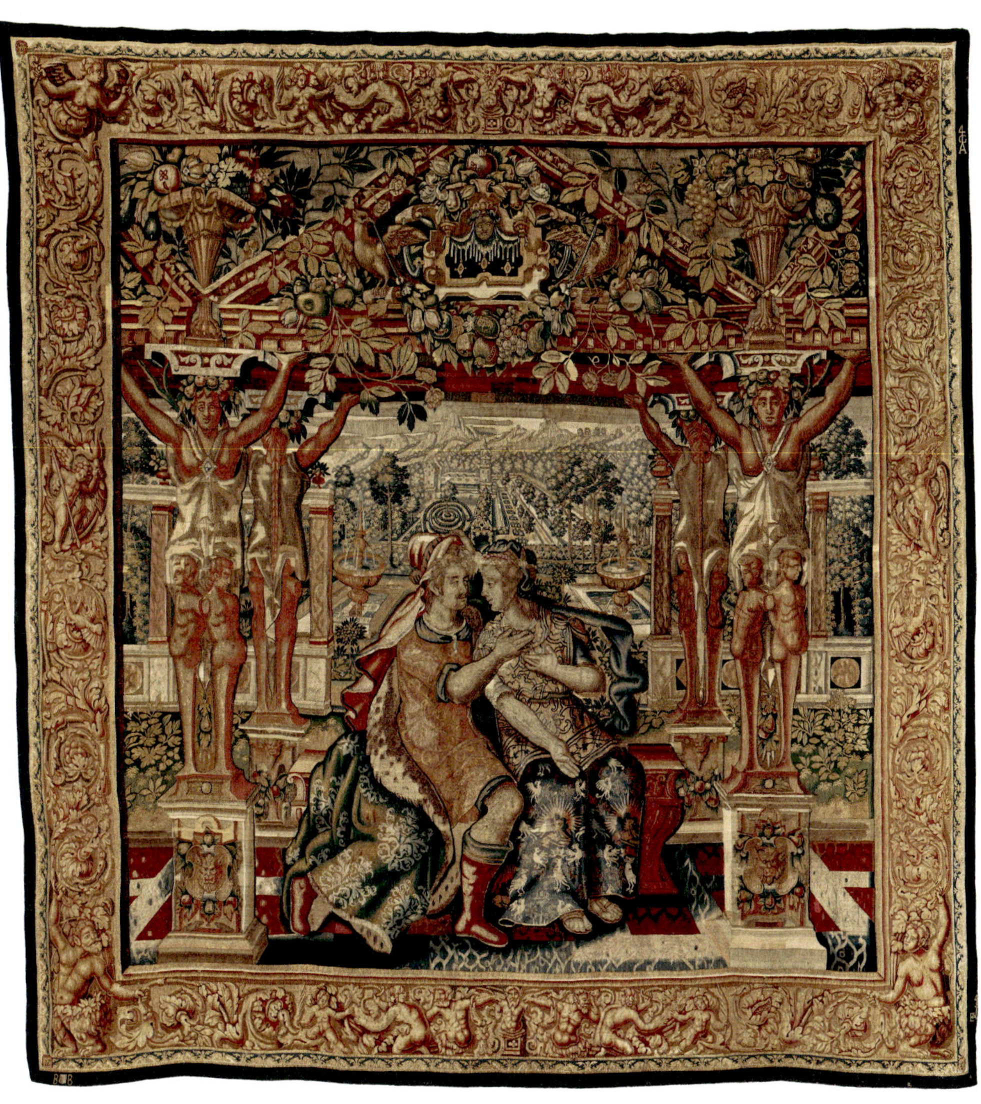

Attributed to Jan Cornelisz., *Vertumnus Throwing off His Disguise*,
first half of the 17th century

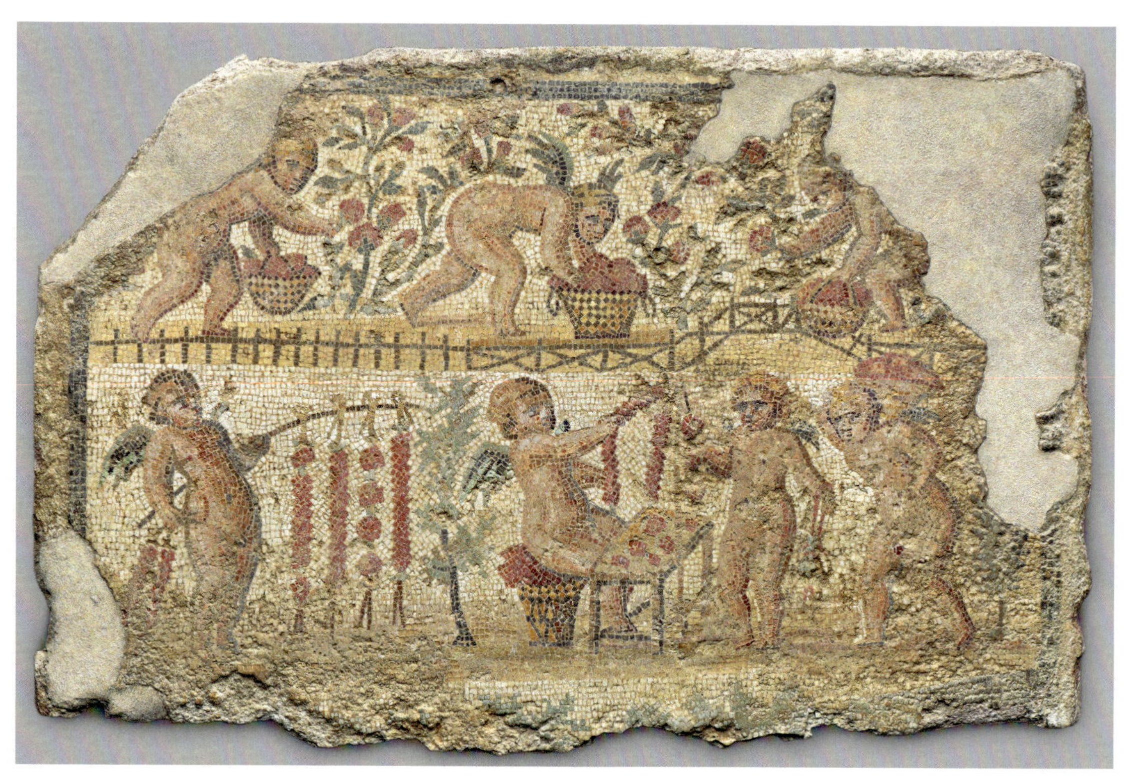

114   Cupids gathering roses in a garden, Roman, late 2nd to mid-3rd century CE

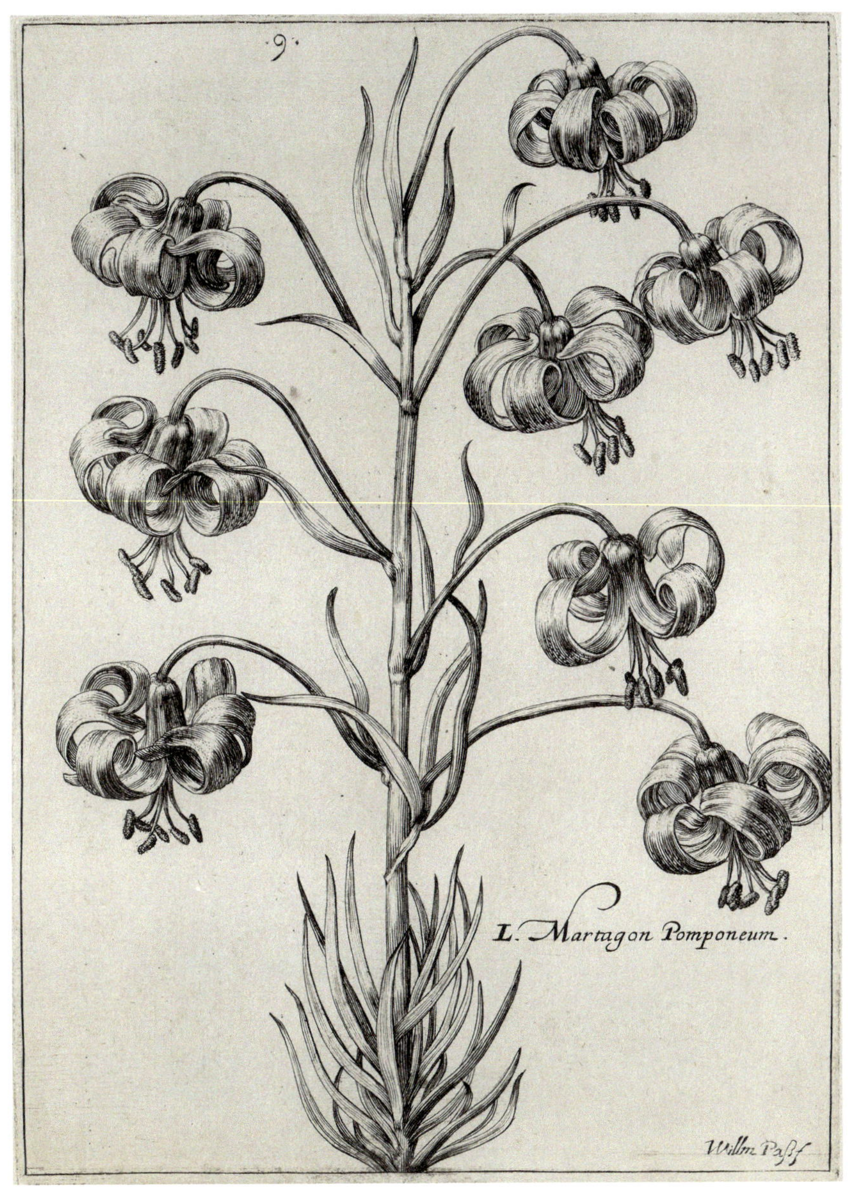

Willem van de Passe, *Martagon Pomponeum*, 1614–17

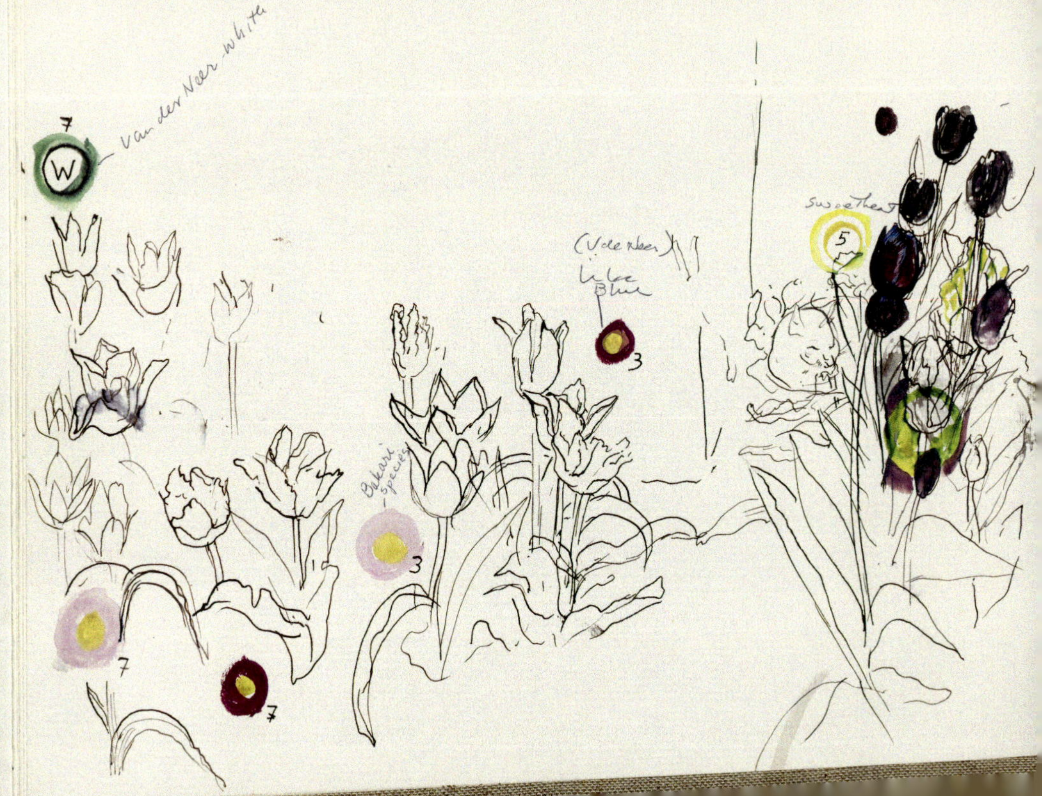
van der Neer white
7
W
(V. de Neer)
Lilac
Blue
3
sweetheart
5
Bakari
species
3
7
7

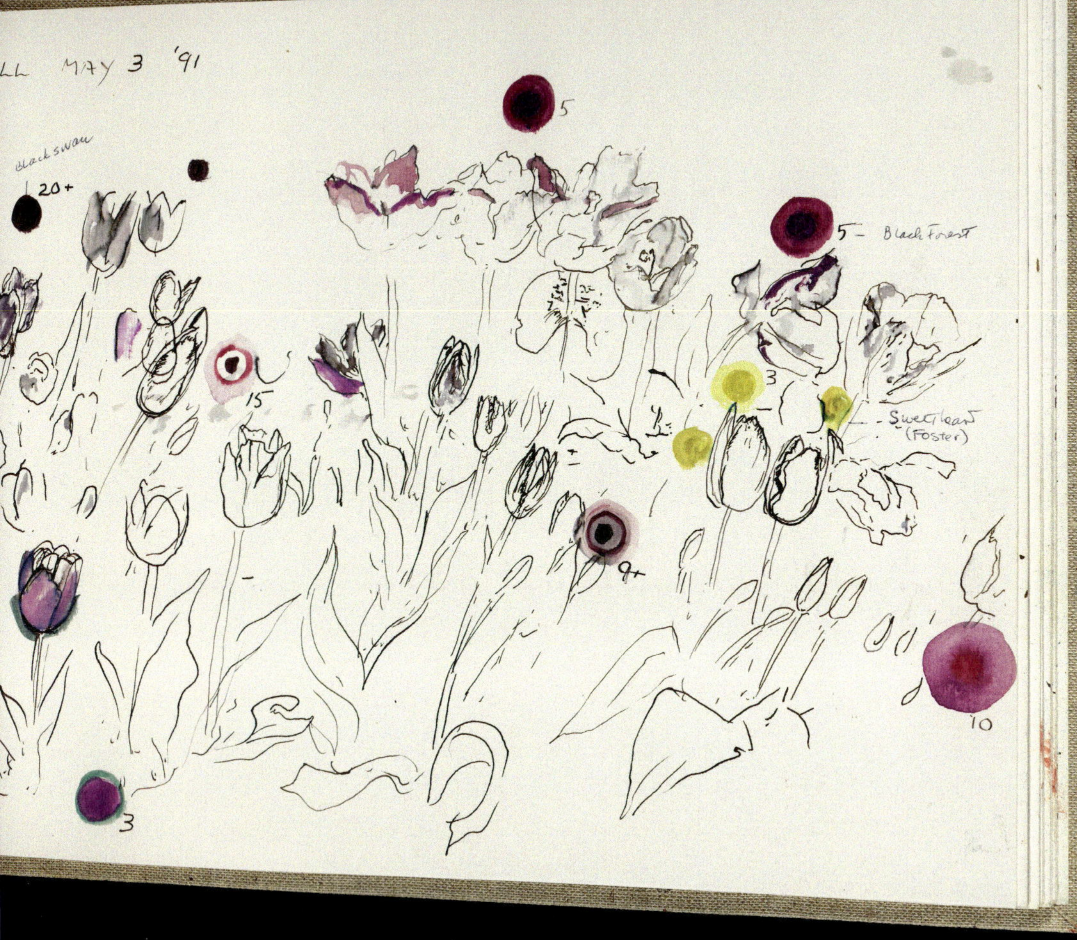
LL MAY 3 '91
5
Black swan
20+
5 — Black Forest
3
15
SweetHeart
(Foster)
9+
10
3

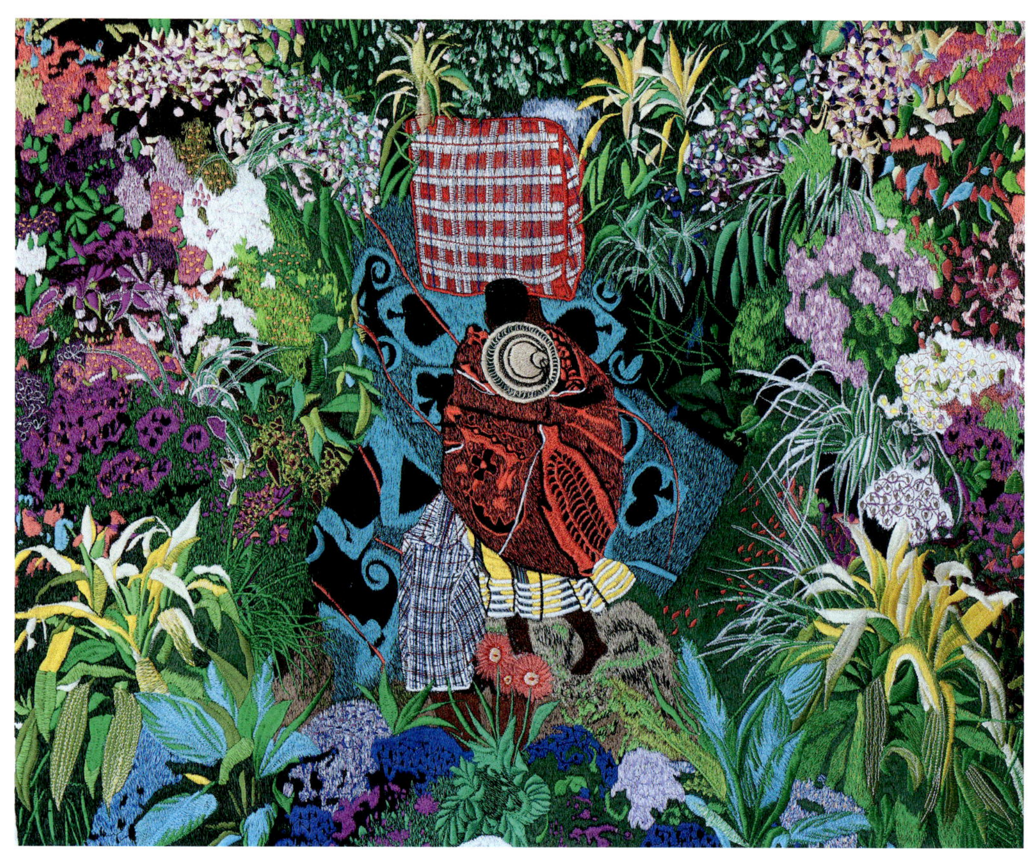

— 71 —
Kimathi Mafafo, *Umtwalo Wami III*, 2019

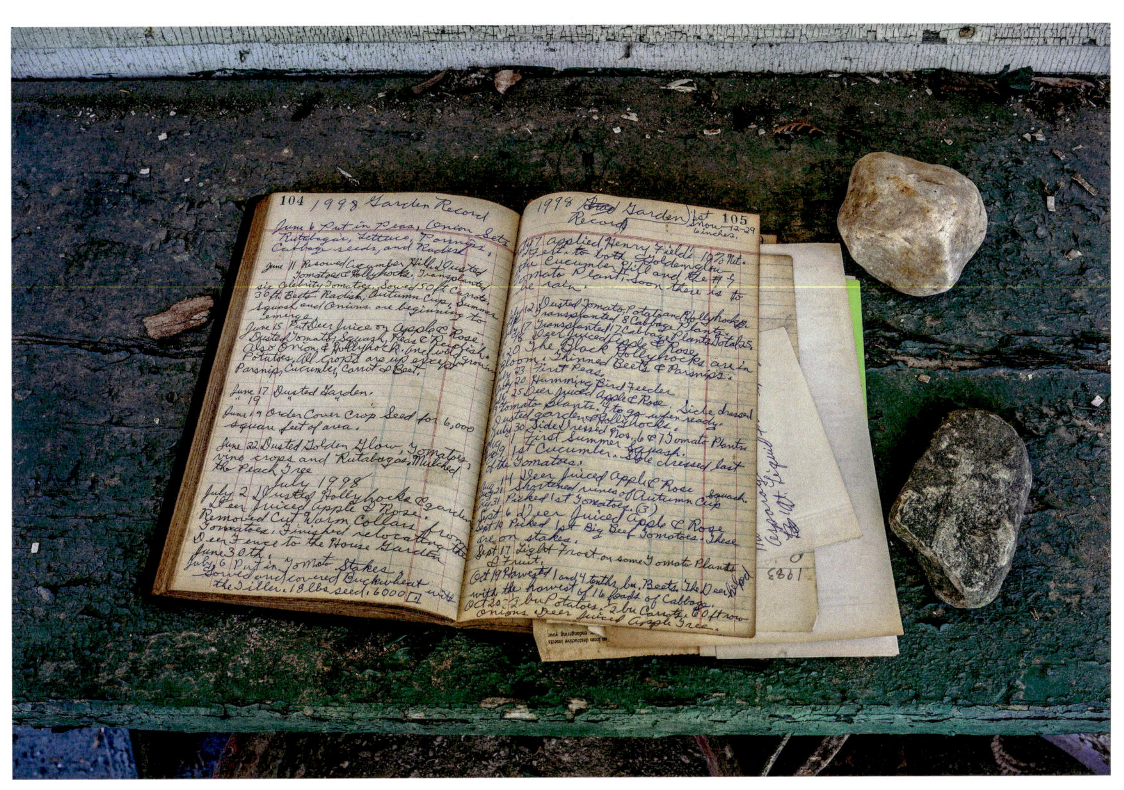

Justin Kimball, *Forest Road, Garden Record*, 2010

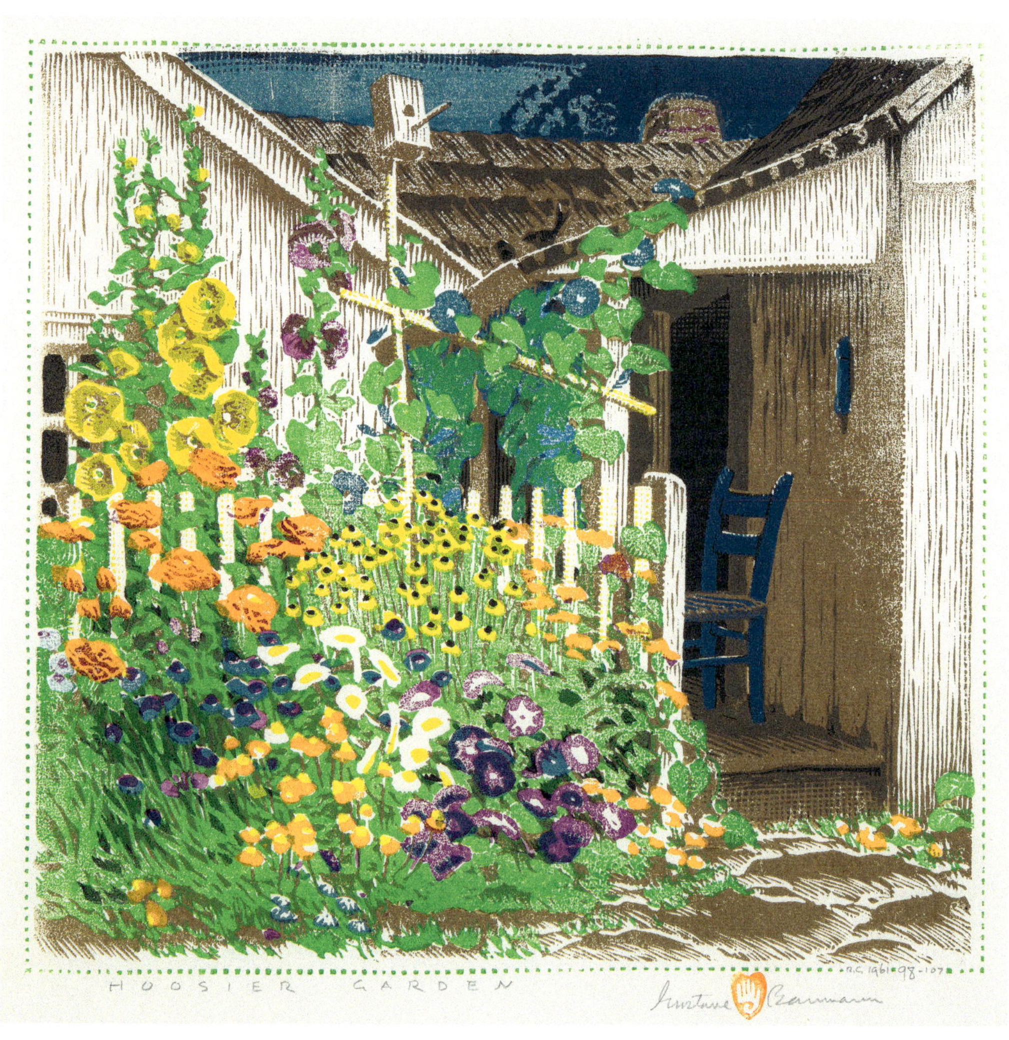

— 73 —

Gustave Baumann, *Hoosier Garden*, 1927

— 74 —

Hilary Pecis, *Hopie in the Garden*, 2021

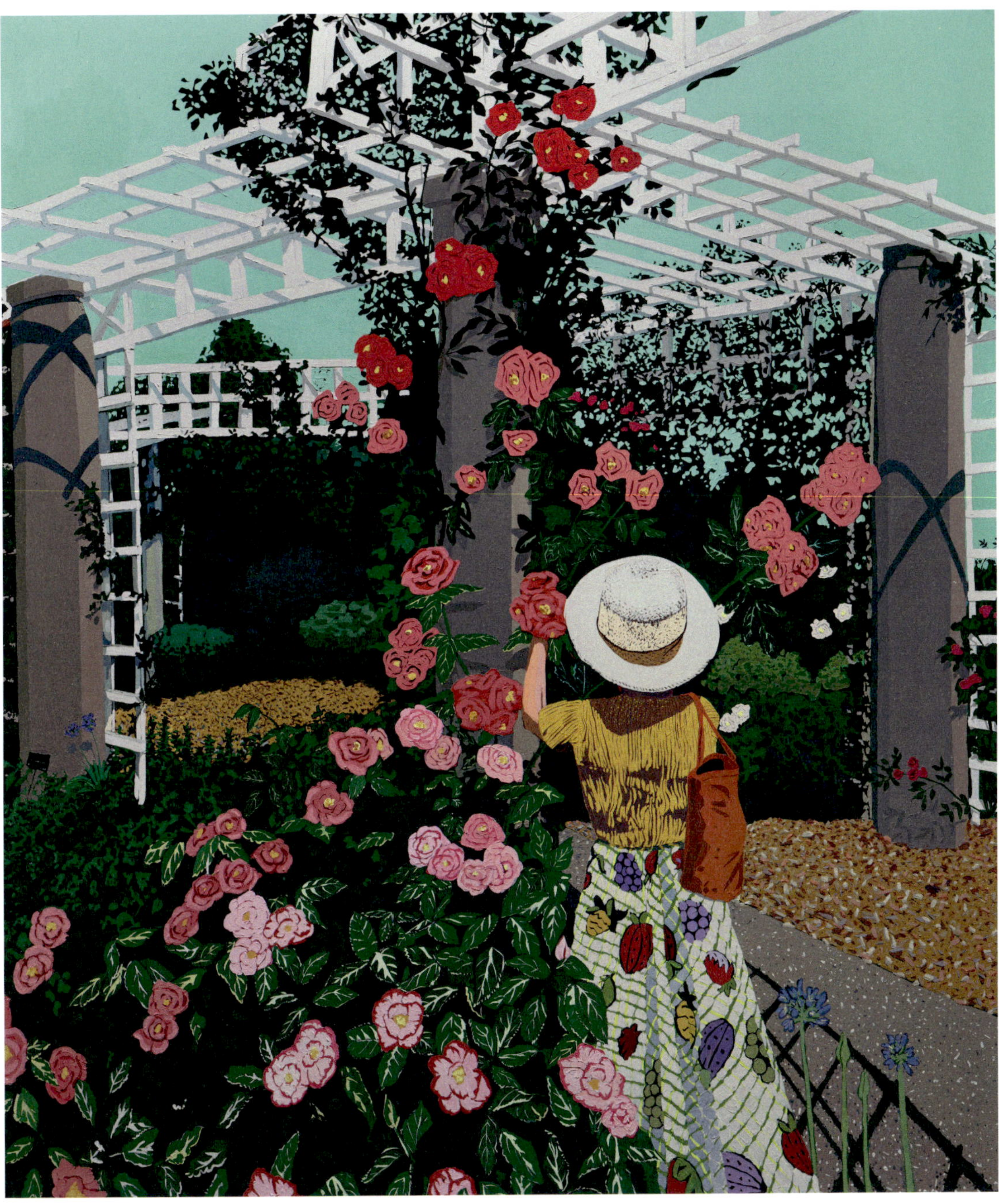

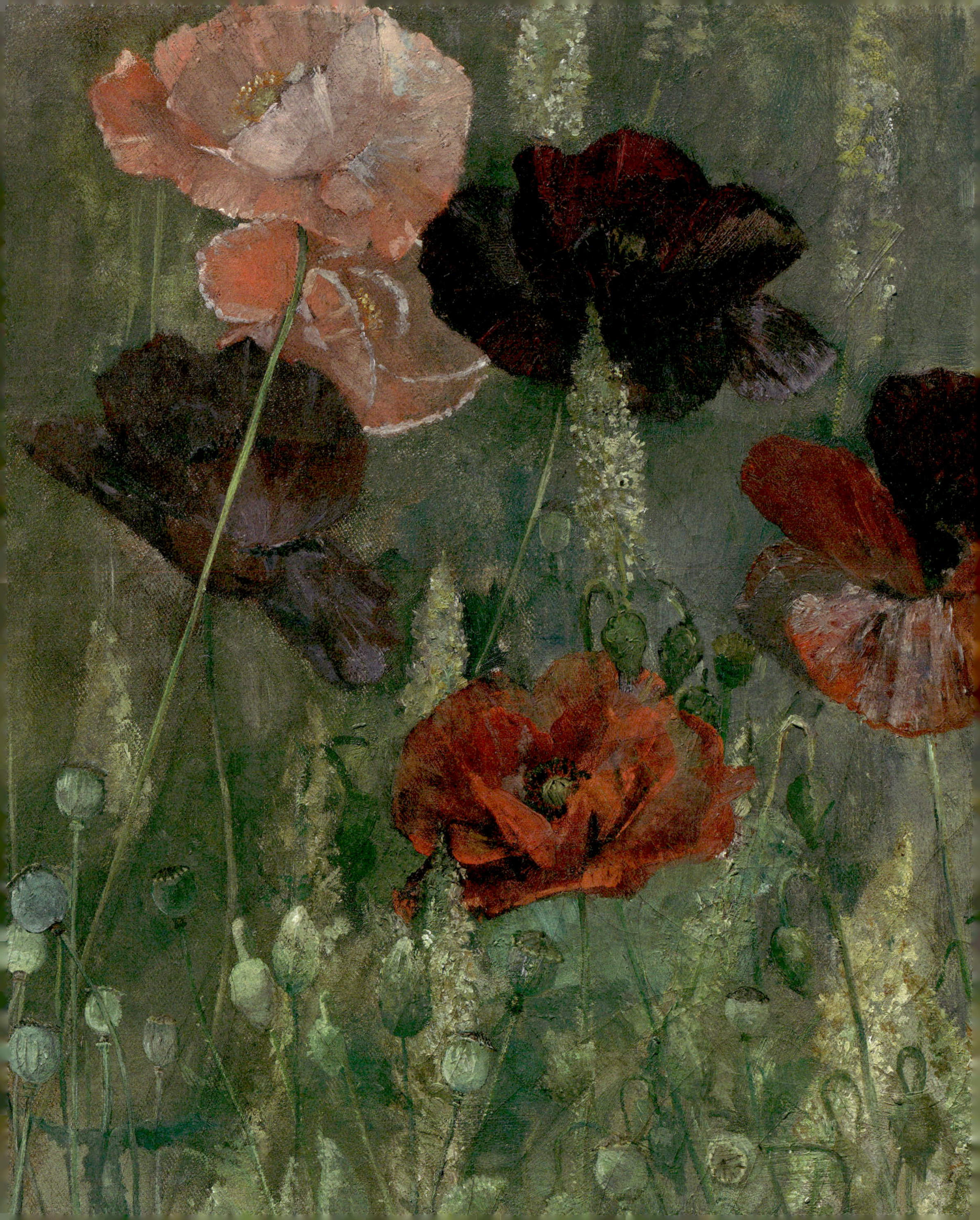

Artists and Gardens

Artists and gardens can be intertwined in different ways. There are artists who depict gardens in their work, through a range of mediums and in different ways, and there are artists who make gardens as part of their artistic practice. For these makers, the garden is the ultimate expression of their craft.

In nineteenth-century North America and Europe, a domestic gardening boom ran parallel with artists working more often out in nature, or *en plein air*. Maria Richards Oakey Dewing, born in New York, trained as a painter in Boston and France, and believed that artists needed to bring their artistic approach to their entire lives to achieve a higher state of being. From 1889 to 1903, Dewing and her husband Thomas (also a painter) spent their summers in an artistic community in Cornish, New Hampshire, where they cultivated a rich garden. Her *Poppies and Italian Mignonette* shows the two flowers growing together in one bed, as they did in her garden (79). This work is a testament to her declaration that any artist attempting to paint from nature should serve "a long apprenticeship in the garden."[1]

Meanwhile, one of the best-known artist-gardeners, Claude Monet, continually turned to his garden at Giverny, outside of Paris, for inspiration. Beginning in 1903, he created a series of paintings of his water garden, with its lily pads and glimmering reflective surfaces (78). The resulting works are variations on the theme under different lighting conditions and show the way in which a garden is never static. For an artist seeking continued inspiration, there is no better source material than a living, breathing, always changing space.

Gardens can also be a place for artists to tell stories about themselves, or to share narratives that may be significant to their lived experiences and working practice. May Morris, an important figure in art embroidery and the Arts and Crafts movement in England at the end of the nineteenth century, was an avid gardener at her home in the Oxford countryside, Kelmscott Manor. She translated this love of the earth and greenery into a set of four *portières*, or curtains, which teem with growth and floral forms (83). Embroidered on a damask called "Oak," the background patterning echoes the vitality of the decoration of fruit trees bearing plums, pomegranates, apples, and cherry blossoms. Inscriptions on the curtains reference either a song about the cuckoo's call in summer, or the way a silkworm feeds on mulberry leaves to create silk, the material used for this ambitious work. The inscriptions' storytelling interwoven with the lush sensory experience of the works further enhances the connection between the artist and the garden in which she found inspiration.

Claudio Eshun unspools his story in a very different way in *Untitled (Our Family's Garden)*. Here Eshun is at center with notebook in hand, and he stages his family frozen in classical poses in their mother's garden outside Worcester, Massachusetts (82). Eshun was born in Ghana, grew up in Italy, and then moved to Massachusetts, where he uses his photography practice to tell the tale of his struggle to reconstruct his identity as a young Black man in a new culture. His mother, the matriarch, sits at the center of the composition, rooting the family in their verdant garden and helping create a sense of connection to the place that balances Eshun's feelings of "alienation, adaptation, and assimilation."[2]

Anthony Green's unusual and perhaps unsettling painting *The Flower Arranger/Early Summer* is characteristic of his work as it shows both the artist himself and a glimpse into his home life in his almost neon green garden (75). Green rarely worked in standard formats, instead preferring irregularly shaped canvases; furthermore, here, he tilted the perspective so that the entire garden is visible behind him, and is seen in full. At just off center, Green himself, is *in* green, and the garden is a reflection of his mind and his work.

A kind of magic happens when artists embrace gardens, either by tending those gardens as places of cyclical or varied inspiration, or as places that reflect their personalities and their artistic instincts. — CLH

— NOTES —

1. Maria Oakey Dewing, "Flower Painters and What the Flower Offers to Art," *Art and Progress* 6 (June 1915): 262.

2. Claudio Eshun, artist's statement about the series *Elegant Alien*, available online at claudioeshun.com.

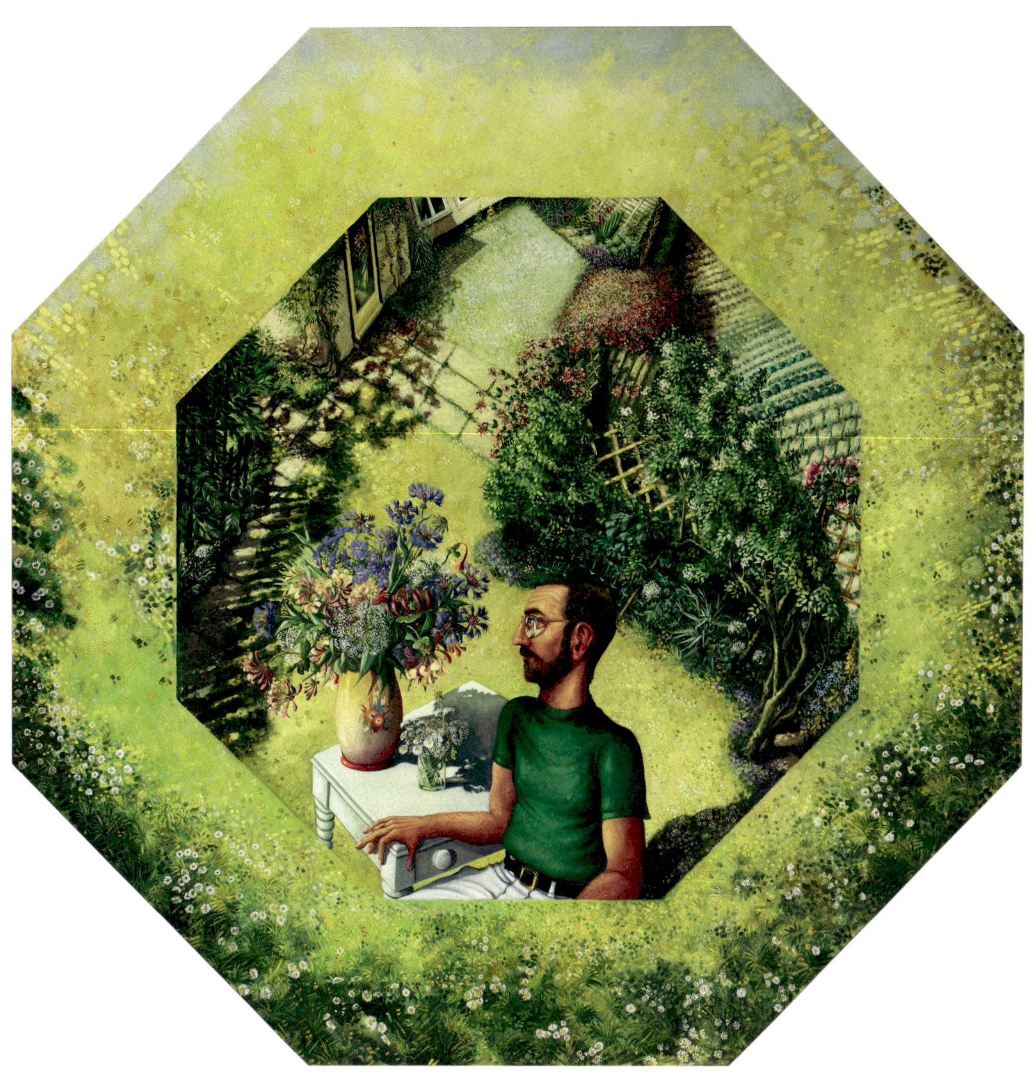

Anthony Green, *The Flower Arranger/Early Summer*, 1982

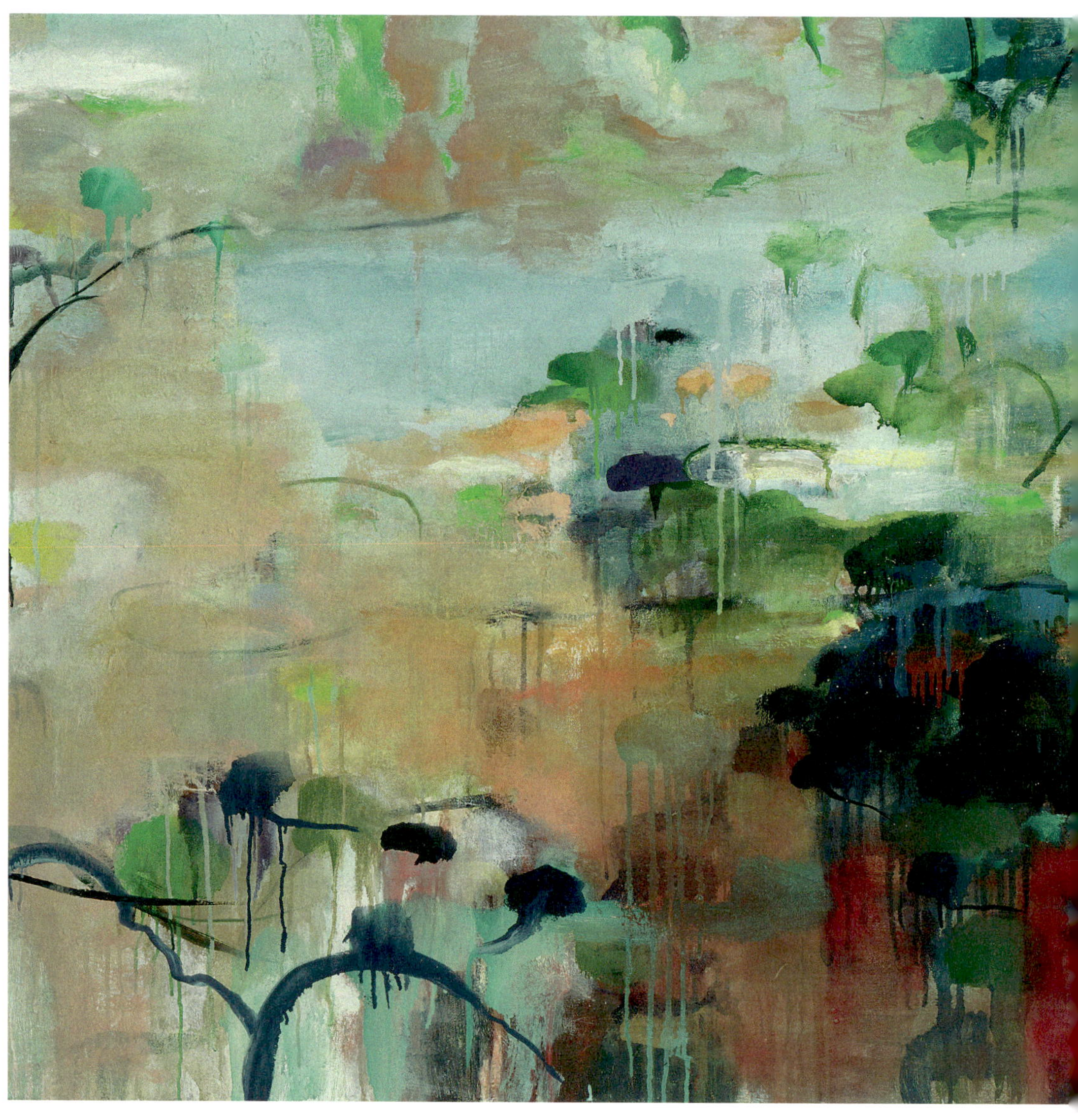

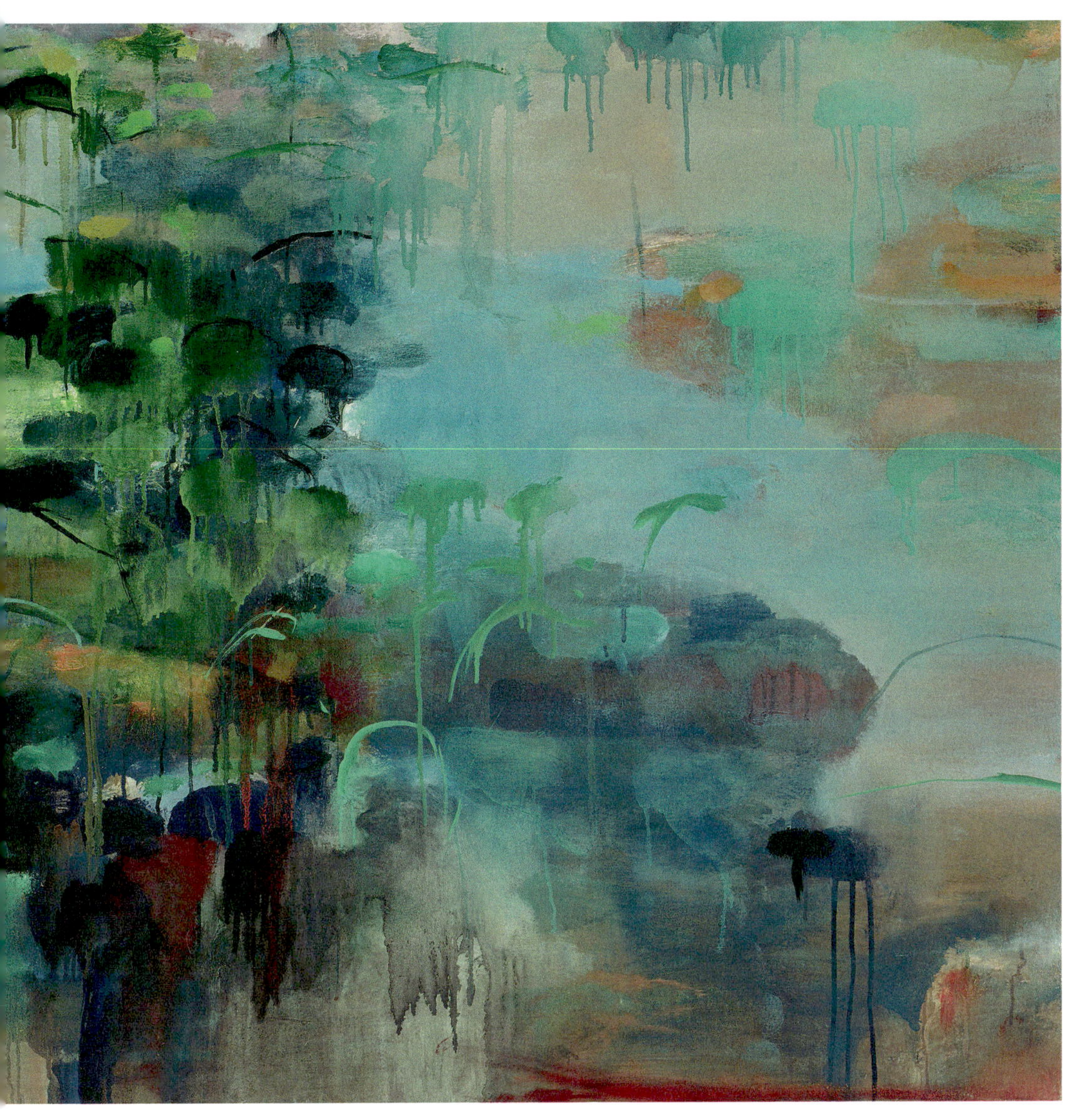

Michael Mazur, *Growth*, 1996–97

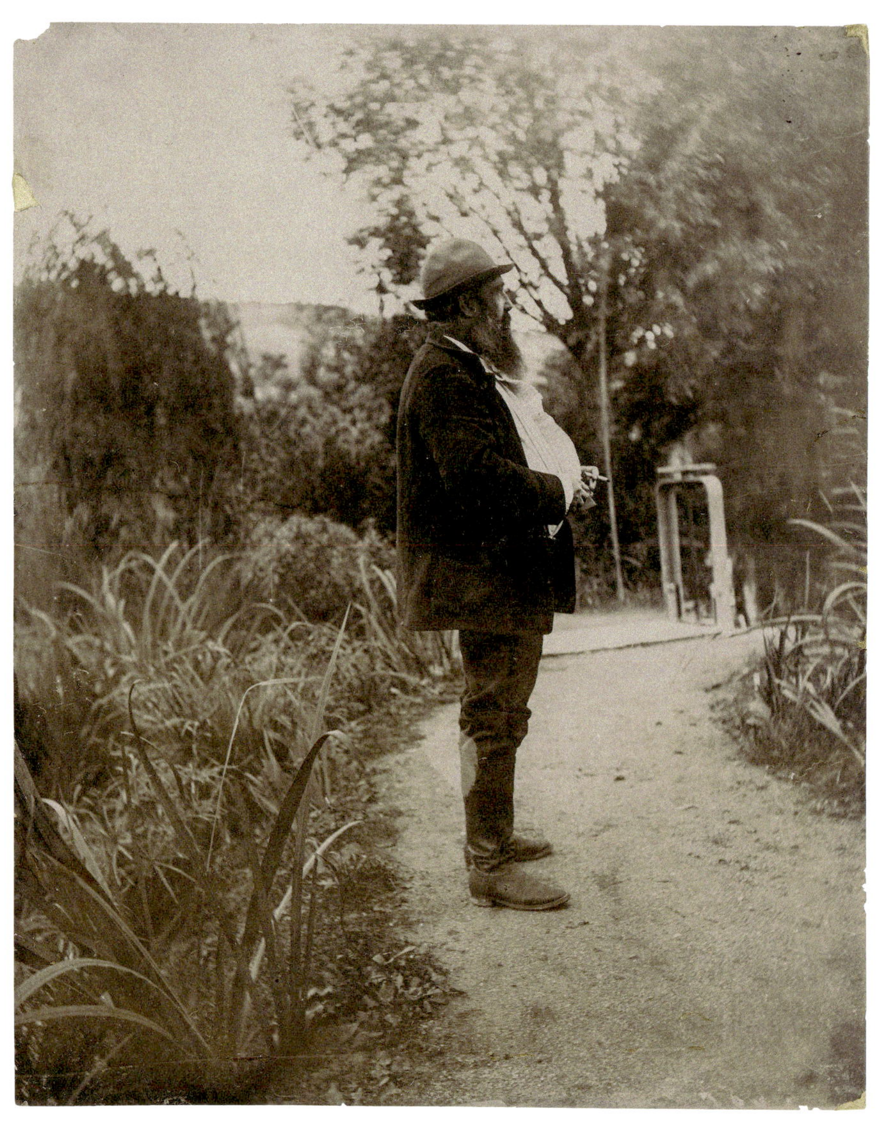

 Lilla Cabot Perry, Monet in his garden, Giverny, 1890–95

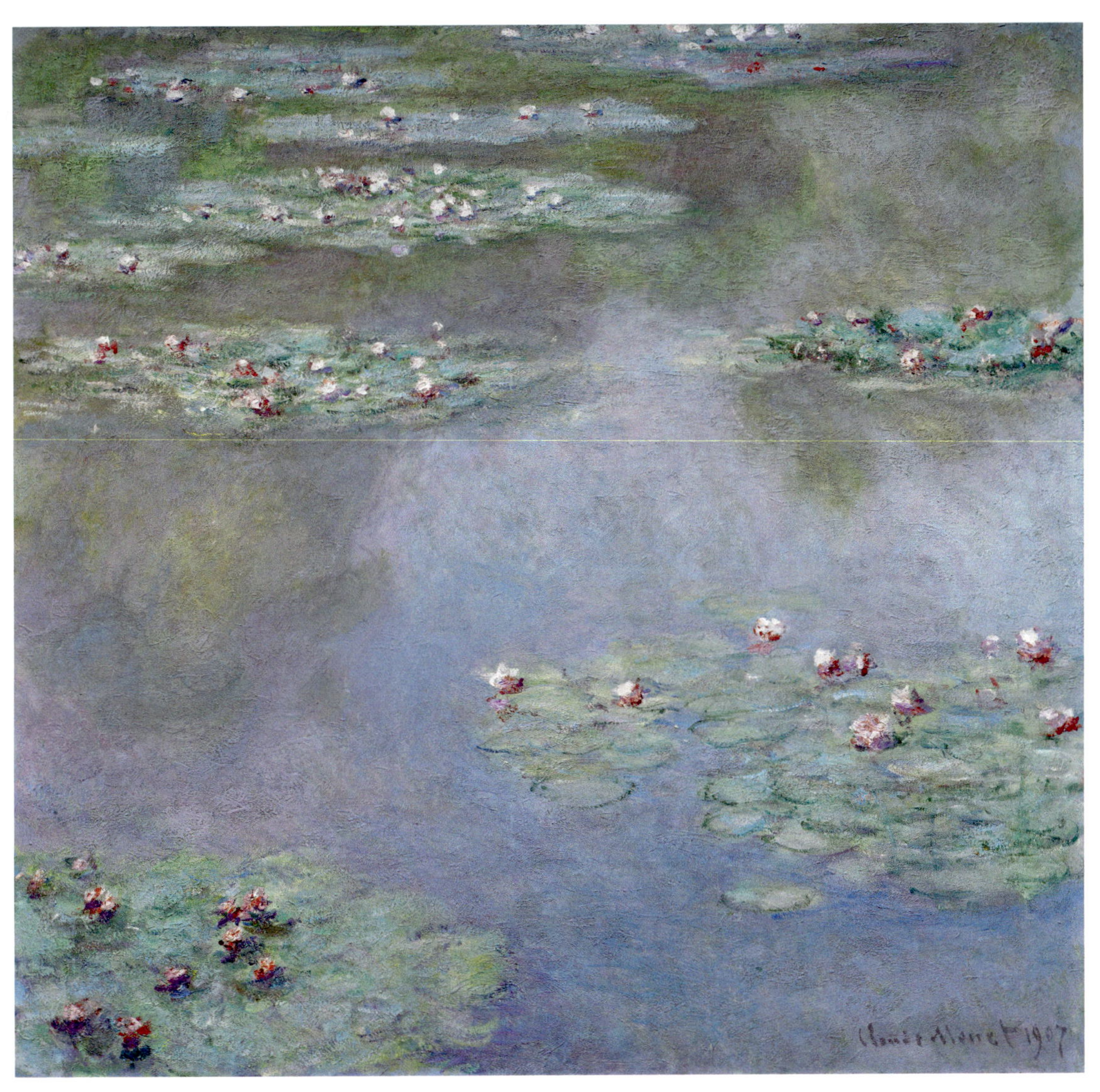

— 78 —

Claude Monet, *Water Lilies*, 1905

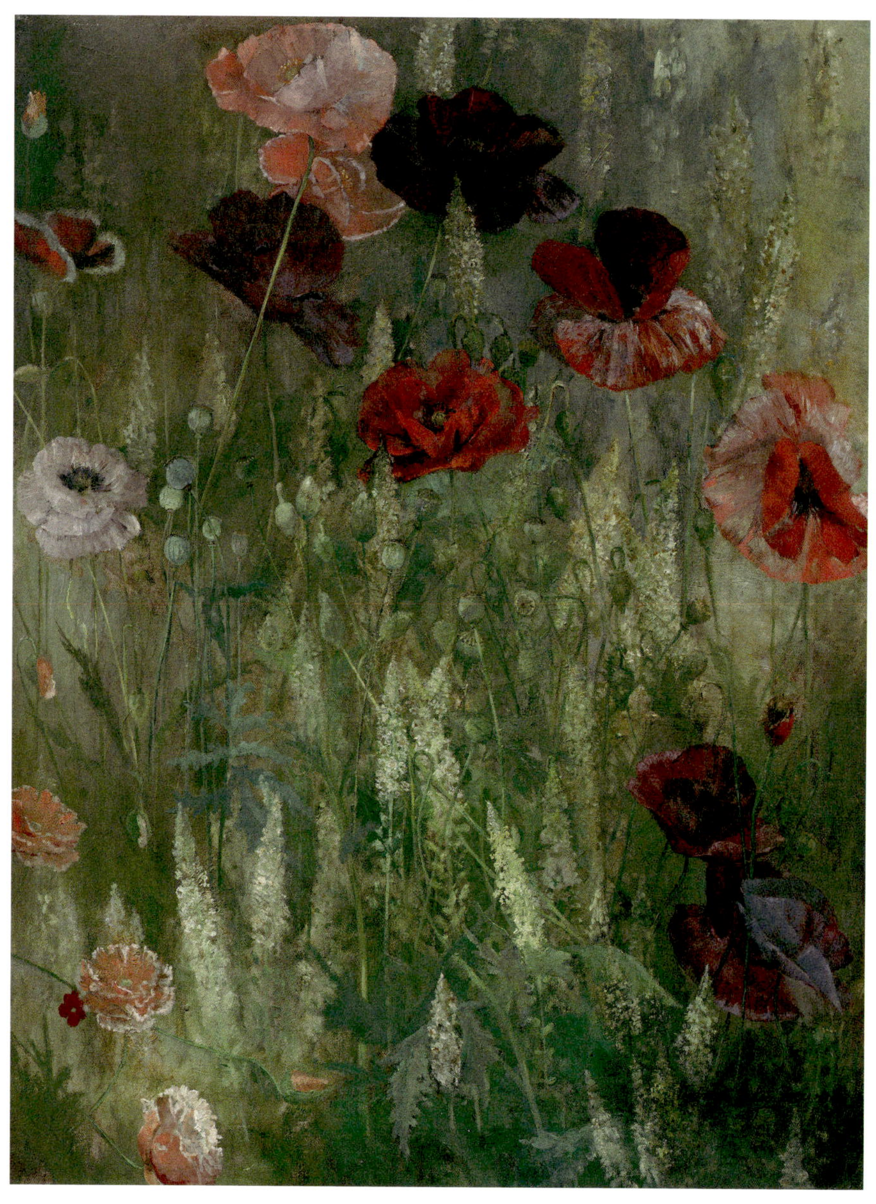

134 Maria Richards Oakey Dewing, *Poppies and Italian Mignonette*, 1891

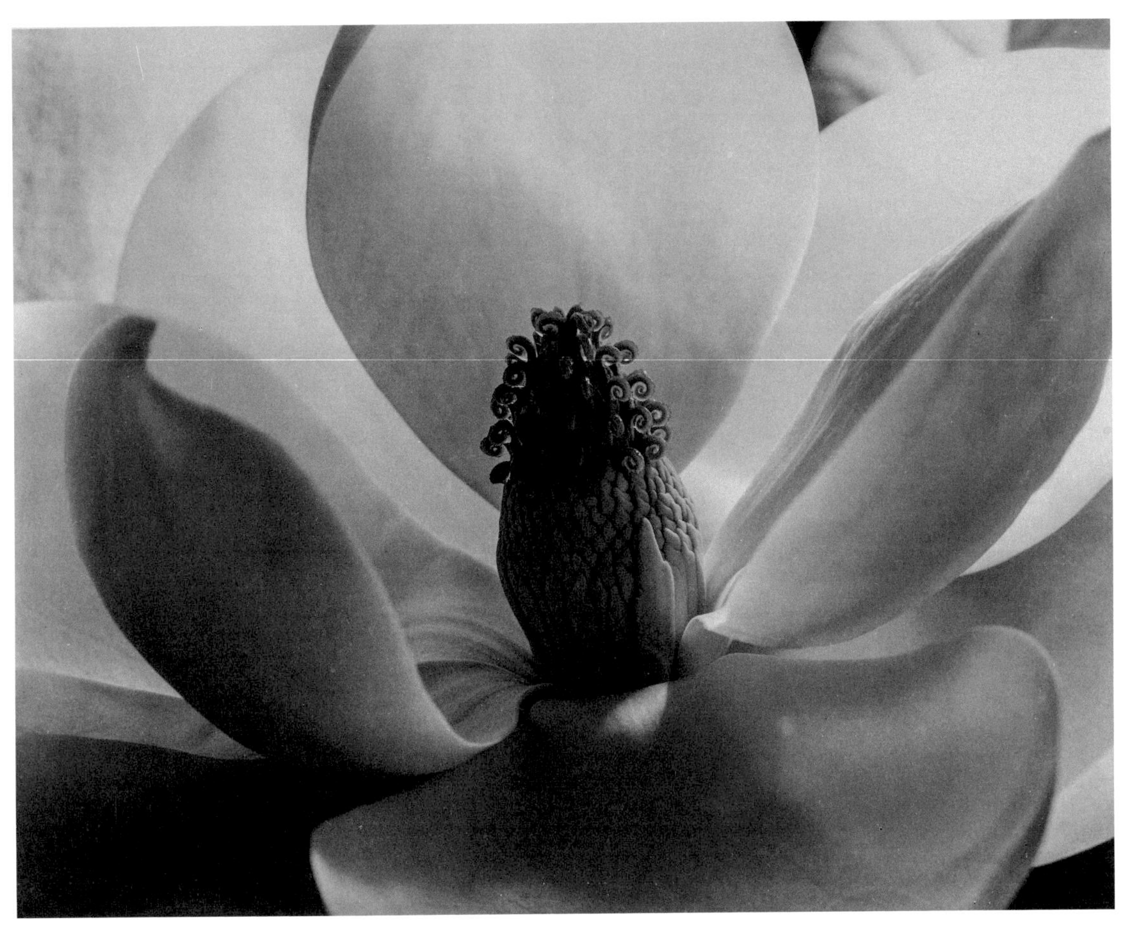

Imogen Cunningham, *Magnolia Blossom*, 1925

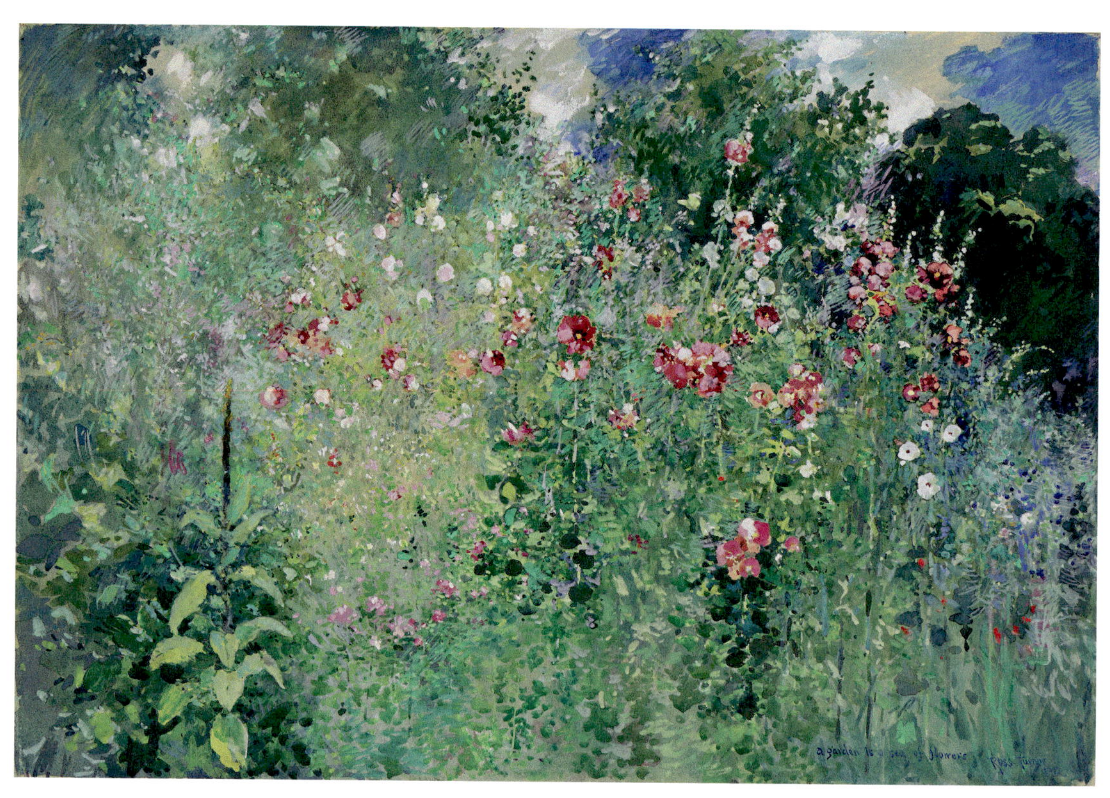

Ross Sterling Turner, *A Garden Is a Sea of Flowers*, 1912

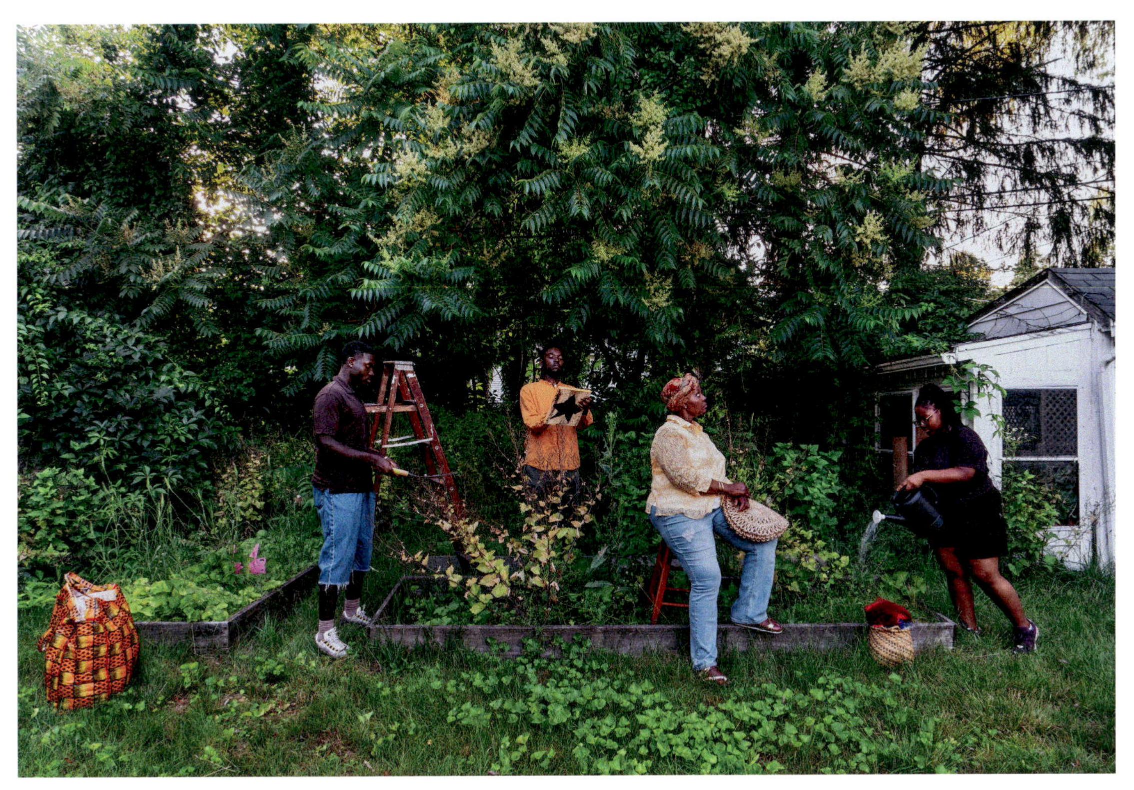

— 82 —

Claudio Eshun, *Untitled (Our Family's Garden)*, 2023

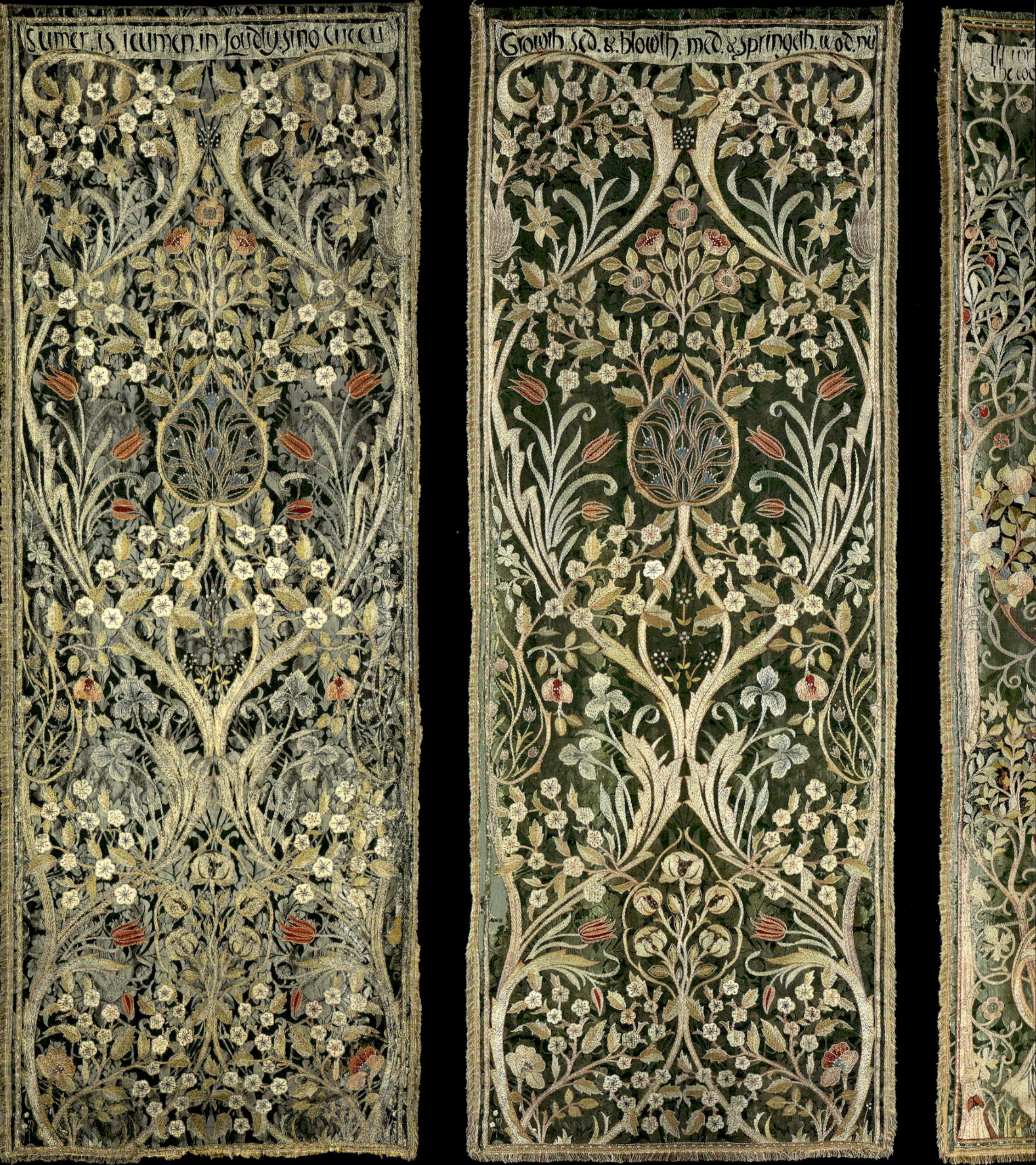

Sumer is icumen in Loudly sing cuccu

Groweth sed & bloweth med & springeth wde nu

Awe wor
the woo

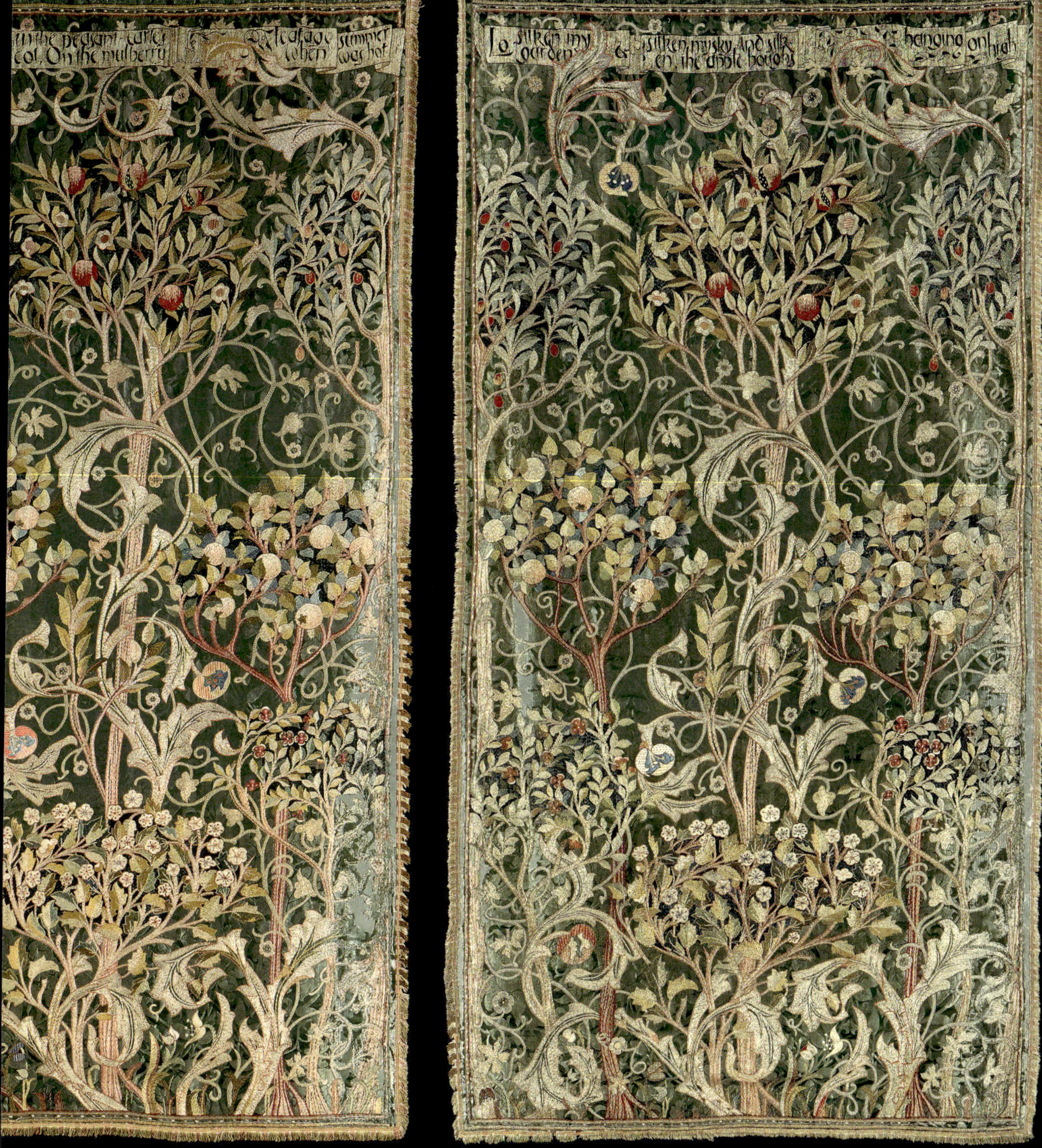

May Morris, Portières, 1892–93

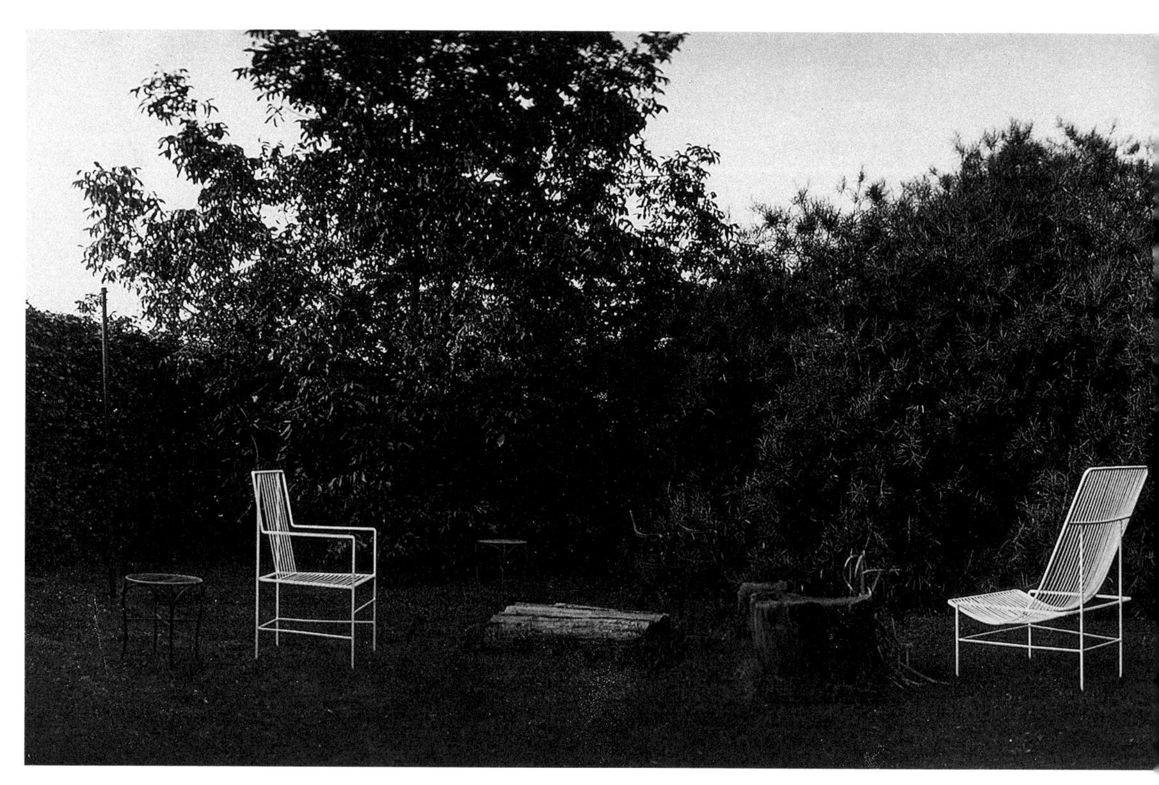

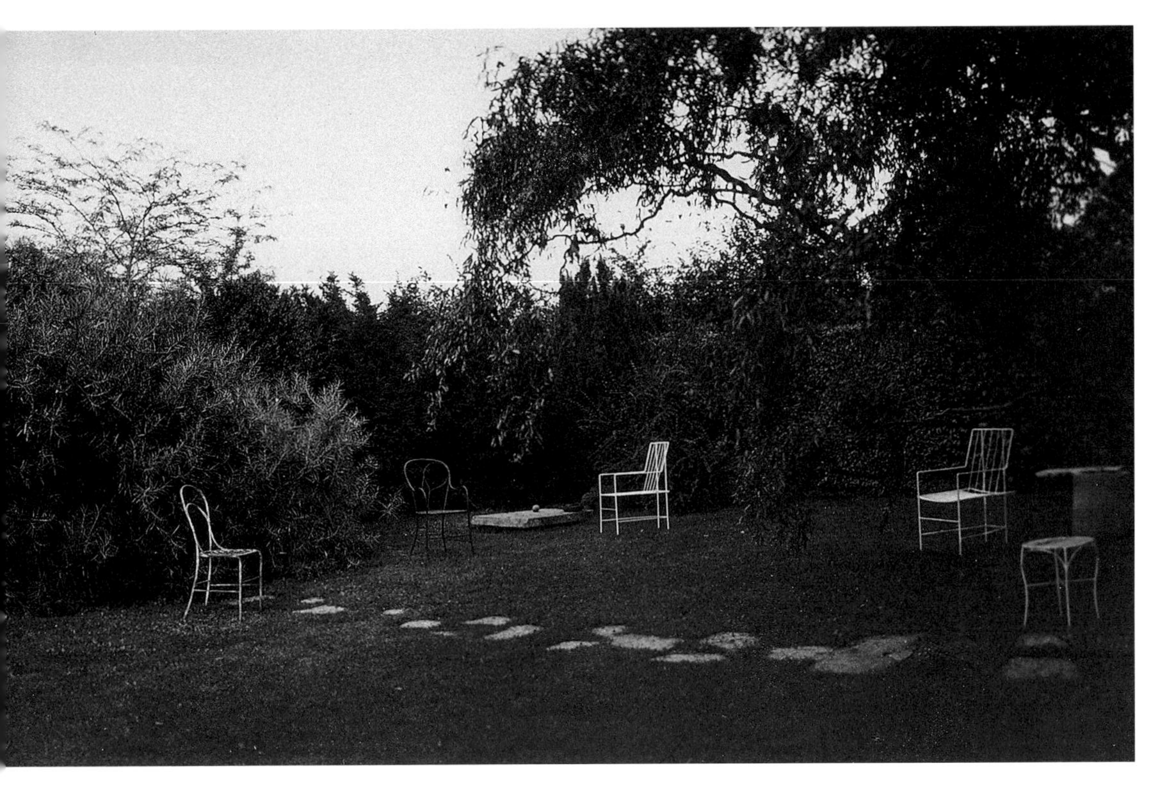

Josef Sudek, *A Walk in the Magic Garden*, 1954

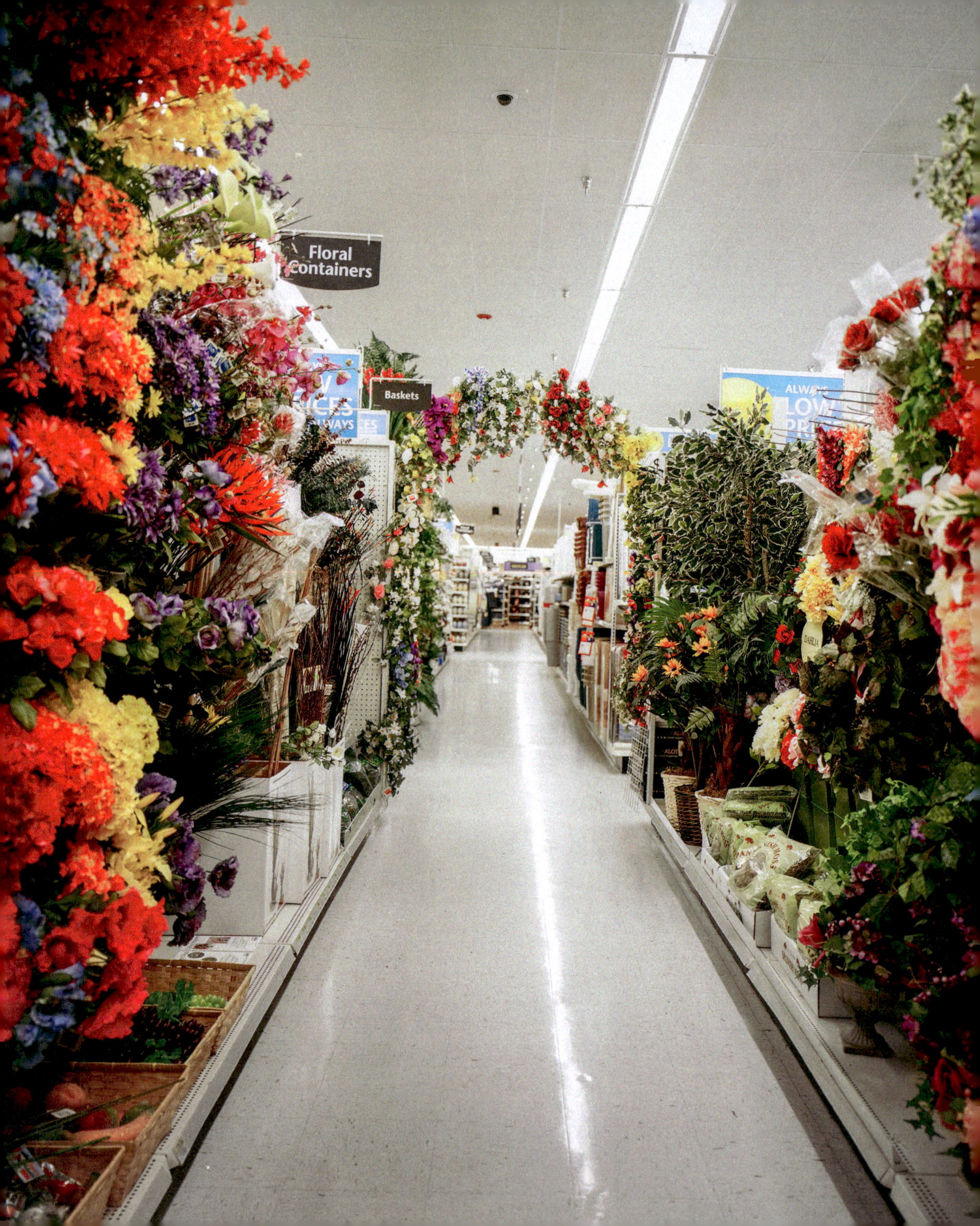

Floral Containers
Baskets
ALWAYS LOW PRICES
PRICES ALWAYS

Taking the Garden with You

Luscious kelly and forest greens, punctuated by bright pops of light pink, red, yellow, orange, and soft cream catch the eye, looking upwards at the face of a female statue, variously identified as the sorceress Armida, Flora, or Pomona (97). The viewer is transported into this rich scene, a space where the beauty and fragrance of the plants were said to have magical powers. When visitors to the 1855 Exposition Universelle in Paris saw this immense wallpaper, displayed by its manufacturer Jules Defossé, they may have fallen head over heels under the spell of Armida and her magical garden. Her story would have been well-known to nineteenth-century viewers, as it came from the epic Renaissance poem by Italian Torquato Tasso, *Jerusalem Delivered*, which had been a popular topic for artists' depictions in the ensuing centuries. Not only an incredible technical feat—each color in the wallpaper was created with a separate printed block—the scale would have made the viewing of this masterpiece a deeply immersive experience.

Defossé wanted to place wallpaper design on par with great painting and hired some of the leading artists of the day to create designs. Artistically, the *Garden of Armida* by Edouard Muller was a success, well regarded by both visitors to the fair and critics. However, as a commercial venture, it was not well suited to domestic interiors due to its shape and size. Ironic, in a way, that a design which sought to bring

the outside world into the homes of clients, should turn out
to be too large and too grand for that purpose.

What does it mean to recreate a garden space inside?
Gardens themselves can exist in many shapes and forms,
and be sources of inspiration for artists to create, interpret,
and reimagine. The act of depicting a garden *away* from
nature is a declaration of just how important these spaces
are to human creativity.

Many also seek ways to bring the garden with them,
wearing clothing or jewelry inspired by blooms or crea-
tures that thrive in the outside world. Legendary couturier
Christian Dior grew up along the northern coast of France
at the Villa Les Rhumbs in Normandy, where spending time
with his mother Madeleine's rose gardens and flowers of
many kinds served as inspiration for his fashion collections.
He later acquired his own home and garden in the south of
France in 1950 and designed pergolas for outdoor sketching
within the garden, so the space could be even more closely
linked to his design practice. His evening dress from 1956
reflects this continued love of roses, though they were not
his favorite flower (92). The lily of the valley had that dis-
tinction, and the superstitious Dior always wore a sprig in
his buttonhole and reportedly sewed dried flowers into
the hem of each haute couture ensemble. The exquisite Lily
of the Valley necklace therefore would have been draped

around the neck of the wearer to bring good luck and happiness, a talismanic linking between a distant garden and the human body (87).

Even after Dior's untimely death in 1957, Yves Saint Laurent, Dior's successor, created a collection for the house in Autumn/Winter 1958 that included pieces both in homage to Dior's love of gardens and Saint Laurent's own interest in nature (93). These gowns, covered in growing, blooming designs—Dior's with bold roses against a pale cream background and Saint Laurent's with small and large flowers densely arrayed in a greenery setting—would make a garden and its vitality seem ever present. These blooms won't fade or drop away, nor will the magical and perfect garden of Armida pass from eternal spring into resting, dormant winter.

David Hilliard's set of five photographs, *Perennial,* captures the permanence and endurance of fake flowers at a Walmart superstore in southern Florida (96). The growth of these blooms is doubly frozen: not only are these flowers not real (how could they grow inside a store with no water and only fluorescent light?), but they are also fixed by Hilliard's camera in their perfect bloom. The human desire for gardens and what they stand for—a sense of growth, feelings of renewal and rebirth, and at their core, their beauty— drives us to seek to bring the garden with us in unusual and touching ways. — CLH

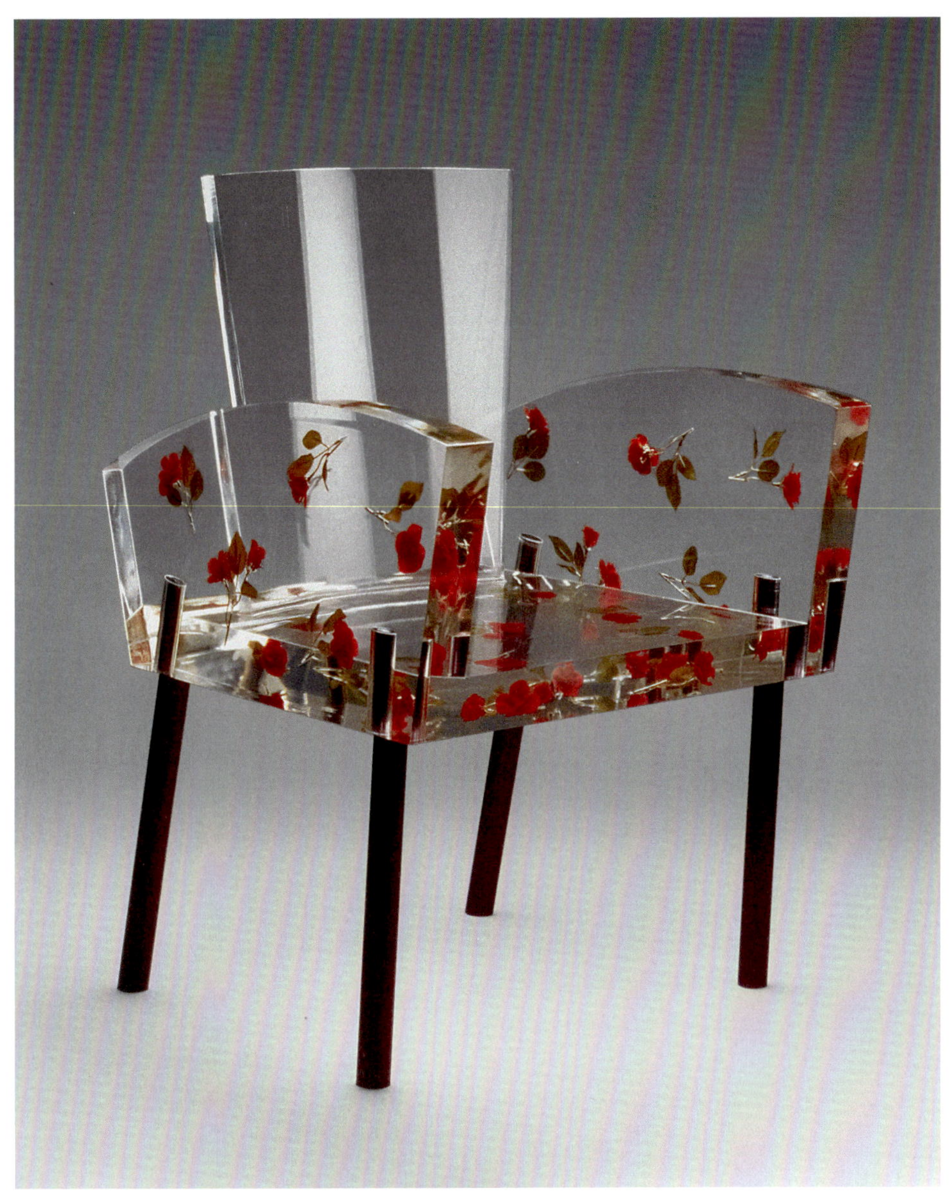

— 85 —
Kuramata Shiro, *Miss Blanche*, designed in 1988

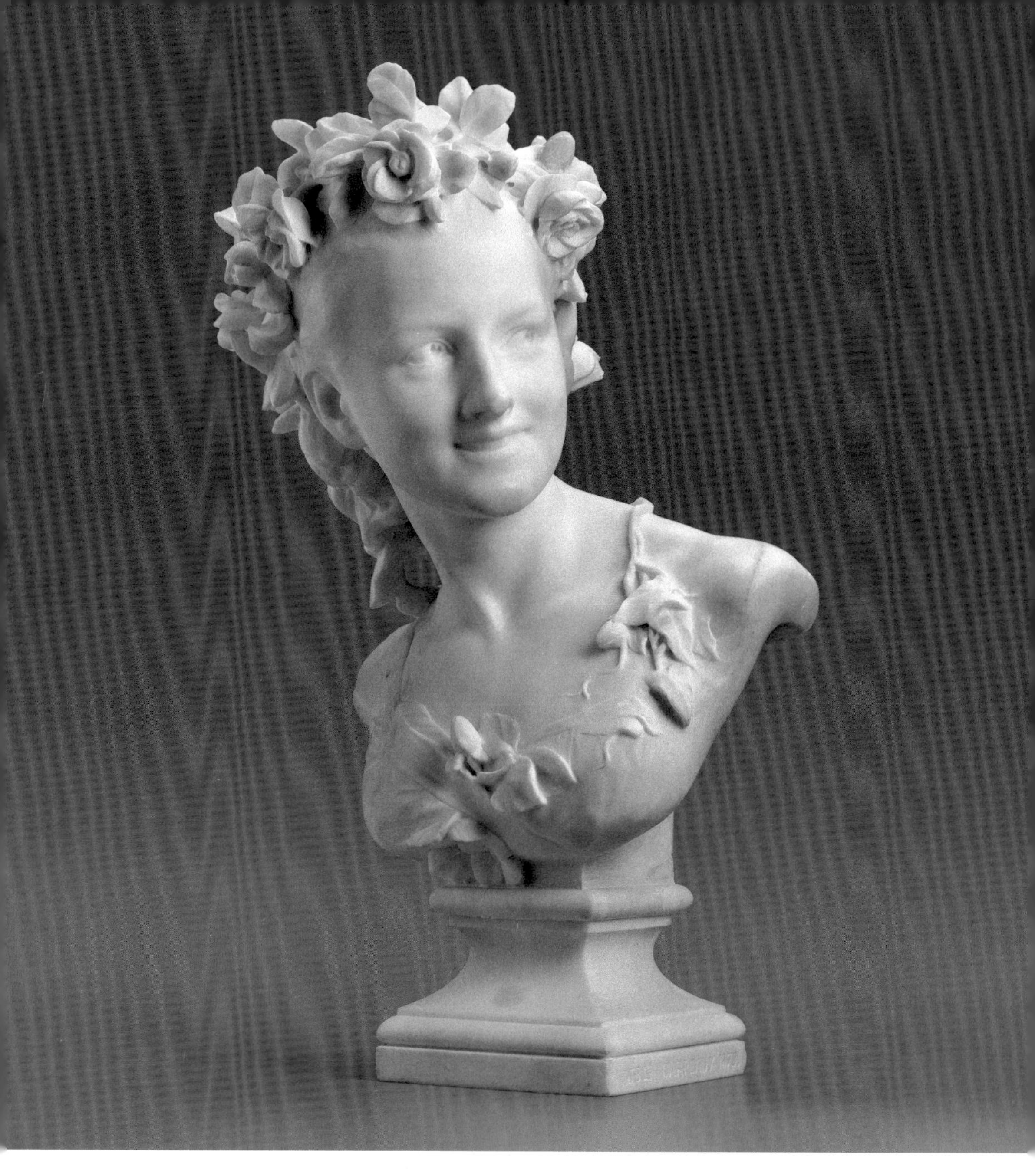

— 86 —
Jean-Baptiste Carpeaux, *La Rieuse aux Roses*, 1874

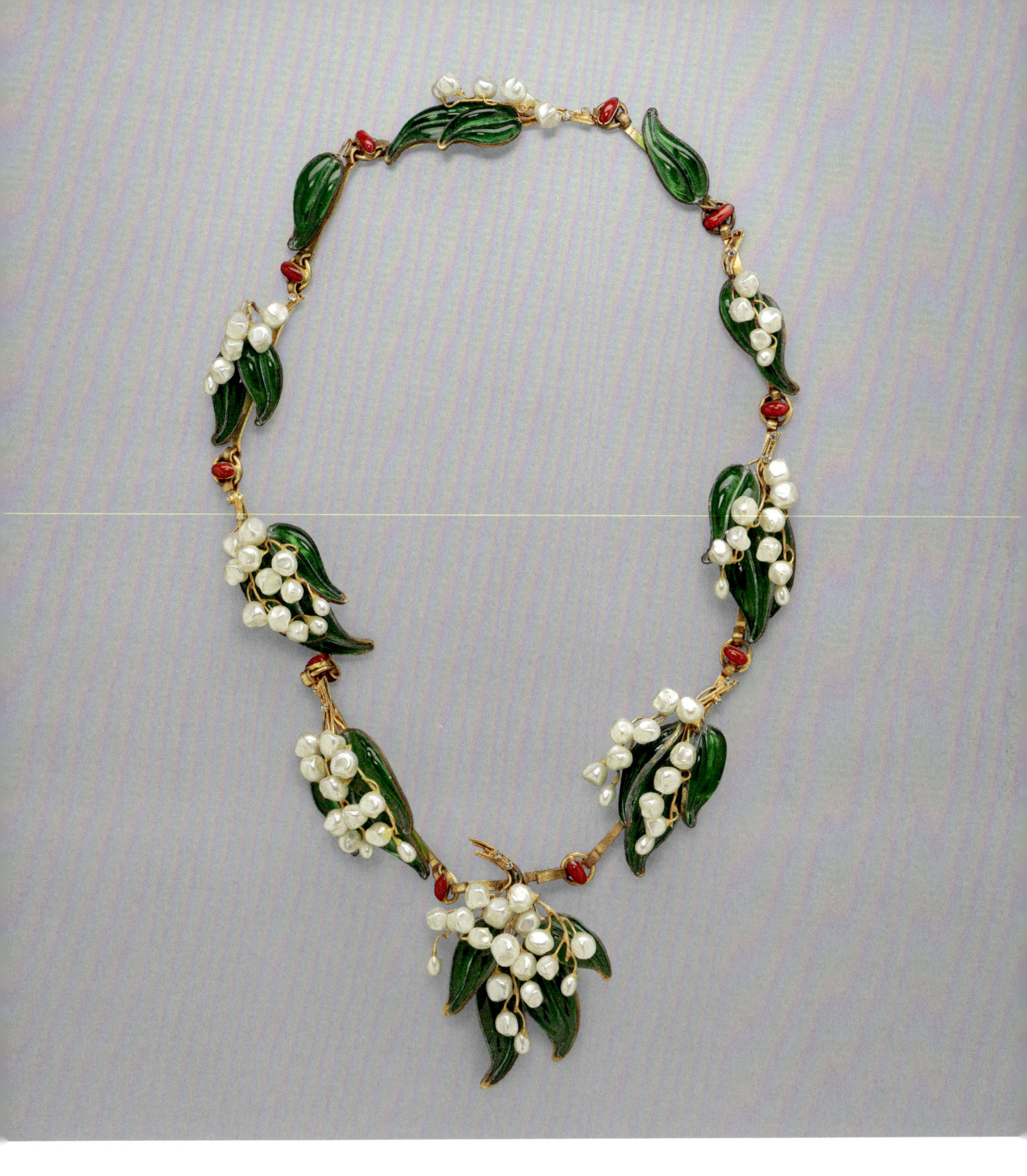

Maison Gripoix for Dior, Lily of the Valley necklace, 1950s

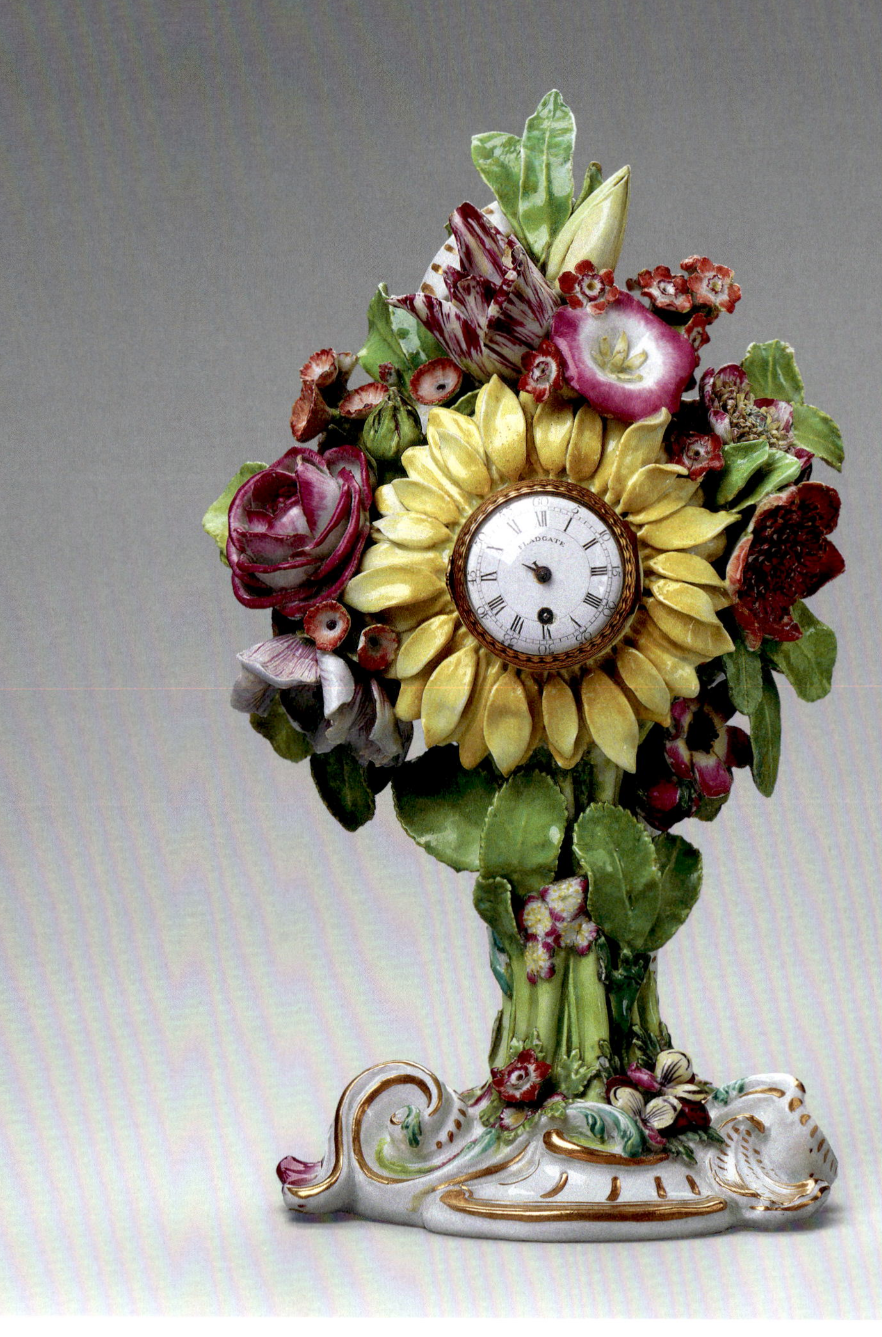

— 88 —

 Chelsea Manufactory, Table clock, about 1761

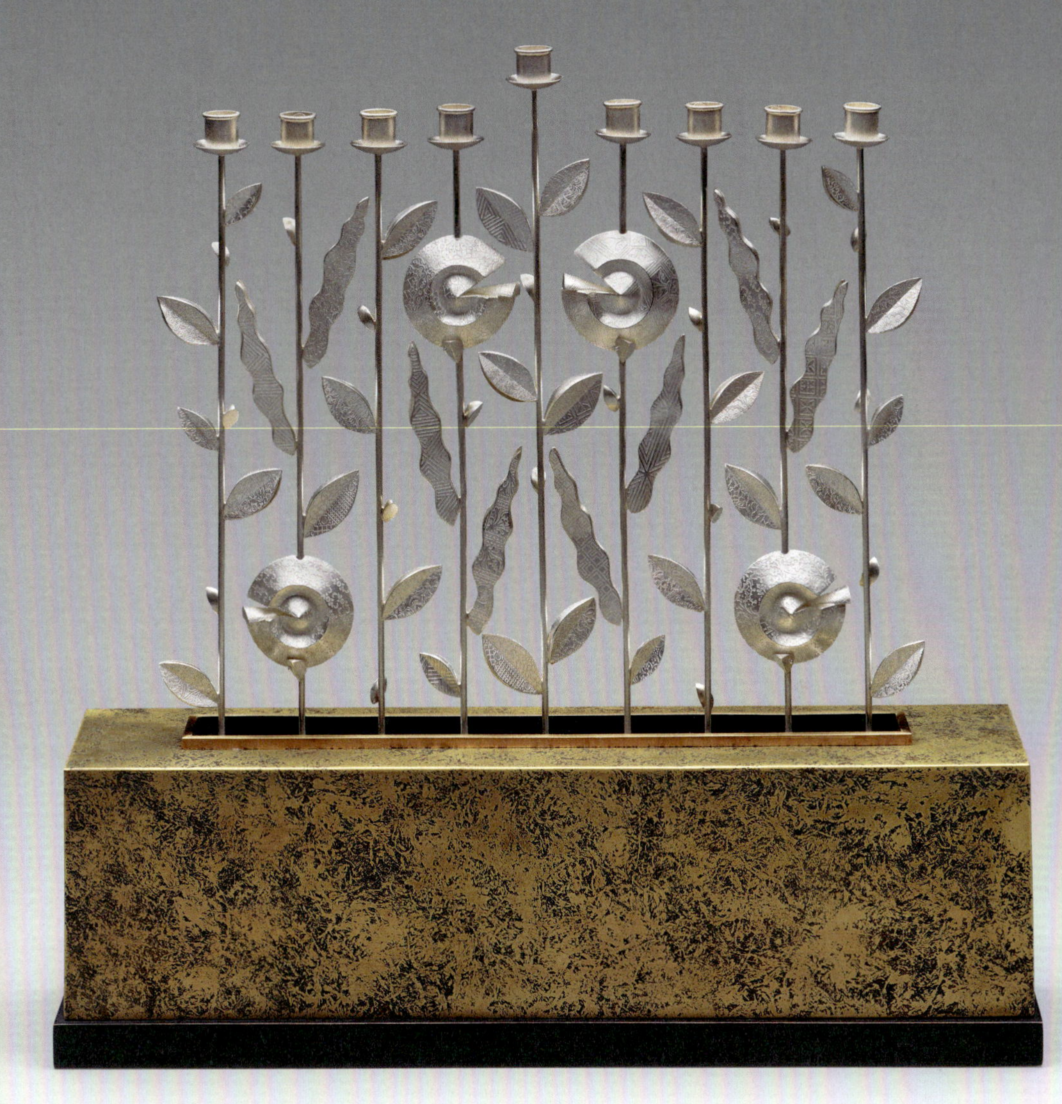

Linda Threadgill, Hanukkah lamp, 1999

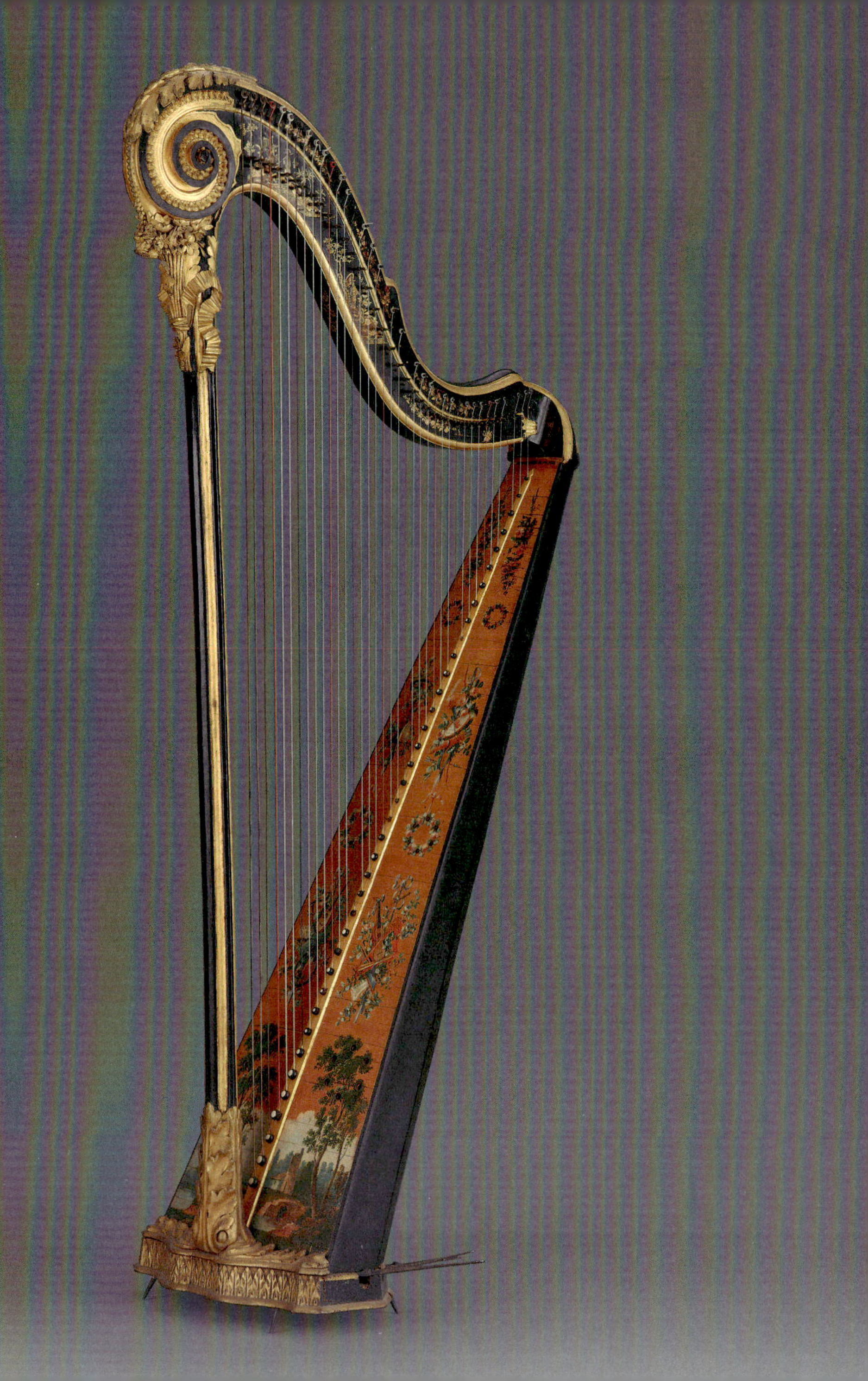

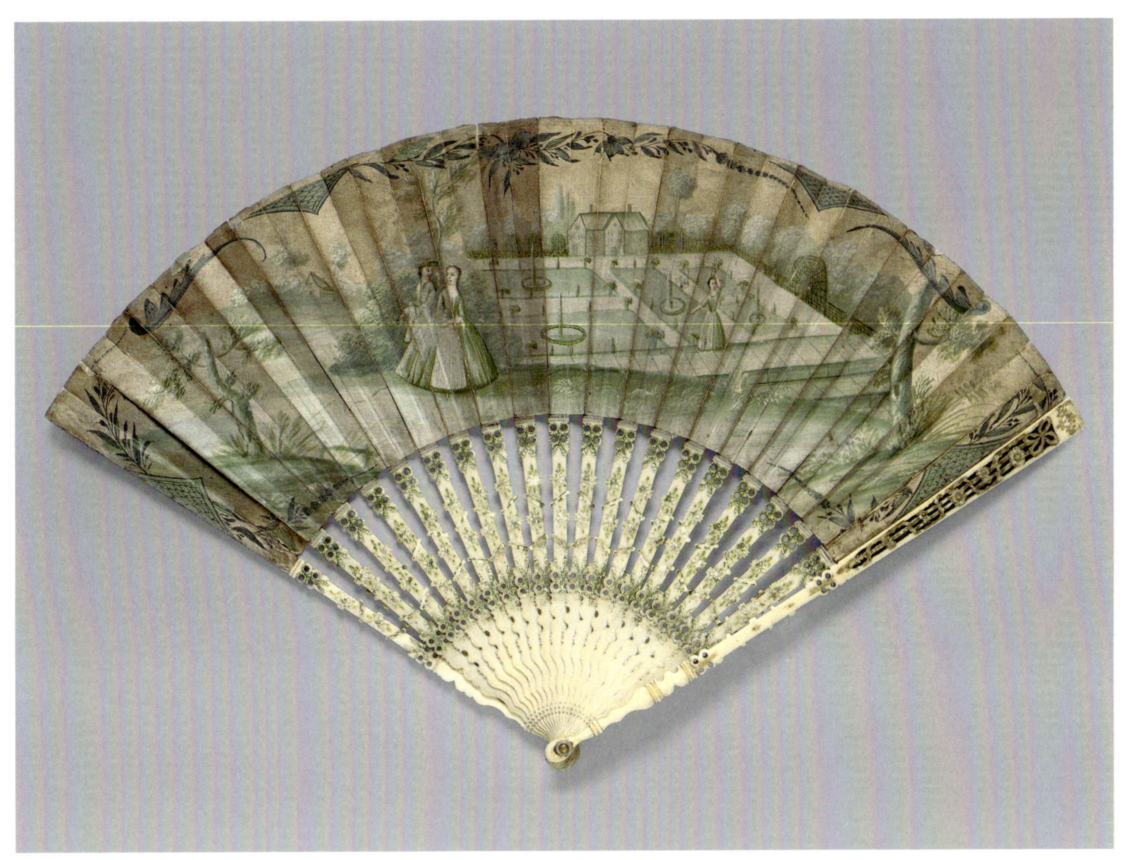

— 90 —
Godefroi Holtzman, Pedal harp, about 1785

— 91 —
Fan, English, 1740s

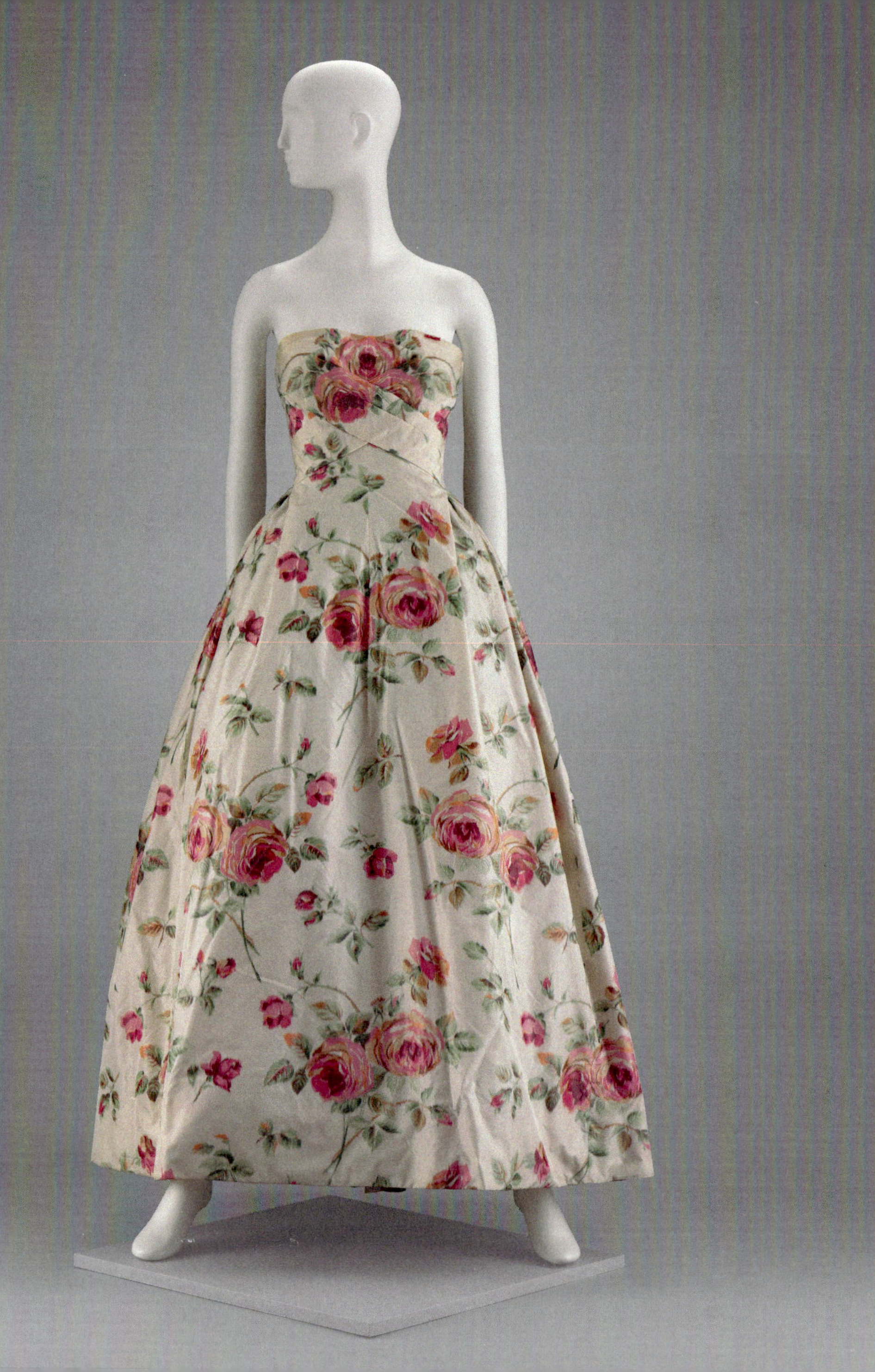

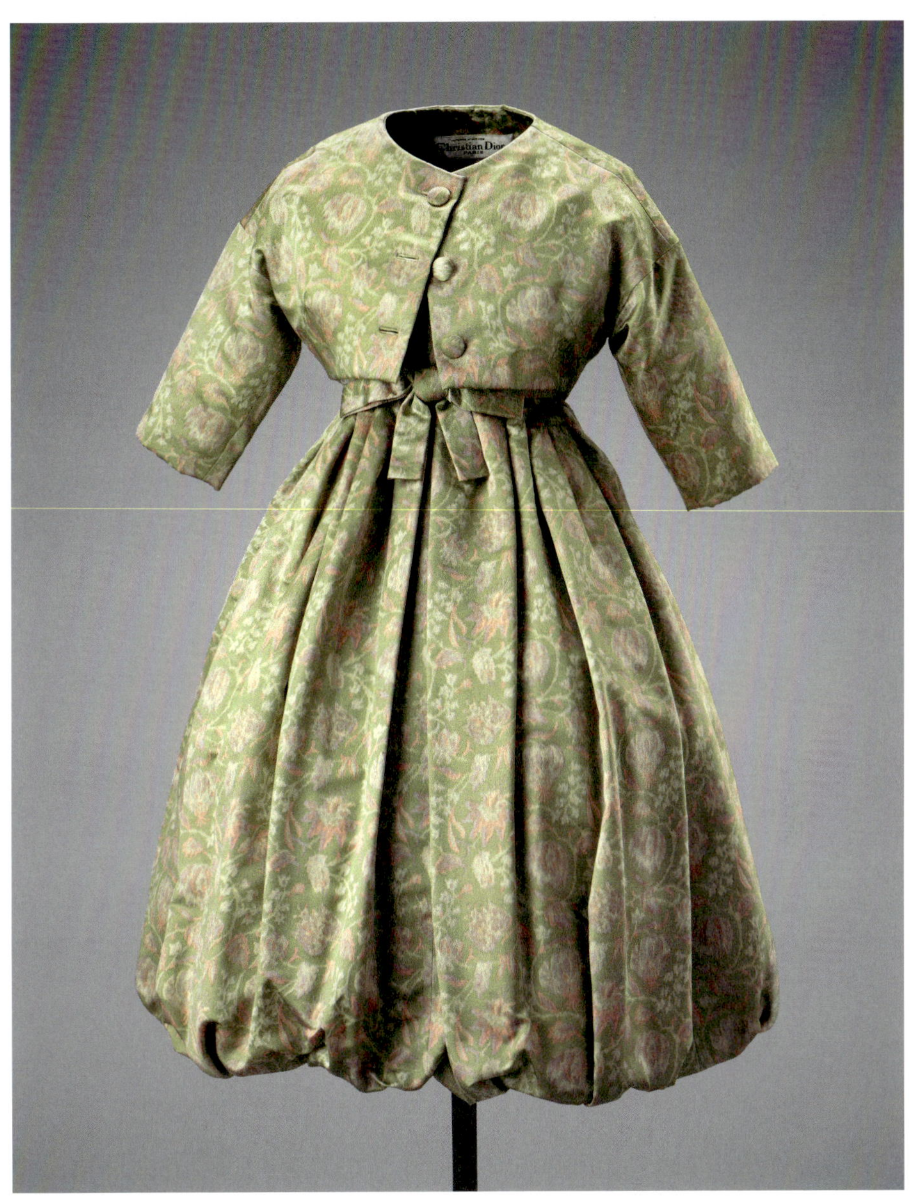

— 92 —
Christian Dior, Evening dress, 1956

— 93 —
Yves Saint Laurent for Dior, Day dress, 1958

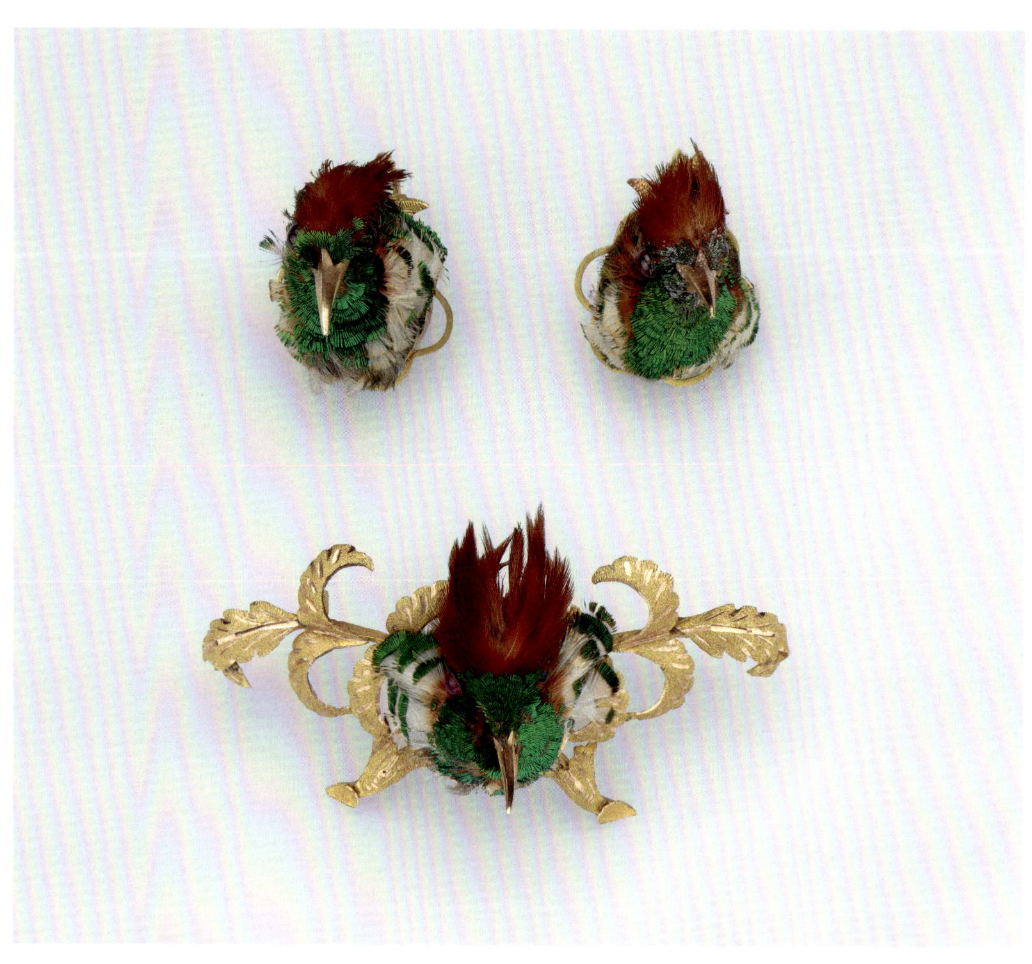

— 94 —

Hummingbird brooch and earrings, English, about 1870

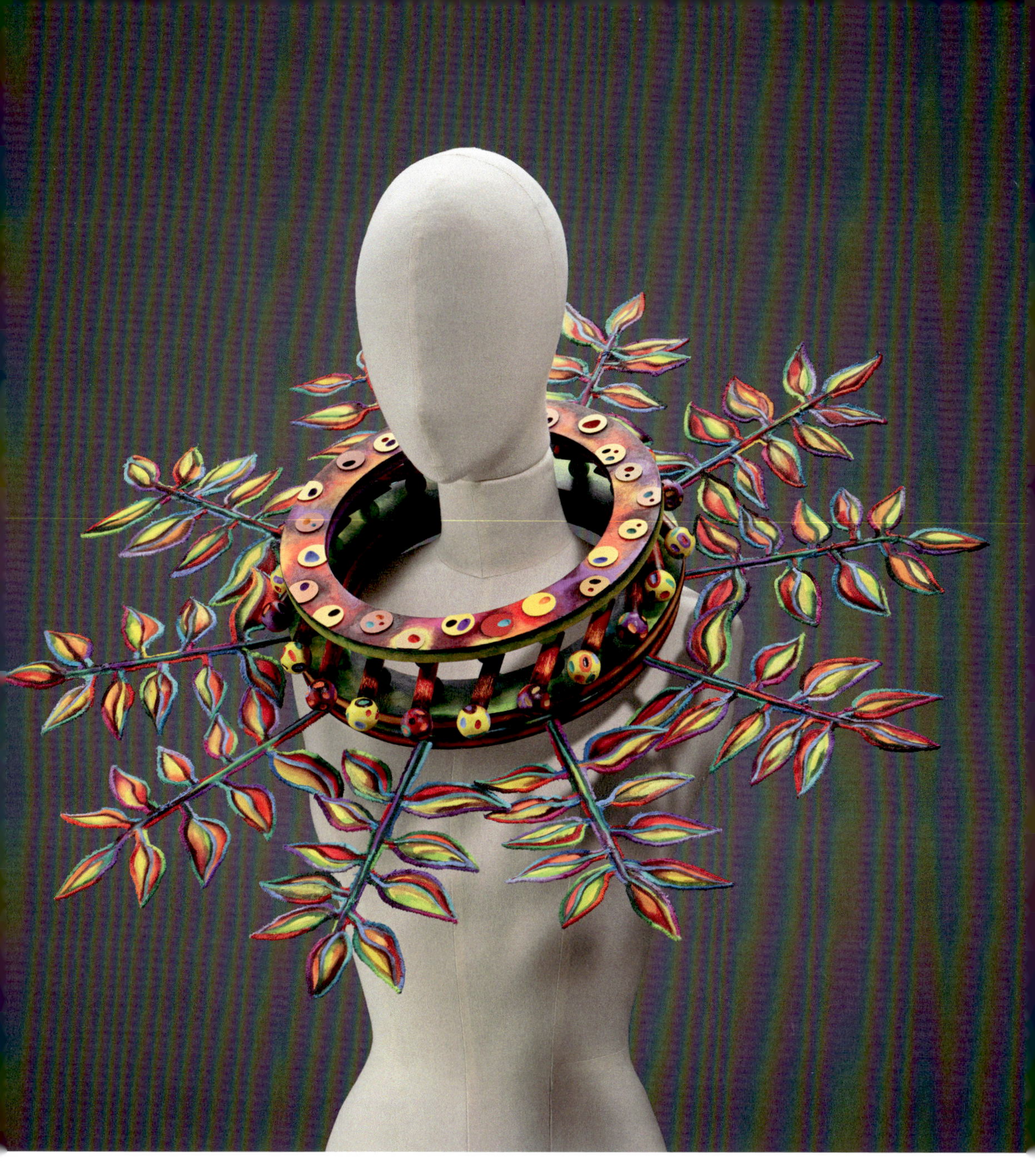

— 95 —

Marjorie Schick, *In Henri's Garden*, 2003

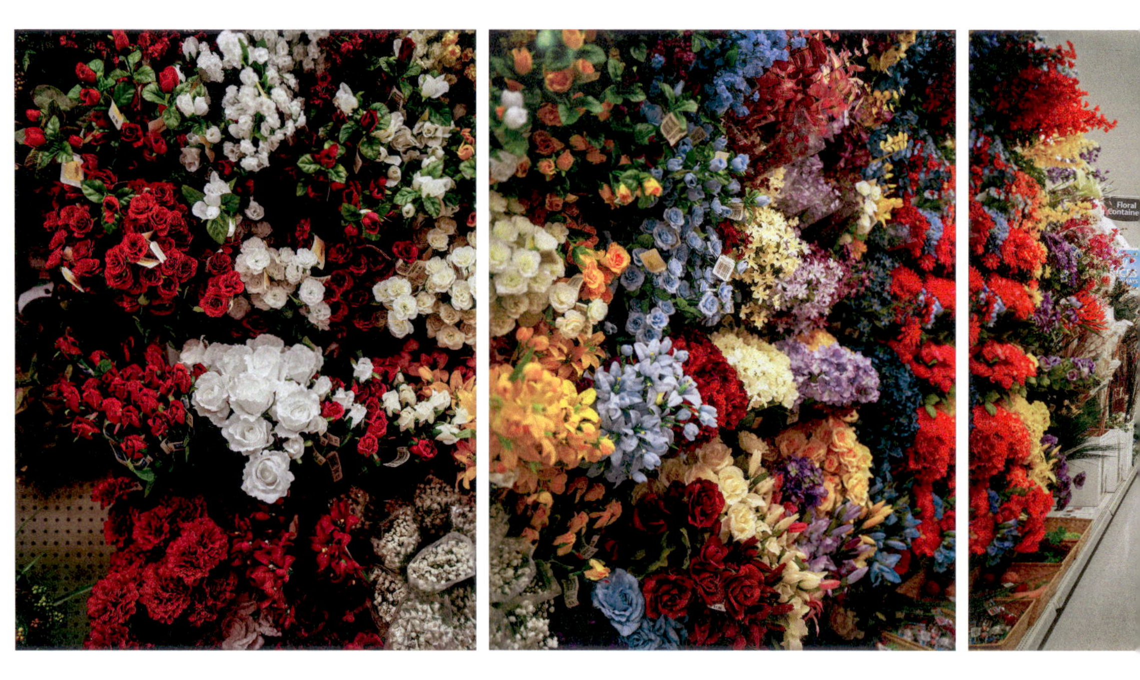

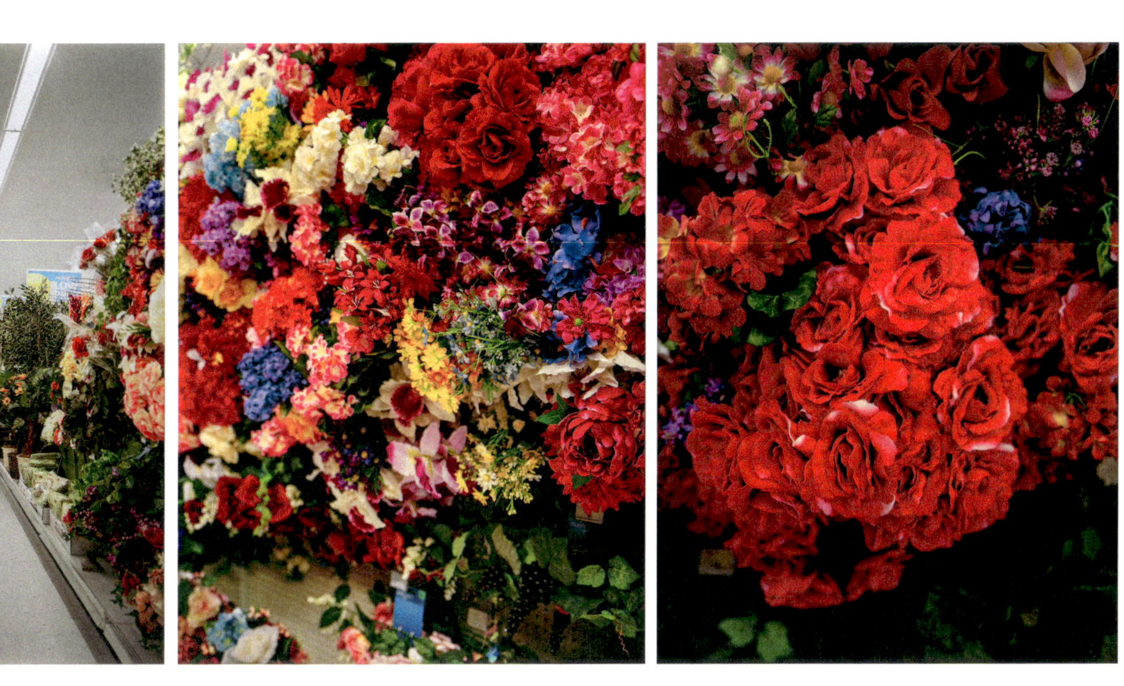

David Hilliard, *Perennial*, 2006

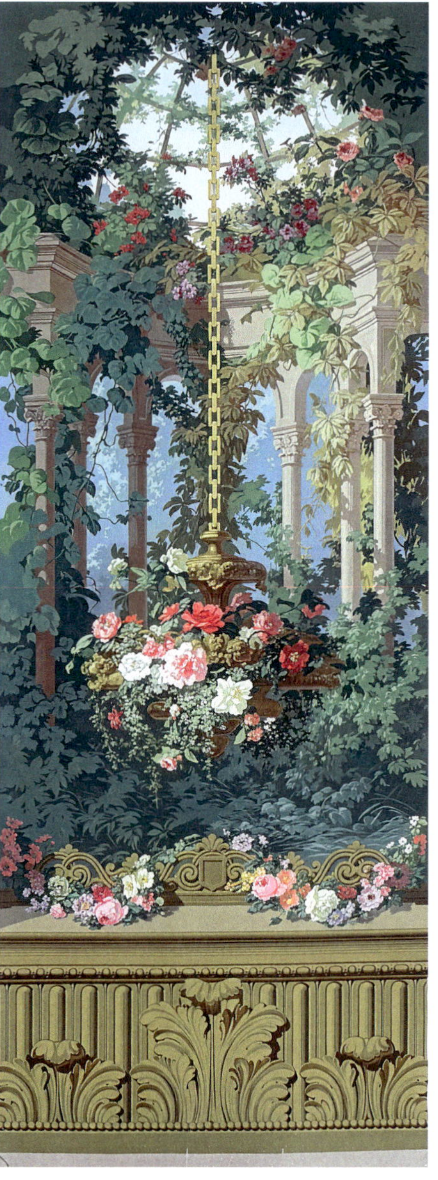
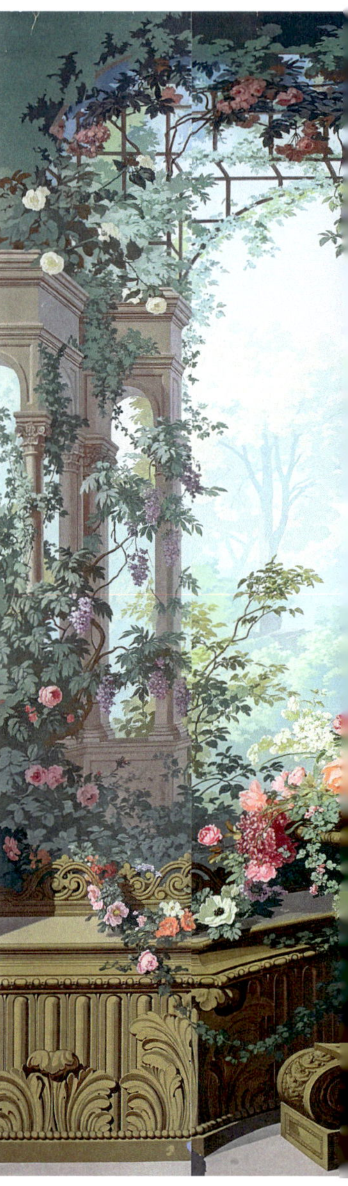

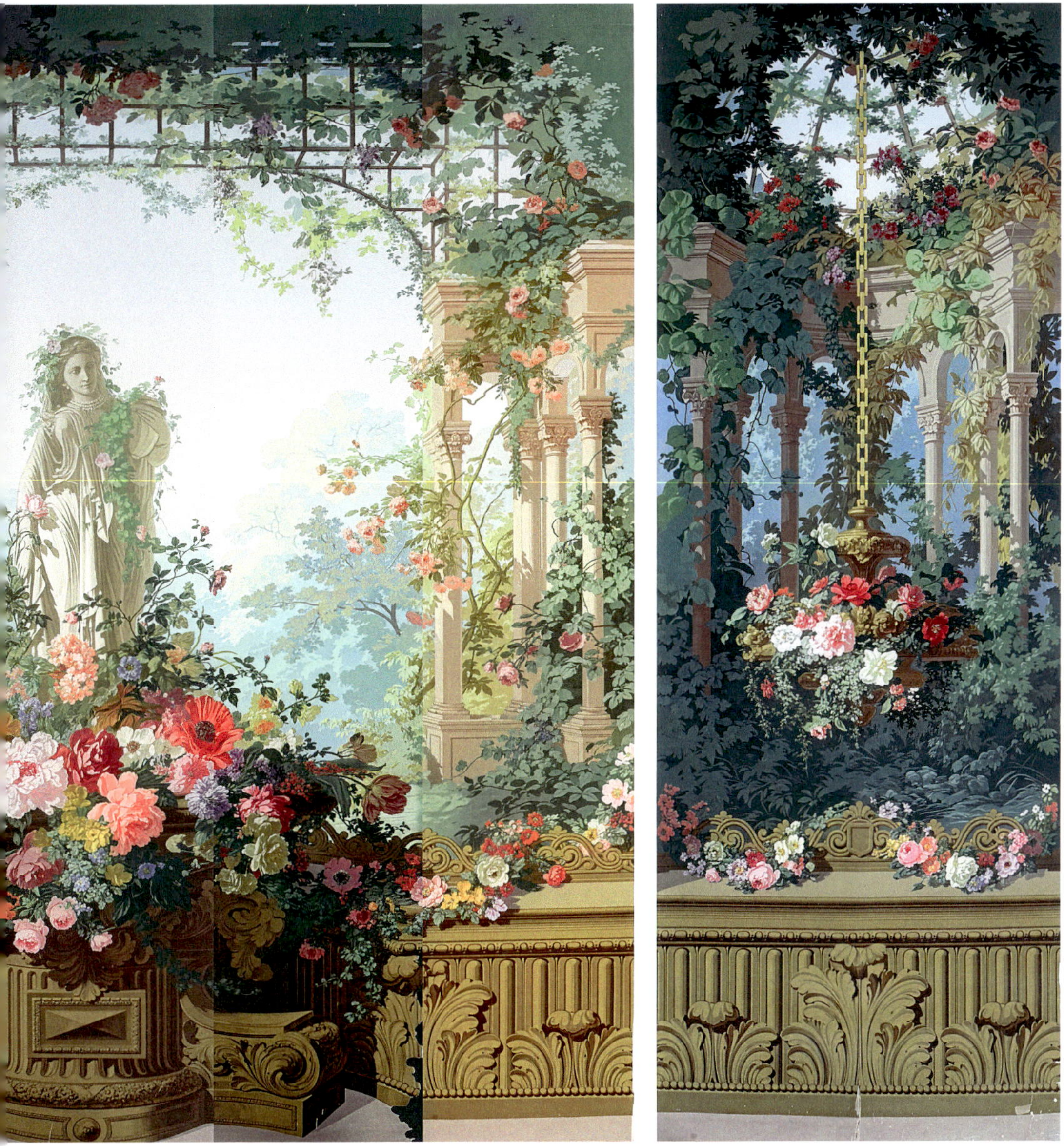

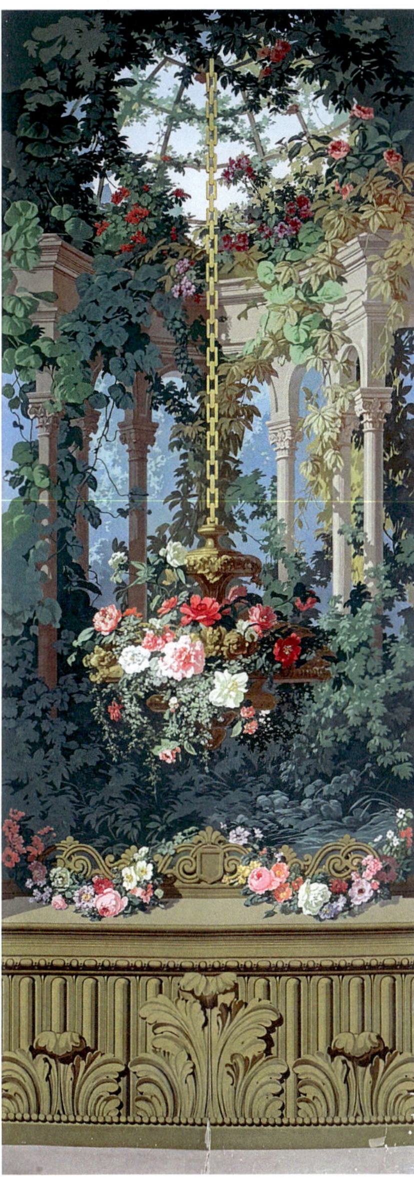

Edouard Muller for Jules Defossé, *Jardin d'Armide*, about 1855

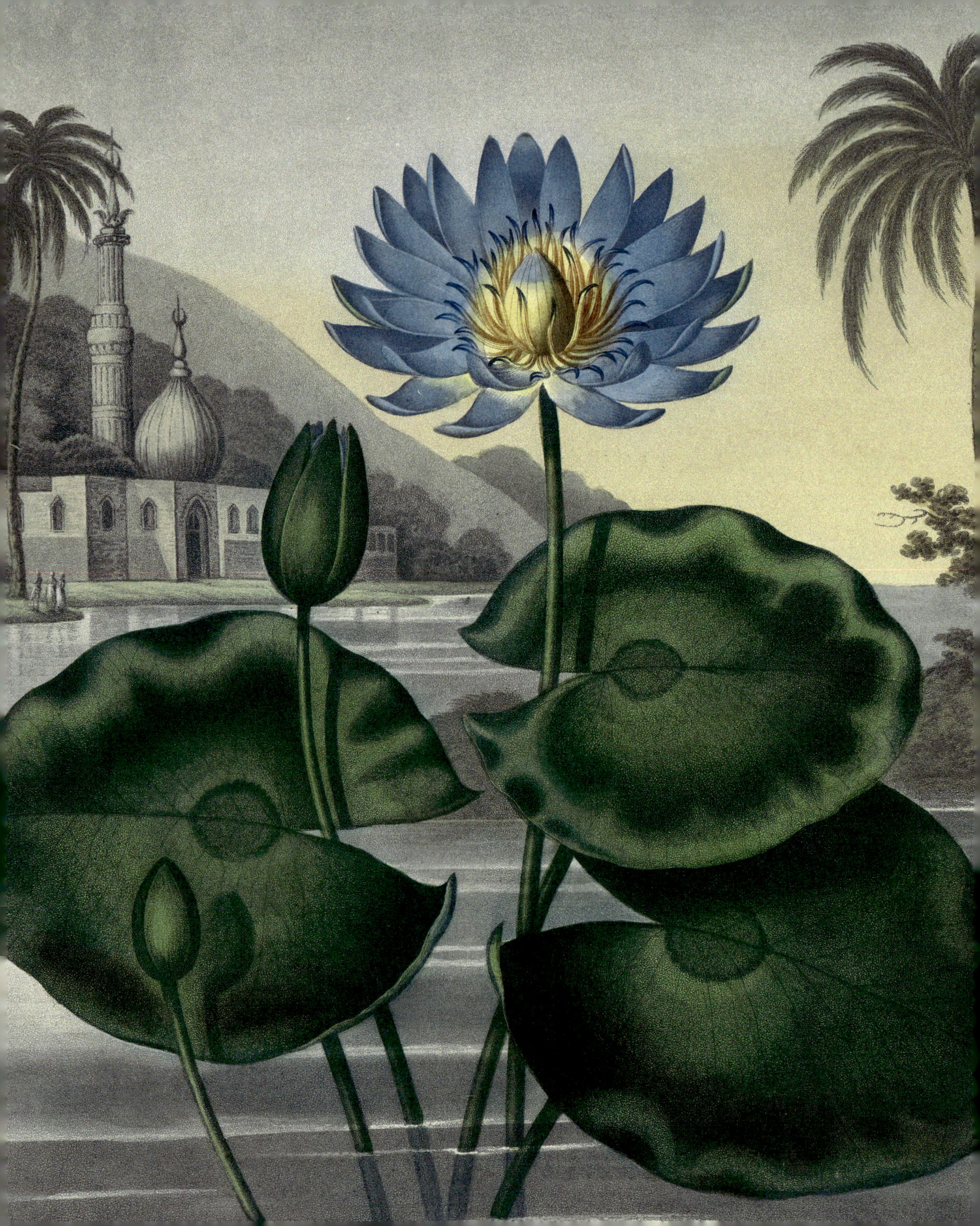

Garden as Stage

Gardens reflect the aspirations of those who care for them, and the resources dedicated to their complex maintenance, from the maximal efficiency of an urban subsistence plot to the dramatic sequencing of a royal estate. Consequently, a garden can be considered a stage, a performance, or both.

A monumental eighteenth-century portrait, honoring a learned woman on her seventieth or eightieth birthday, centers the venerable sitter in the staged setting of her private garden (102). Seated in front of a portable framed landscape painting, she projects a serene majesty. Surrounded by books and objets d'art, accessories typically associated with male scholars, her position of social and intellectual power is amplified by multiple visual references to longevity and prosperity. The refined environment of her garden provides a holistic platform for honor and celebration.

A garden of scale can be the ultimate setting to perform control over nature. Vast garden complexes, some the size of cities, were developed during the Safavid period (1500–1736) in what is today Iran. The lush garden border of a sumptuous silk carpet from the period frames a dramatic hunting scene (99). Stepping onto the carpet—a privilege reserved for a very select few—invites engagement with the unfolding drama alongside the court spectators in their verdant enclosure.

A spectacular porcelain service documenting plant specimens from Josephine Bonaparte's renowned botanical garden at Malmaison, her private residence outside of Paris, provides another mode of sensory encounter with nature (103). A gift from the Sèvres Porcelain Manufactory, which hoped to secure Josephine's patronage, the service is now recognized as a unique artistic expression of human control over nature. Josephine, an amateur botanist and patron of the natural sciences, benefited from seemingly unlimited access to specimens from around the world, courtesy of her privileged position as Napoleon Bonaparte's wife with direct access to a global trade network. Plants and trees from six continents were grown in the gardens and greenhouses at Malmaison, many of which were documented by renowned flower painter Pierre-Joseph Redouté, former court artist to Marie Antoinette, Queen of France (1755–1793). Redouté's fine botanical watercolors of the plants at Malmaison formed the basis for the decoration of the porcelain service (104). Each exquisitely rendered specimen serves as a potent reminder of Josephine's passion for the natural sciences and her ability to pursue it on a global scale. The very latest in botanical scientific knowledge was captured in a most unexpected and luxurious fashion— a testament to the ambitions of the maker and the patron.

A contemporaneous effort to document botany from life is seen in *The Temple of Flora*, the third part of Dr. Robert John Thornton's *New illustration of the sexual system of Carolus von Linnaeus*, an ambitious print publication created between 1799 and 1807 (100). Thornton engaged a number of artists and engravers to create over thirty images depicting plants in their natural setting, at the time still considered an innovative approach to botanical illustration. Thornton's artists used various printing and coloring techniques to create dramatic images with the respective plant in the near foreground, set against a superficially appropriate but imaginary landscape. Considered one of the most memorable botanical print projects of its time, the publication brought Thornton fame rather than fortune, due to the high production costs, but remains one of the most recognizable and distinctive artistic projects through its poetic framework and extravagant ambition. Its visual power continues to resonate today.

Nearly two hundred years after the publication of *The Temple of Flora*, American printmaker Jim Dine, at the suggestion of his first wife and passionate gardener Nancy

Thornton's *Temple of Flora* presented plants both familiar and new, the latter due to the extensive colonial networks and the associated global plant trade. While the original was a celebration of imperial power and national dominance, Dine's iteration provokes reflection on the part of the reader, inviting engagement with concepts of earth as communal paradise. On one plate, project director and poet Andrew Hoyem asks the readers "as Gardeners and gamekeepers of Eden" to contemplate if "it is not Paradise enough?" — MM

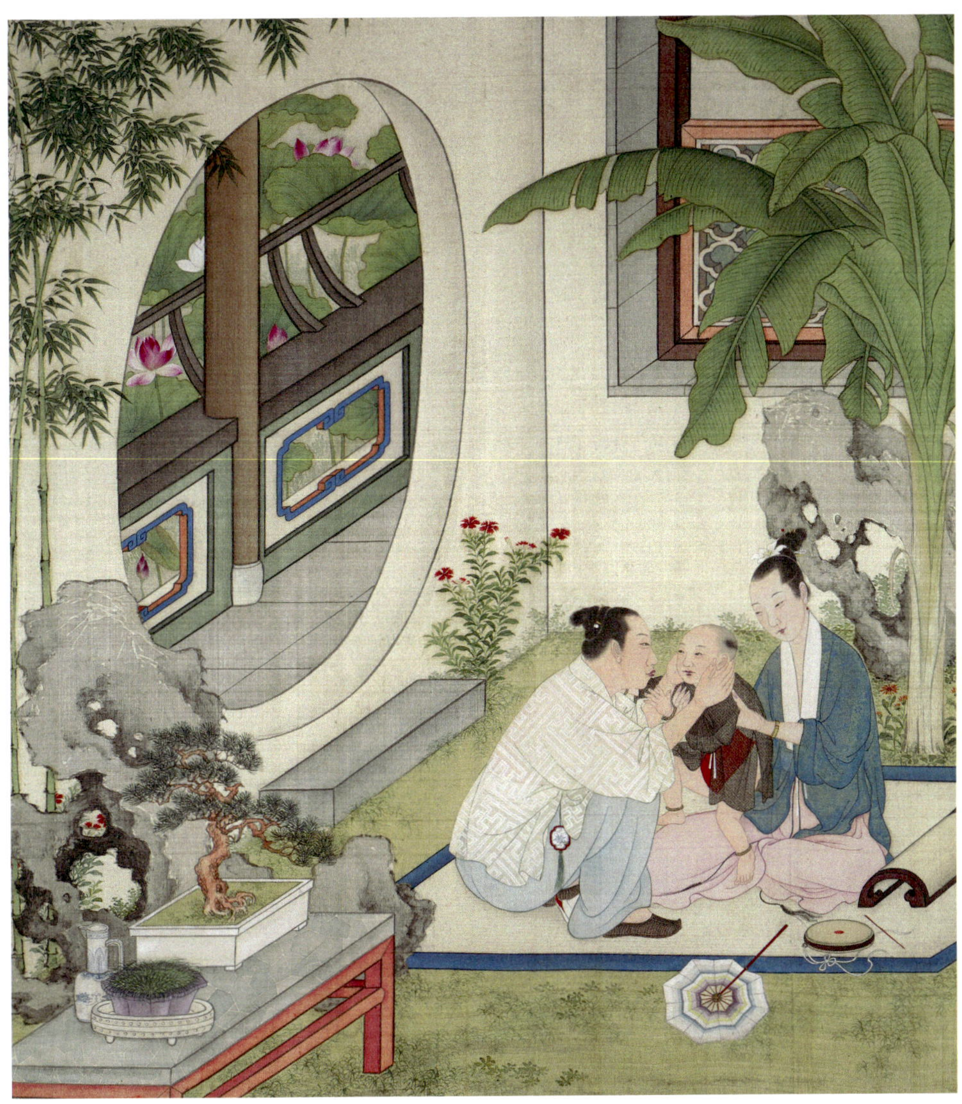

Domestic scenes from an opulent household palace,
Chinese, third quarter of the 18th century

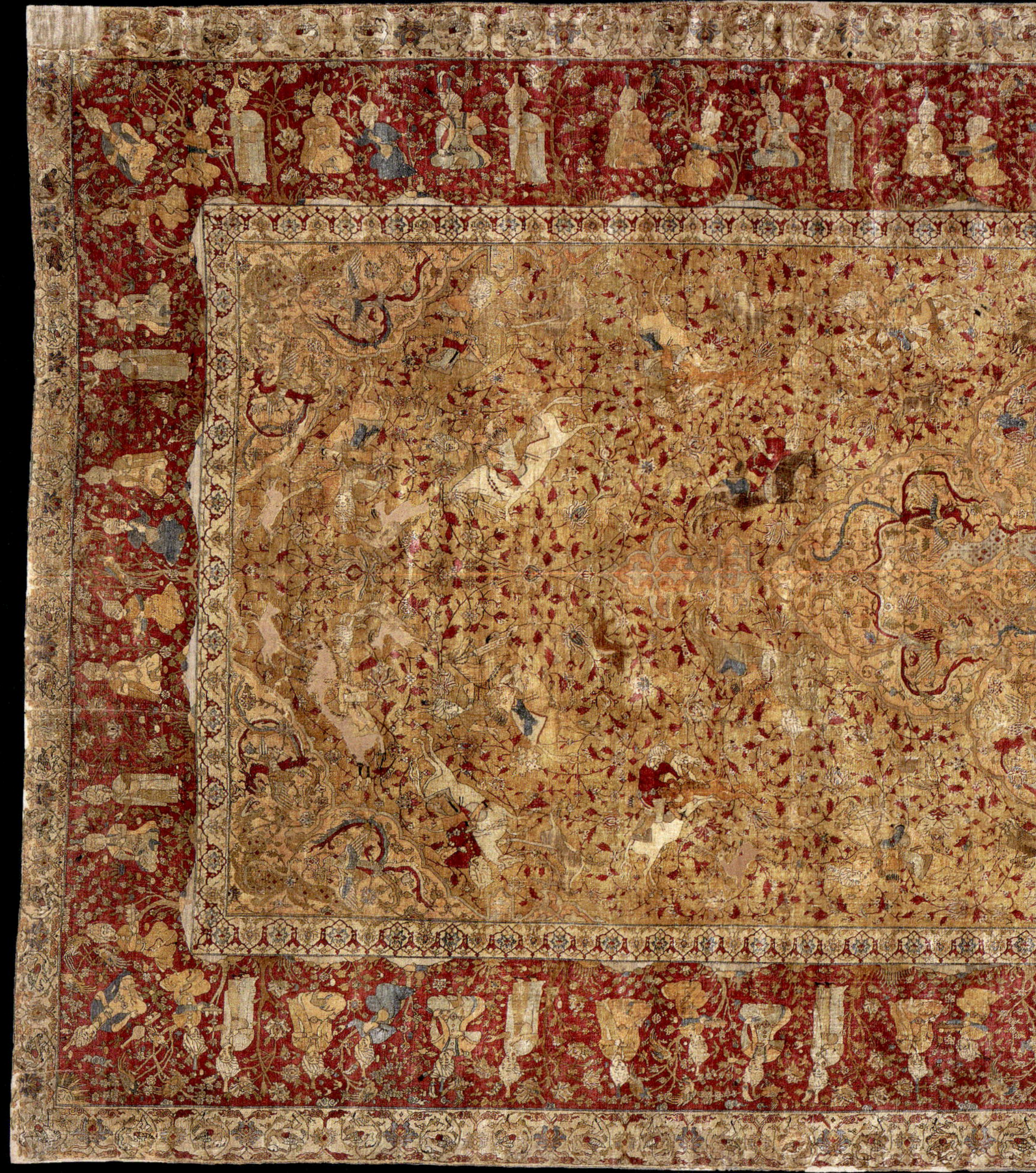

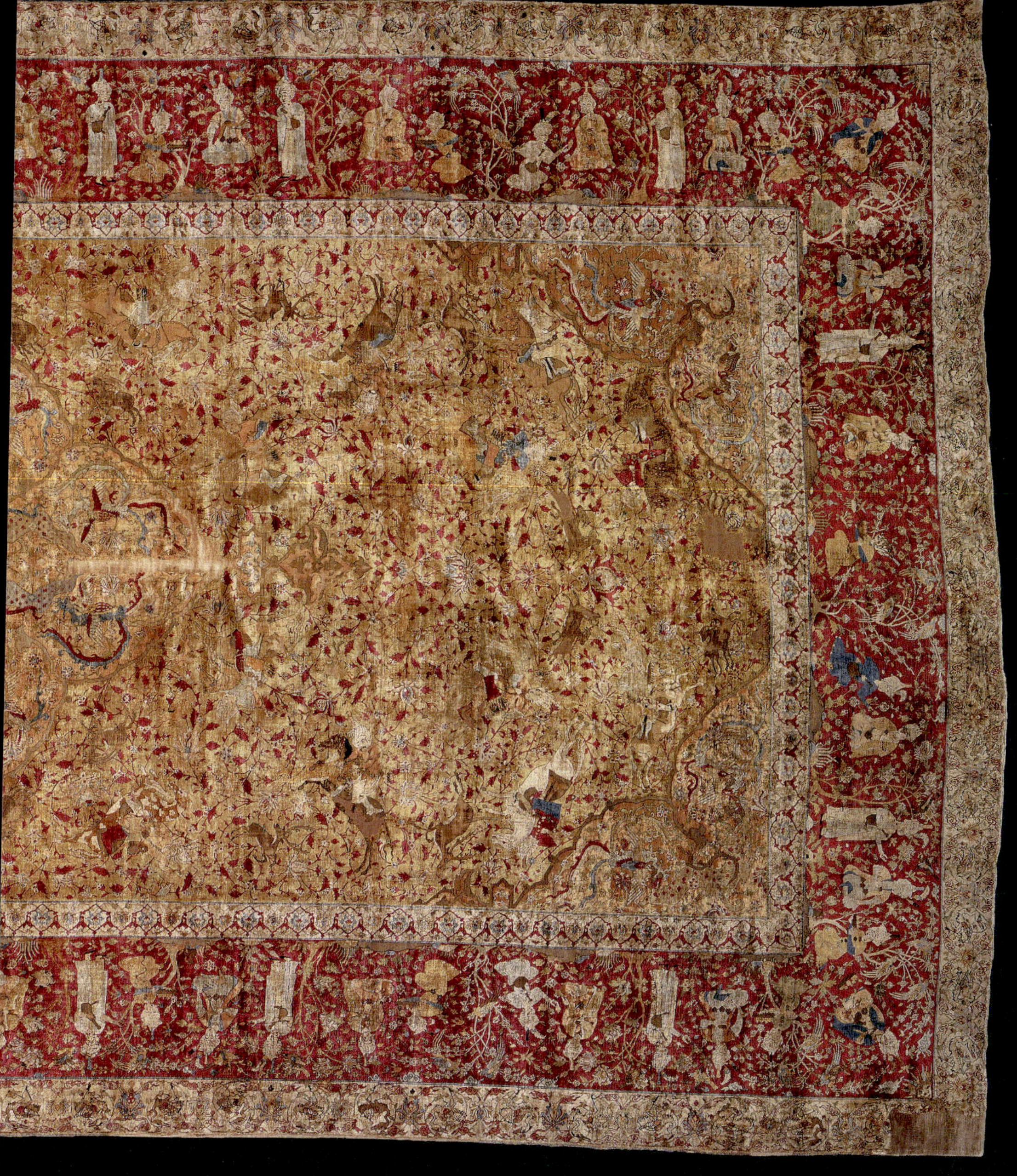

— 99 —
Probably designed by Aqa Mirak and Sultan Muhammad, Hunting carpet, about 1530

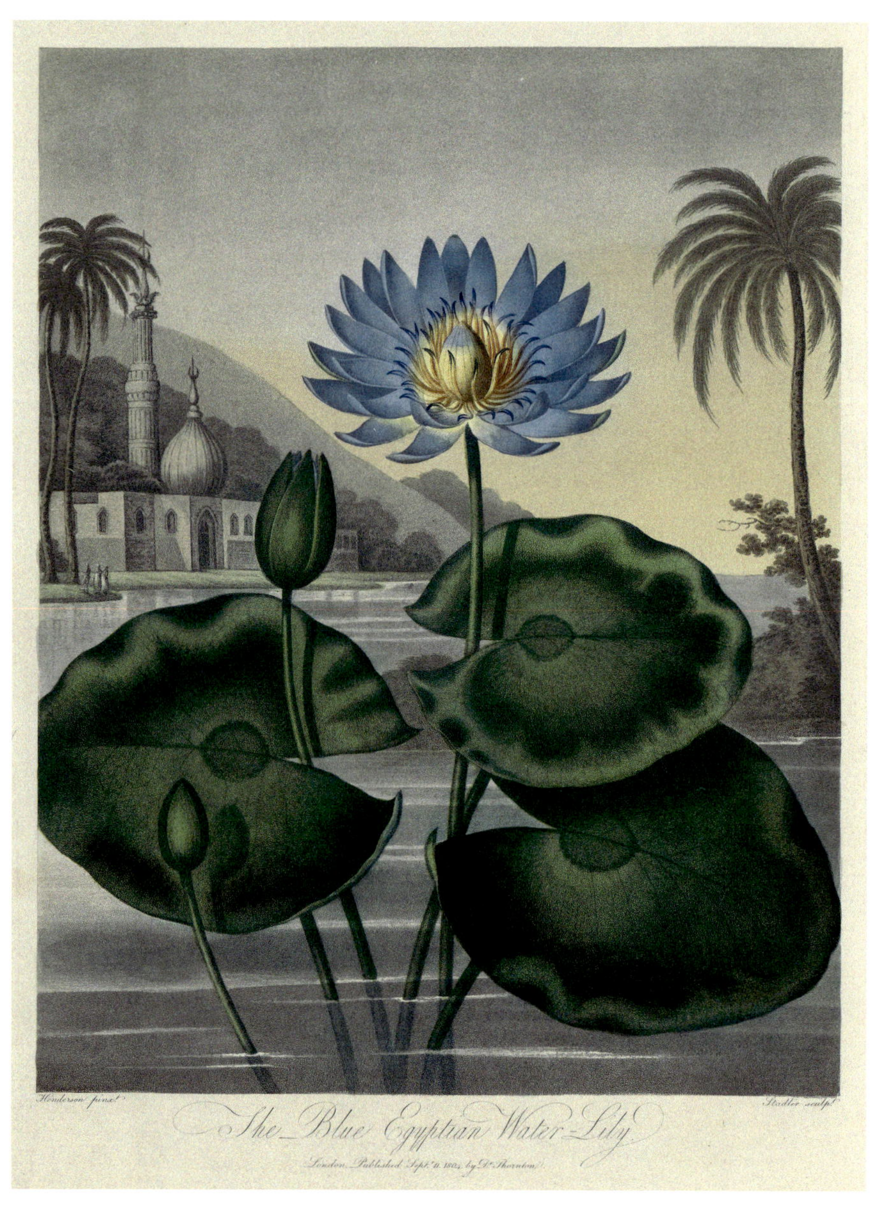

— 100 —

Joseph Constantine Stadler after Peter Charles Henderson,
The Blue Egyptian Water Lily, 1804

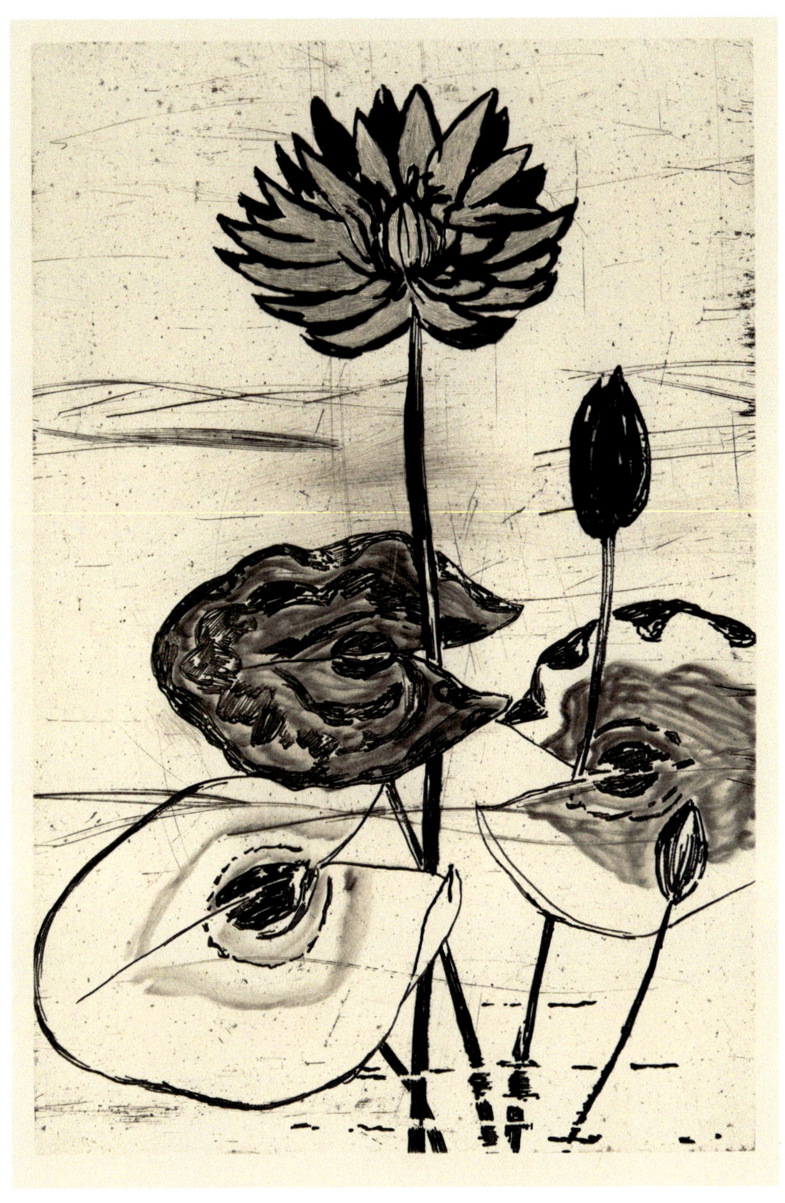

Jim Dine, *The Temple of Flora, Plate XIII: Blue Egyptian Water Lily*, 1984

Birthday portrait of a lady, Chinese, late 18th century

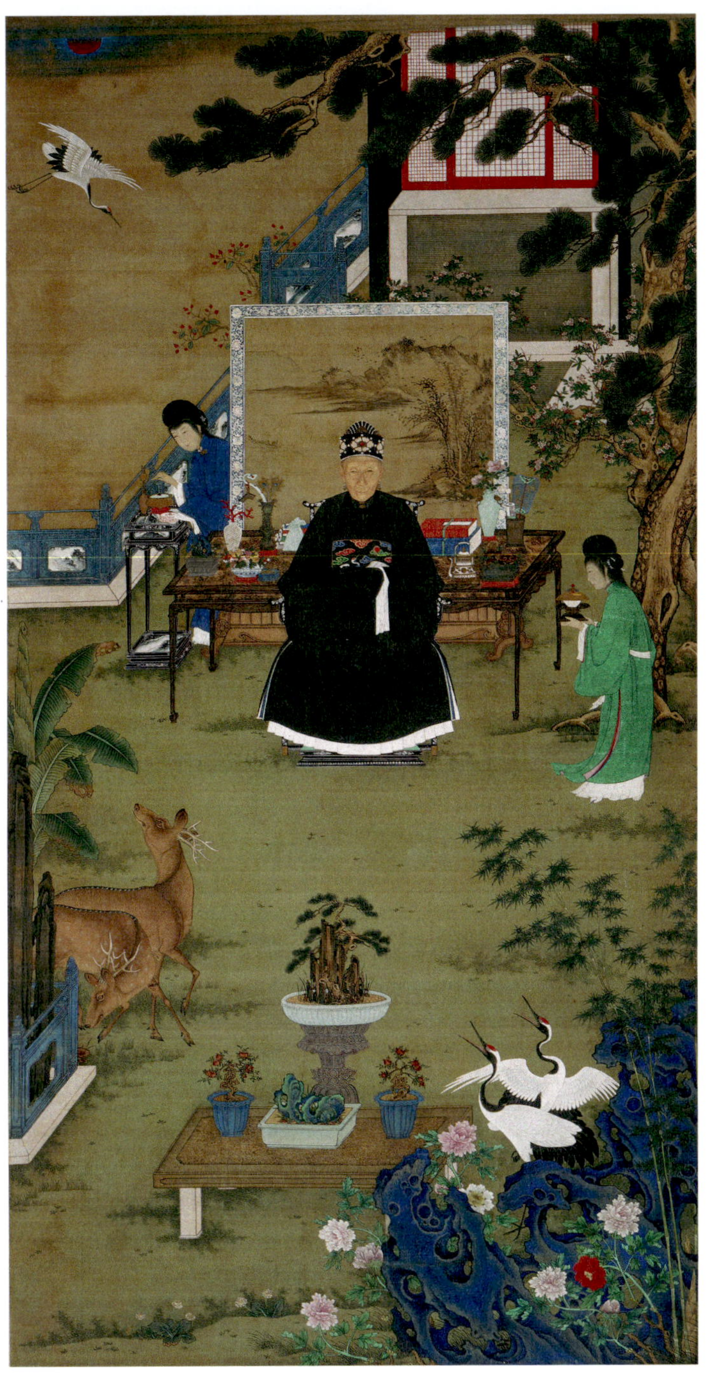

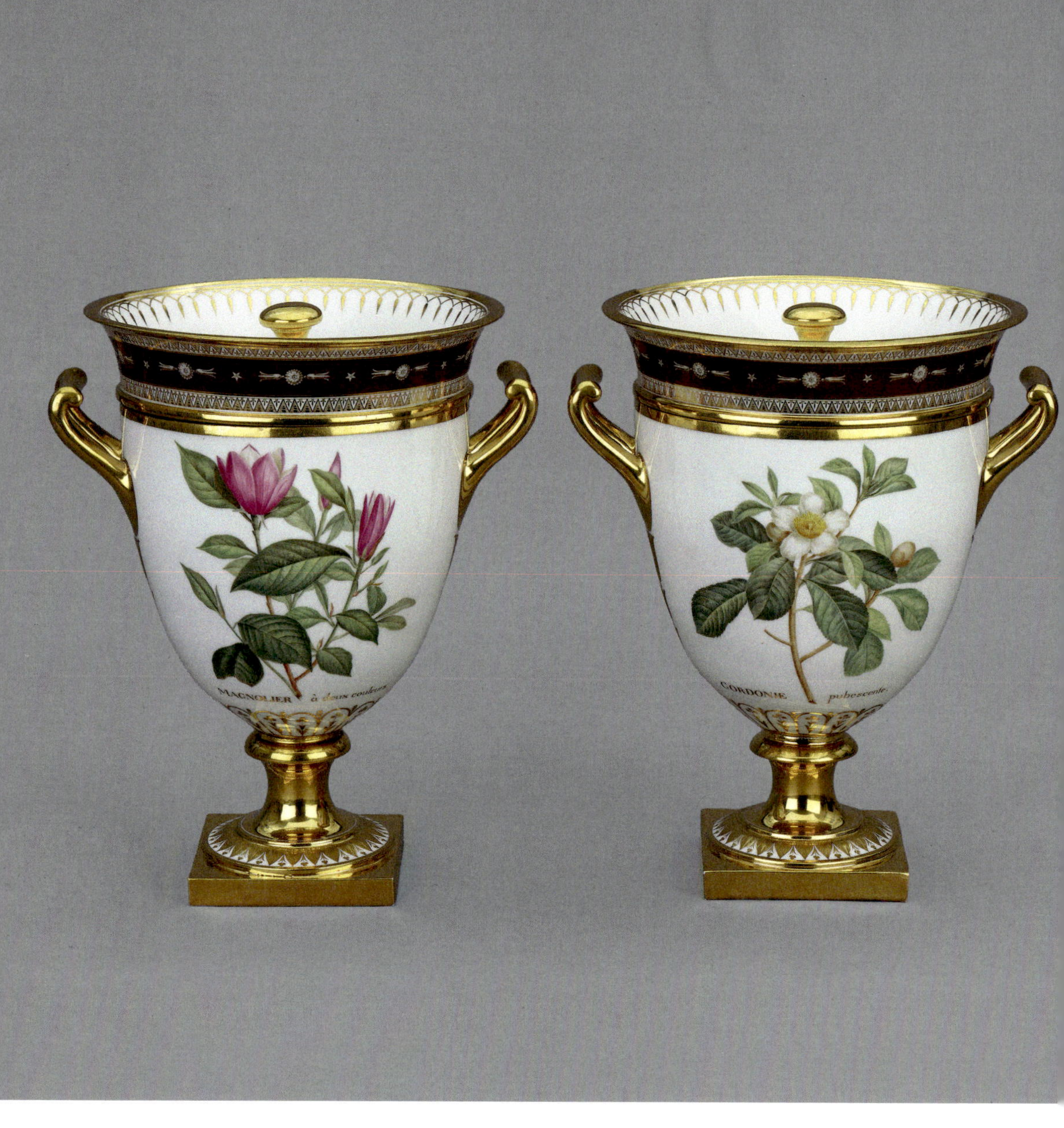

— 103 —
Sèvres Manufactory,
Ice cream coolers, 1803–04

— 104 —
Pierre-Joseph Redouté,
Albuca Minor, 1802

178

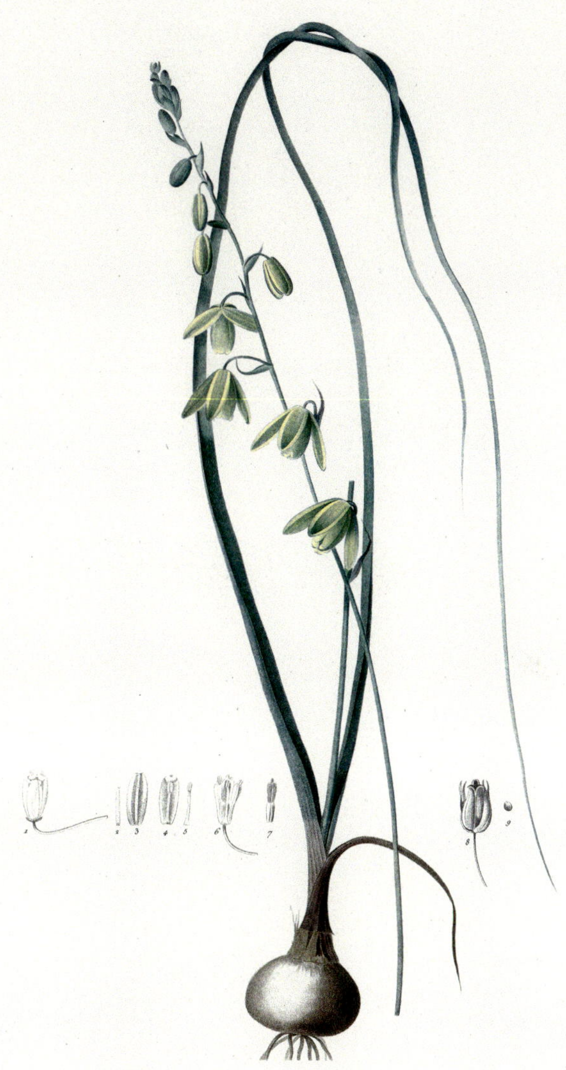

Albuca Minor.   *Albuca Jaunâtre.*

P. J. Redouté pinx.   Lemercier sculp.   Tassaert direx.

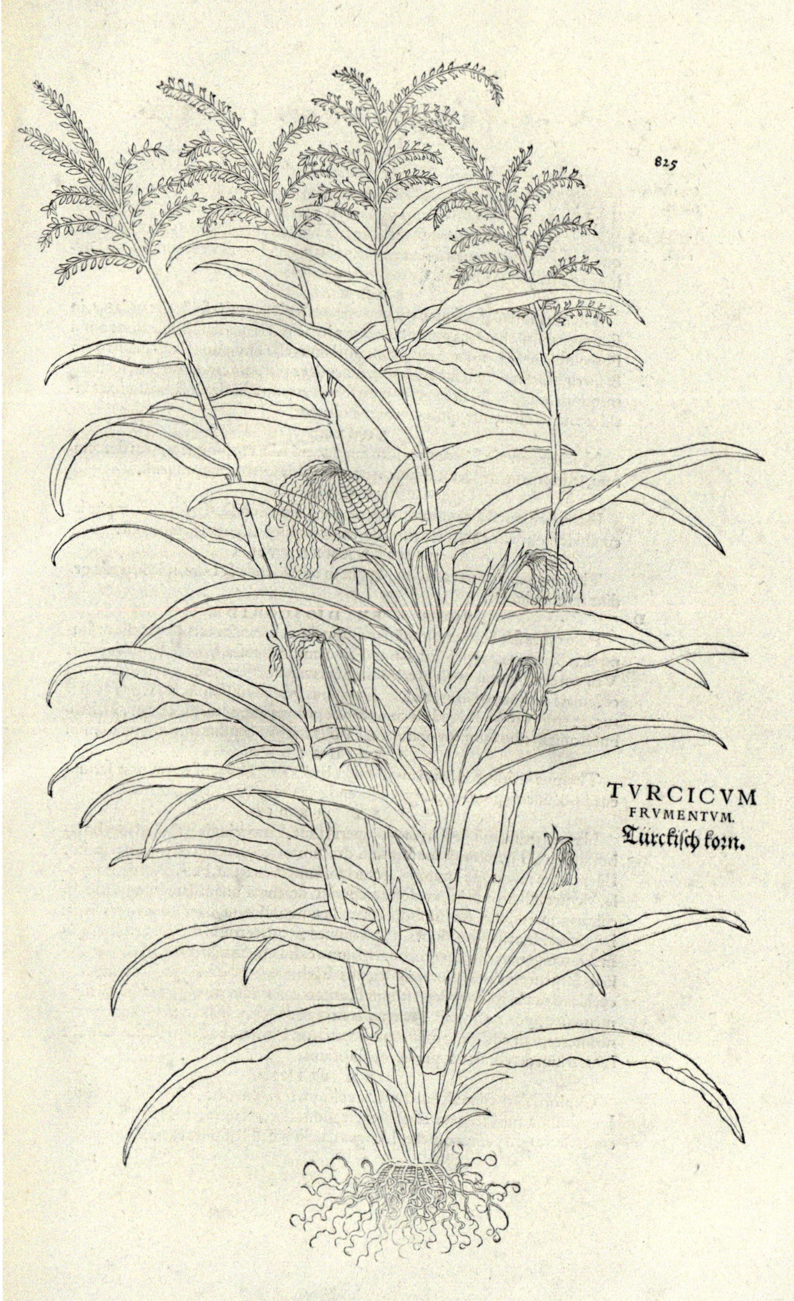
TVRCICVM
FRVMENTVM.
Türckisch korn.

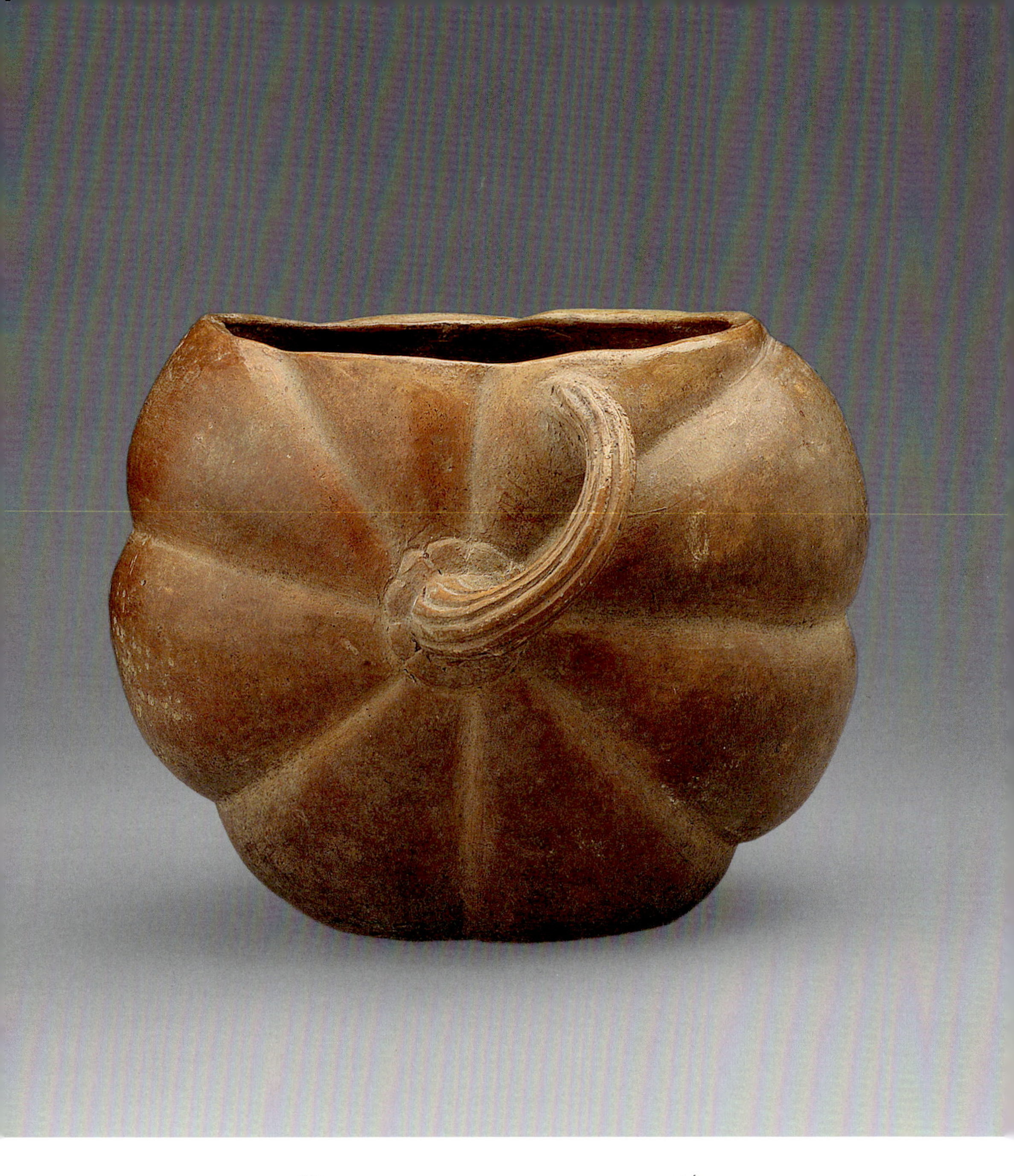

— 105 —
Turcicum Frumentum, German, 1542

— 106 —
Squash effigy dish, Maya, 650–850 CE

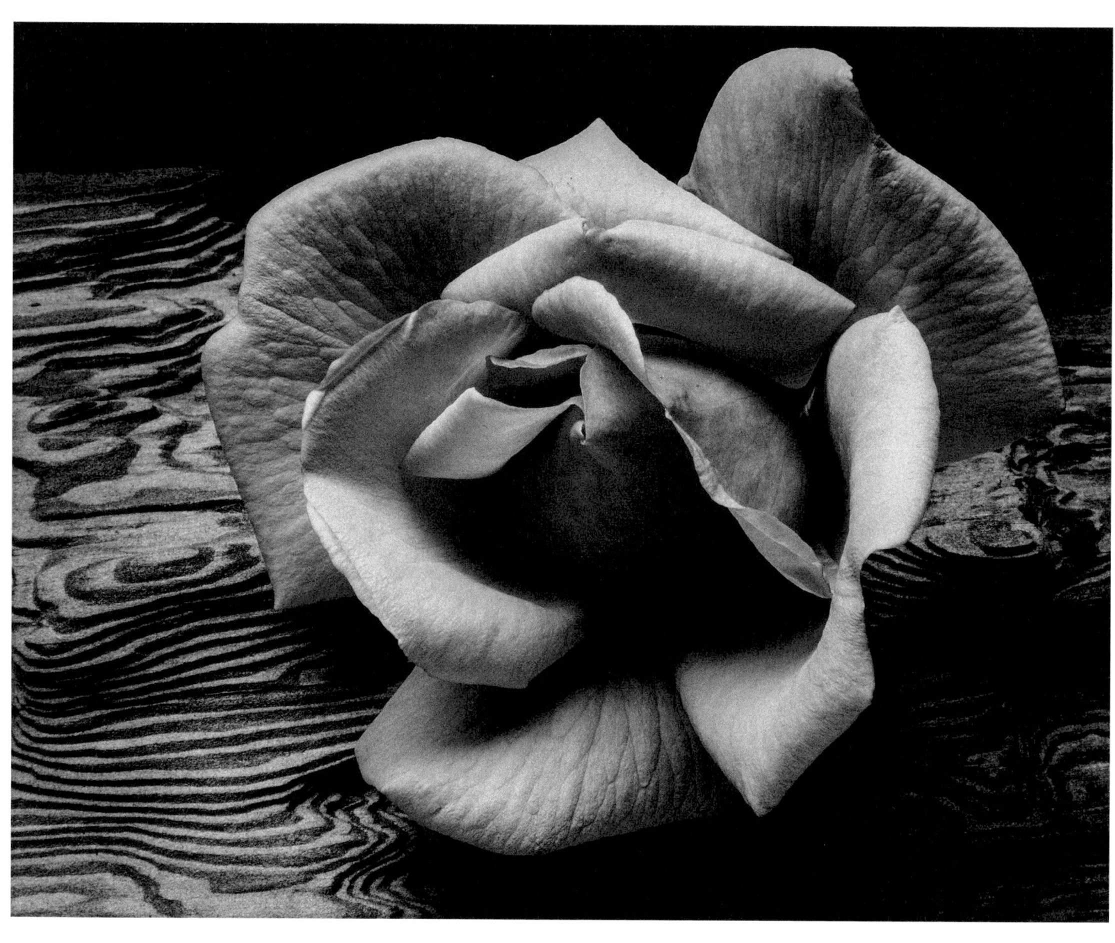

— 107 —
Ansel Adams, *Rose and Driftwood,
San Francisco*, about 1932

— 108 —
Vik Muniz, *White Brazilian Orchid*, 2010

182

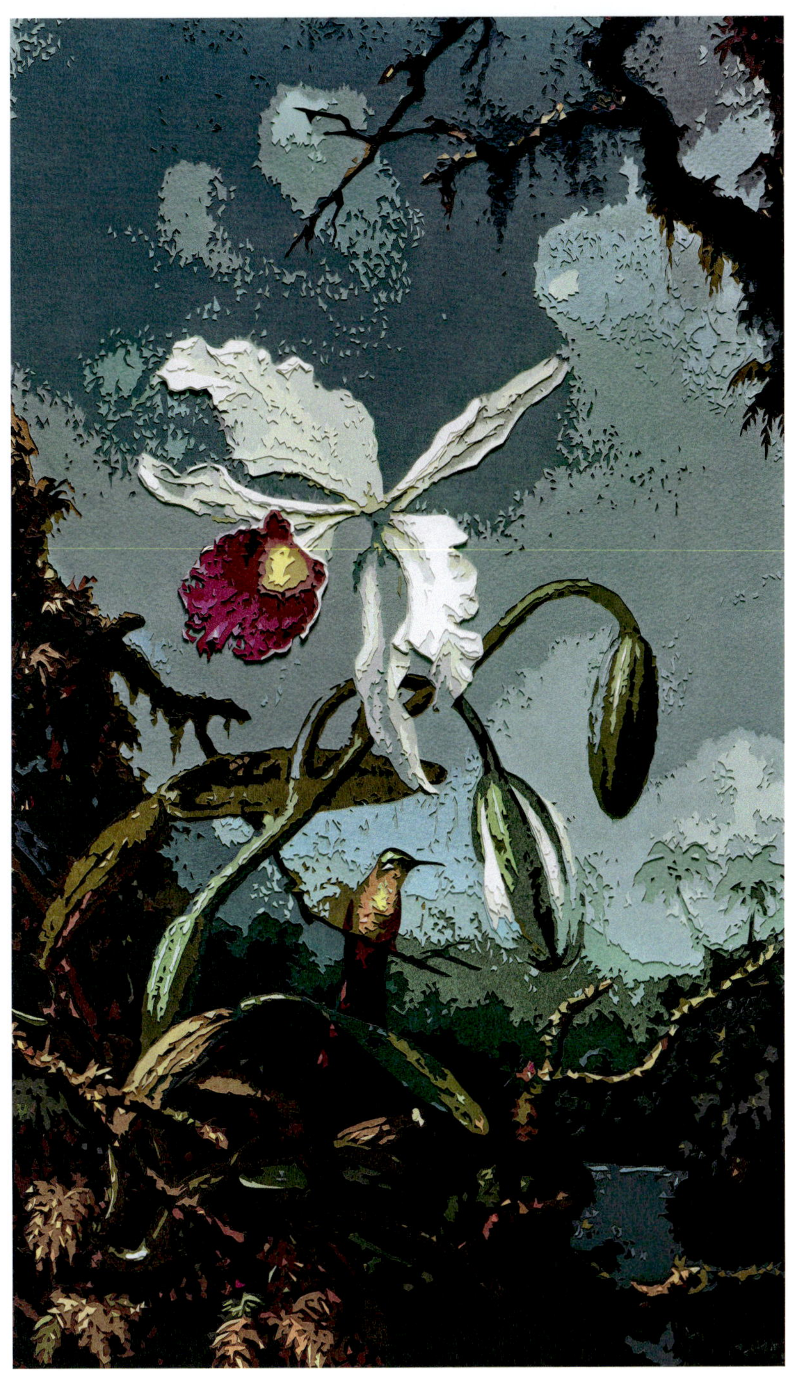

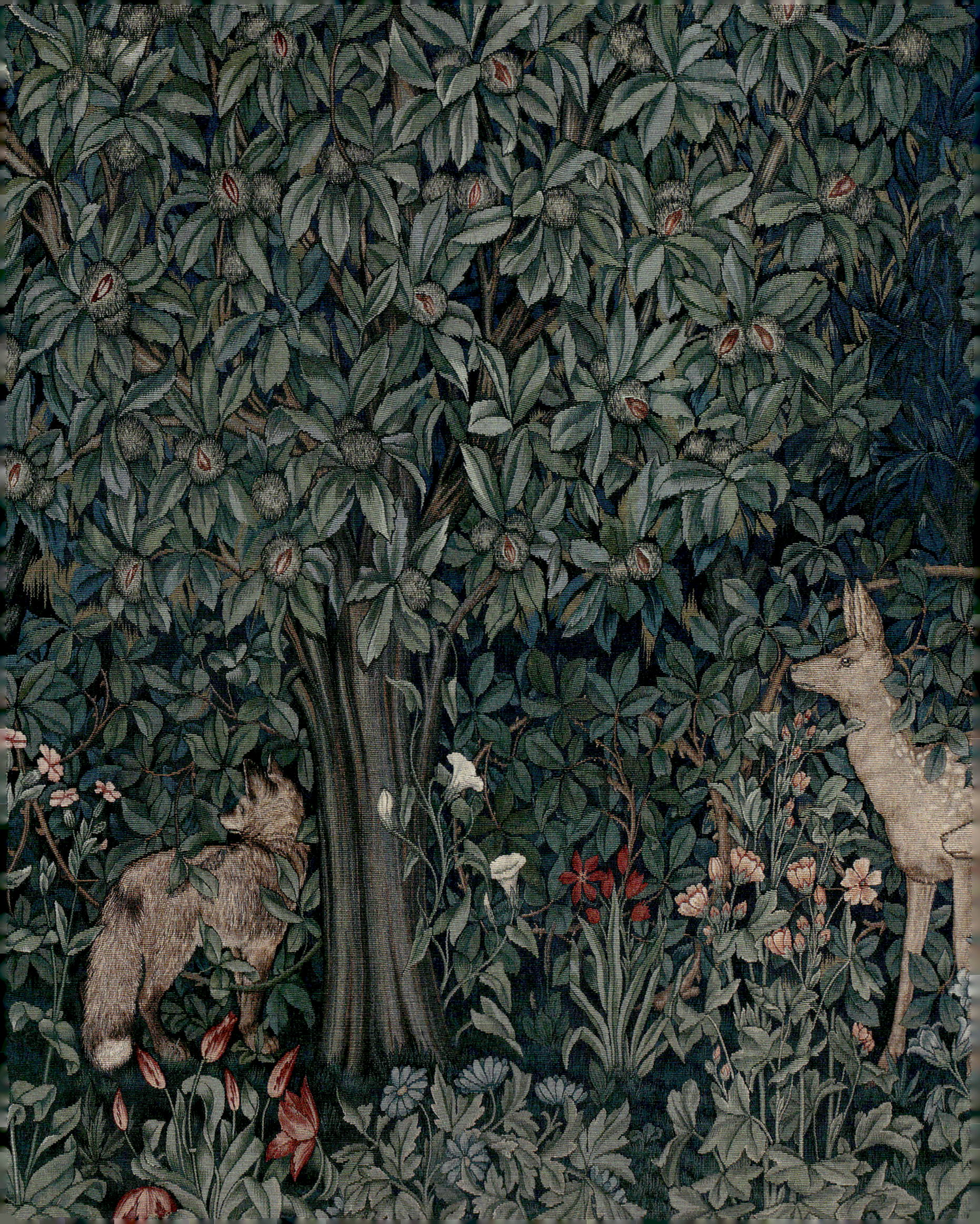

Gardens Real and Imagined

Due to their cyclical nature, gardens inherently speak to the future—future seasons, future growth, and ultimately, future change. Artists have looked to gardens as solace in the face of this change, as a form of critique, and as a harbinger of the future.

Arts and Crafts designers and social reformers such as William Morris, active in England during the second half of the nineteenth century, sought refuge in the natural world of their gardens. Faced with sweeping societal transformation brought on by the Industrial Revolution, Morris and his circle modeled their work on their conception of Medieval ideals, with an emphasis on hand crafts and domestic pieces, like the greenery tapestry produced at Merton Abbey workshop outside London in 1892 (114). Morris described such tapestries as "the noblest of the weaving arts" and saw in them a model for making art more broadly available to the public and uplifting for all.[1] The tapestry's densely wooded forest, replete with rabbits, fox, and deer, perfectly illustrates the designer's call for a return to the natural world when confronted with the burgeoning growth of cities. Nature's riches are further represented in the foreground with the delicate array of flowering plants, ranging from foxgloves to wild strawberries, daisies to bluebells.

Almost exactly a century later, photographer Gregory Crewdson's series *Natural Wonders* seems a far cry from

William Morris's utopian vision of a bucolic woodland. Inspired by diorama displays in natural history museums and the eerie, dreamlike settings of director David Lynch's films, Crewdson's tabletop creations focus on the unsettling beauty of American suburbia and its thin veneer of normalcy (109). Rows of cookie-cutter houses, empty streets, manicured lawns and gardens appear to have been invaded by a marauding army of insects and other animals, their progress unhampered by the presence of people in Crewdson's photographs. His apocalyptic landscapes, devoid of human beings, speak to an idea of gardens as microcosms of the larger natural world, one that in Crewdson's eyes has taken a much darker and disquieting turn toward the future.

The impact of human activity on the land can be measured in cultivated spaces, and even gardens of a modest scale demonstrate signs of climate change. They have become bellwethers of fluctuations in the environment, such as the hotter, drier summers and warmer, wetter winters that many parts of the world have experienced with growing frequency. With gardeners on the front lines of an issue that promises to have huge implications for everyone on earth, not just in the distant future but even in the near term, it may also be that gardens are an ideal platform for envisioning a better world.

Extreme weather events—in the form of droughts, storms, floods, and fires—and significant stressors on the ecological balance of the environment such as the steady rise of temperatures and shifting climate zones, have meant some environments are no longer suited to the plants that once flourished in them. Photographer Graciela Iturbide was invited to document the ethnobotanical garden in Oaxaca in central Mexico in 1998 (111). There she discovered native plants, many of them literally on life support, cared for cared for by the local people. Iturbide's haunting portraits of these ailing succulents and venerable cacti, with their handmade splints and bandages and hanging IVs, have a melancholy beauty that speaks to their strength and resilience, as well as the challenging conditions that they and their caretakers face to survive.

Mary Mattingly is another contemporary artist who has had a longstanding interest in seeking out ways to represent ancient geologic time, fragile ecosystems, and the visible marks of climate change on natural habitats. Her focus on the human impact on landscapes led her to create a Dr. Seuss–like series of glowing otherworldly gardens centered on futuristic plants and flowers that turn out to be much more than initially meets the eye. *Magnetic Field* appears to be set in a world upside down; although the moon shines brightly in the sky above, the plants below seem to be growing underwater (113).

Writing in the late 1990s, the self-described "gardenist" Gilles Clément defined earth as a "planetary garden" that requires careful tending, and declared that all of the world's inhabitants must be not only responsible gardeners but also "guardians" of this planet.[2] Clément also pointed out that gardens are spaces in which many diverse forms of life are brought together and taught to adapt in order to co-exist. For Clément, the natural environment should be treated with the same careful attention and stewardship as the networks of human communities. — KEH

— NOTES —

1. William Morris, "Textiles," *Journal of the Society of Arts* 36 (November, 18, 1887): 1133.

2. Gilles Clément, *The Planetary Garden and Other Writings* (Penn Studies in Landscape Architecture, 2015).

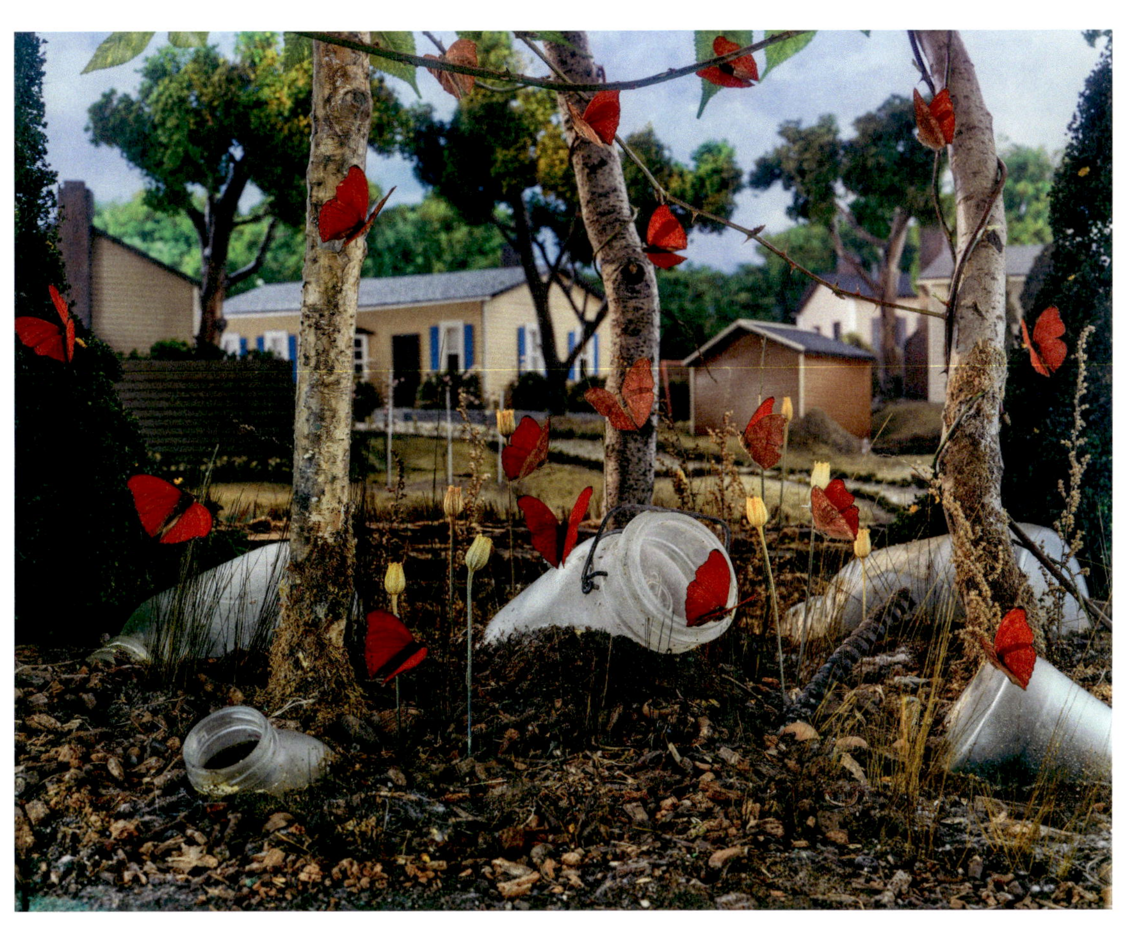

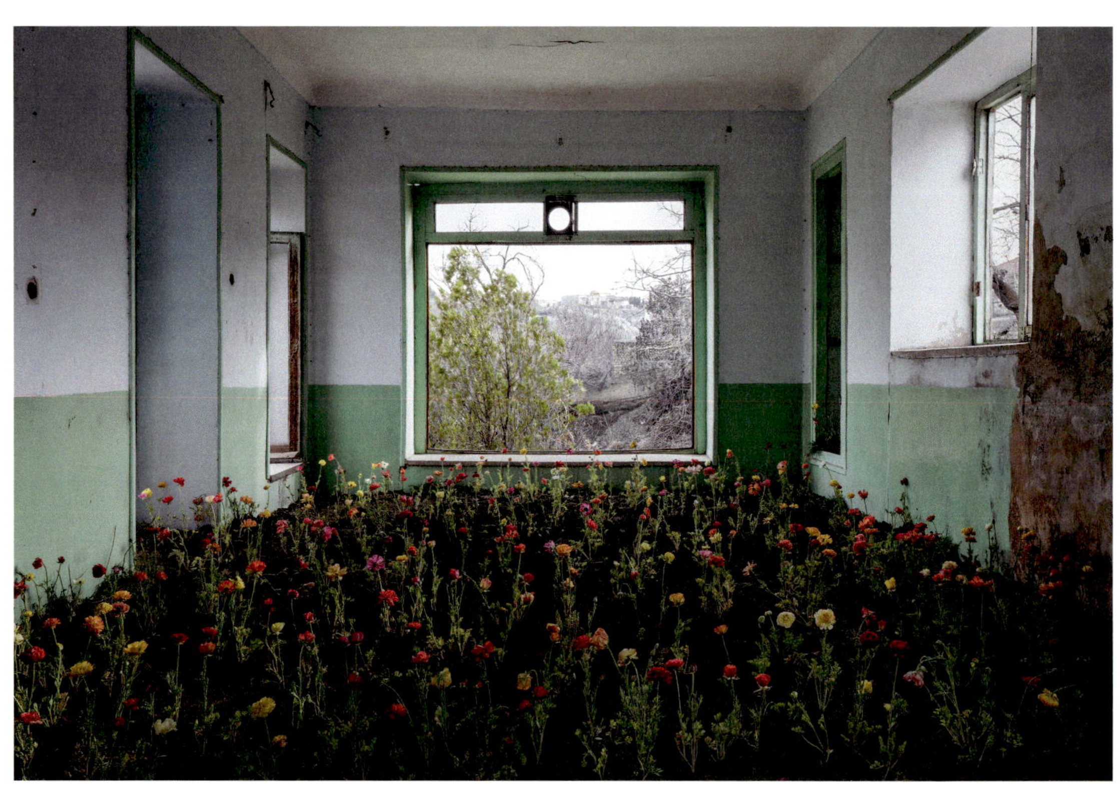

— 110 —

Gohar Dashti, *Untitled*, 2017

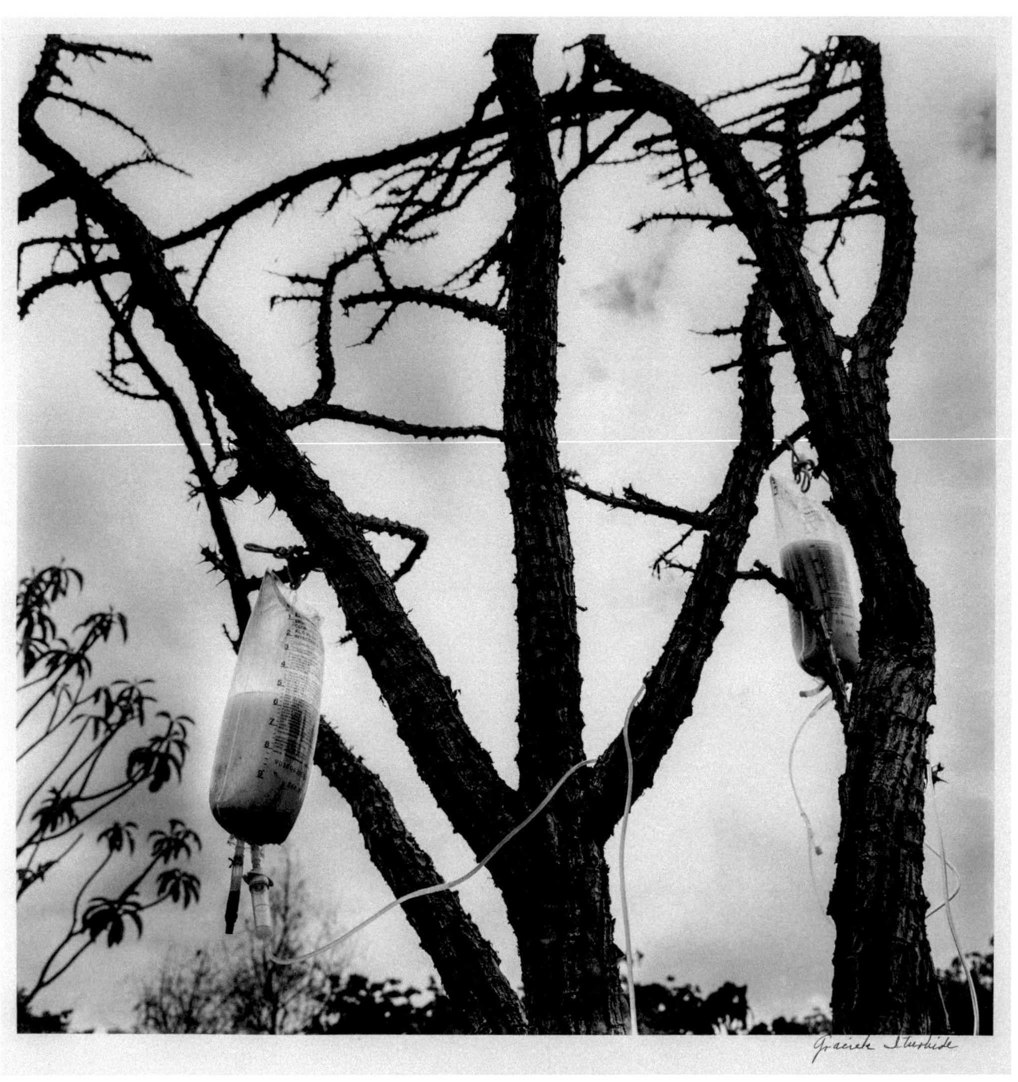

— 111 —

Graciela Iturbide, *Jardín botánico, Oaxaca, México*, 2002

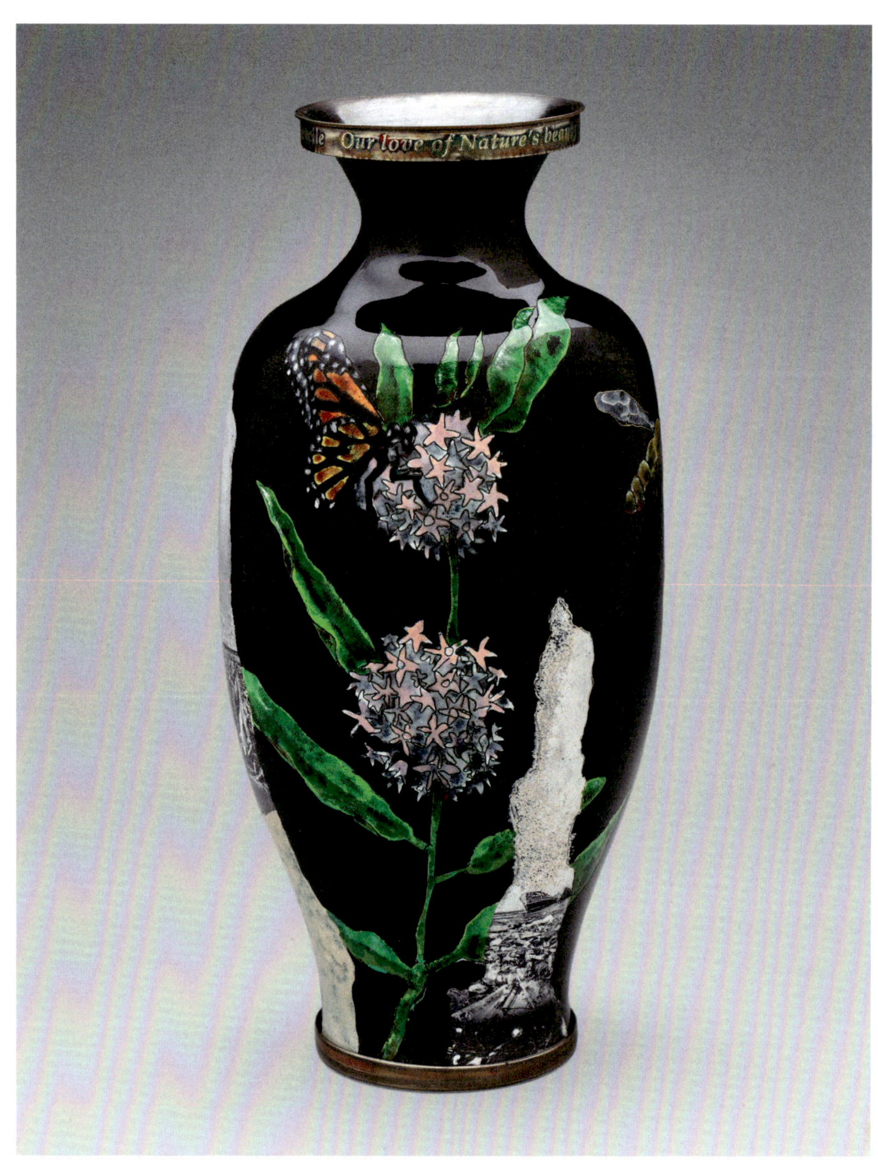

Harlan W. Butt, *Extinction Vessel #6: Veneer*, 2020

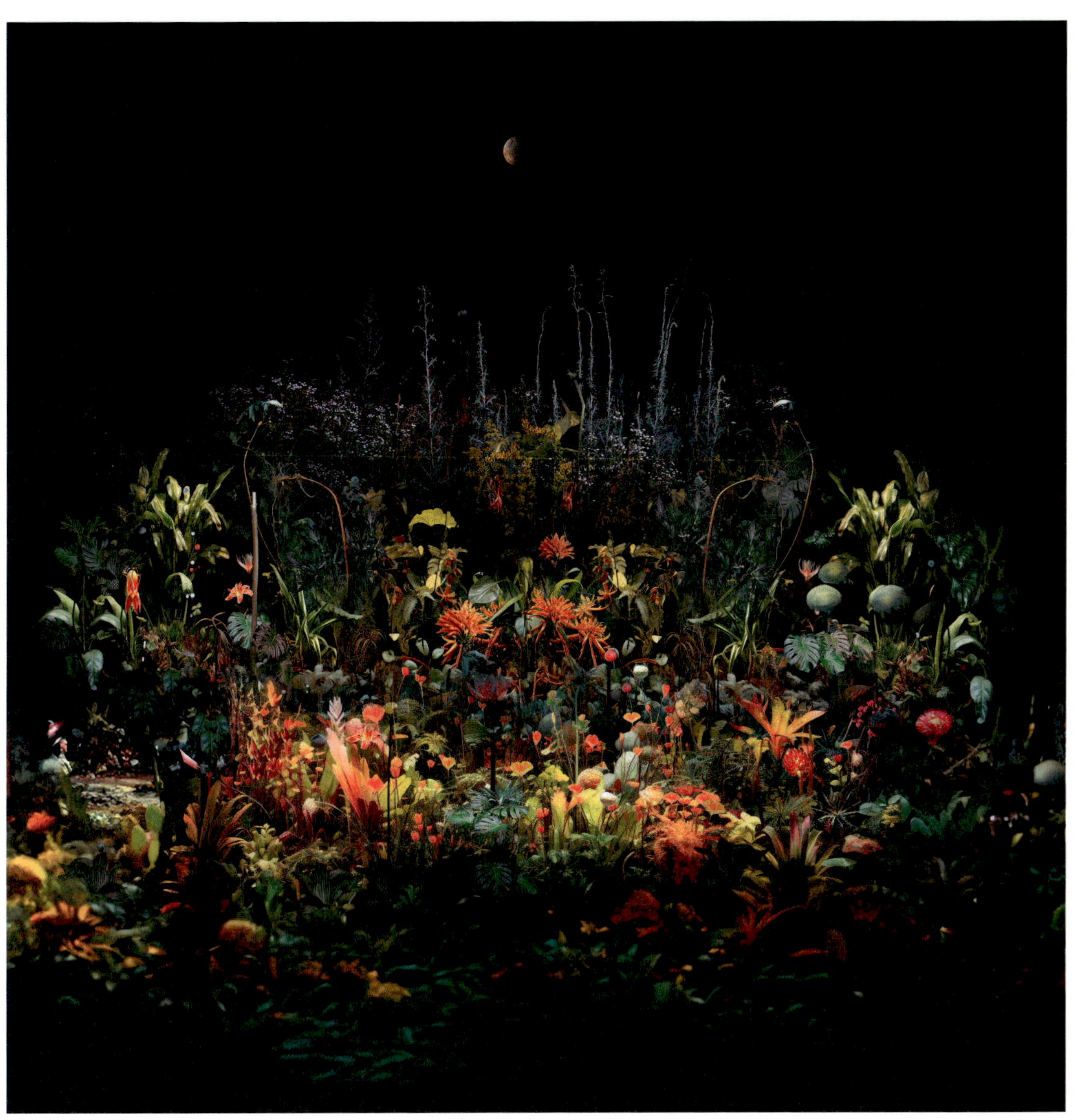

Mary Mattingly, *Magnetic Field*, 2023

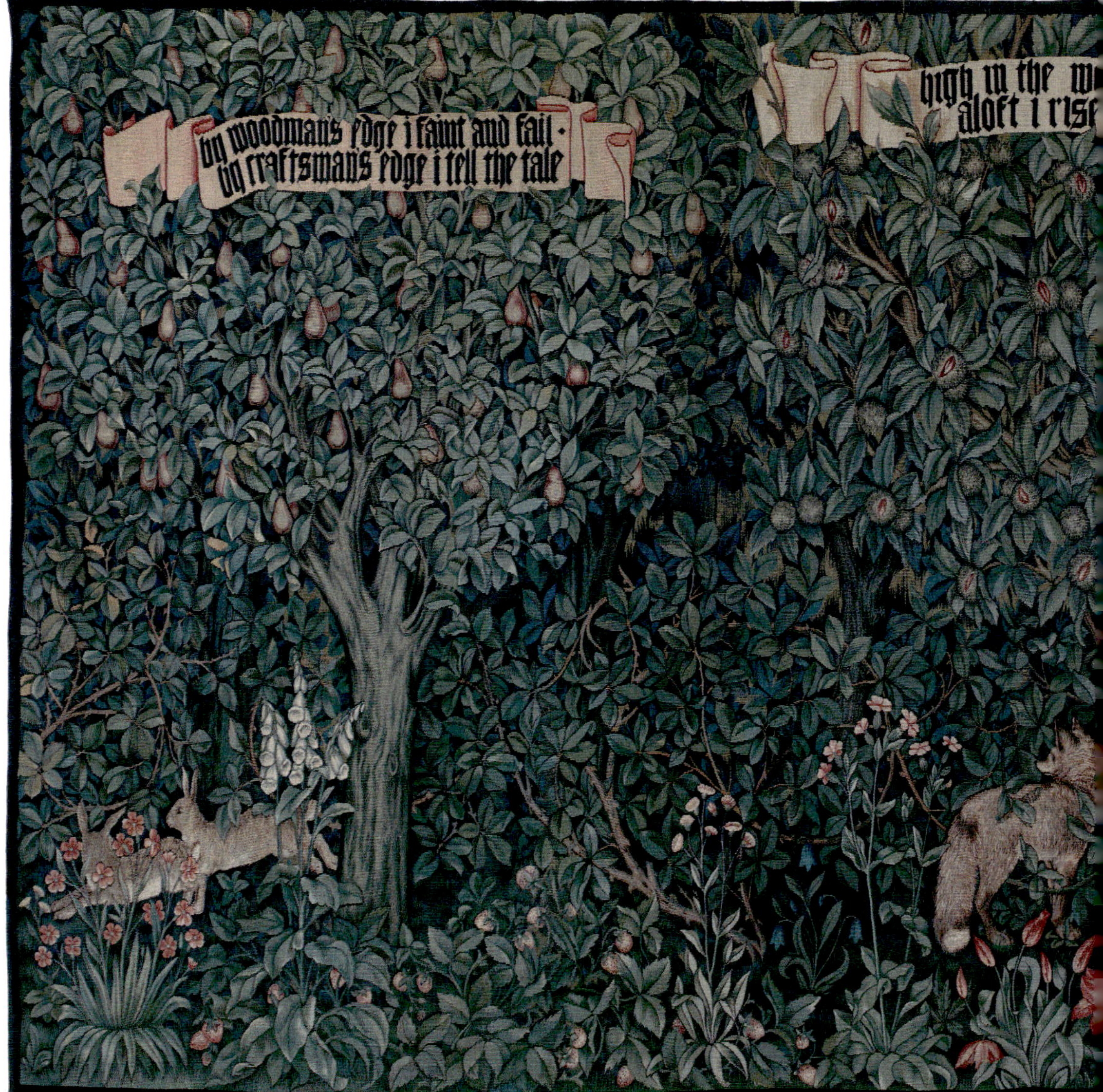
by woodman's edge i faint and fail ·
by craftsman's edge i tell the tale
high in the wood
aloft i rise

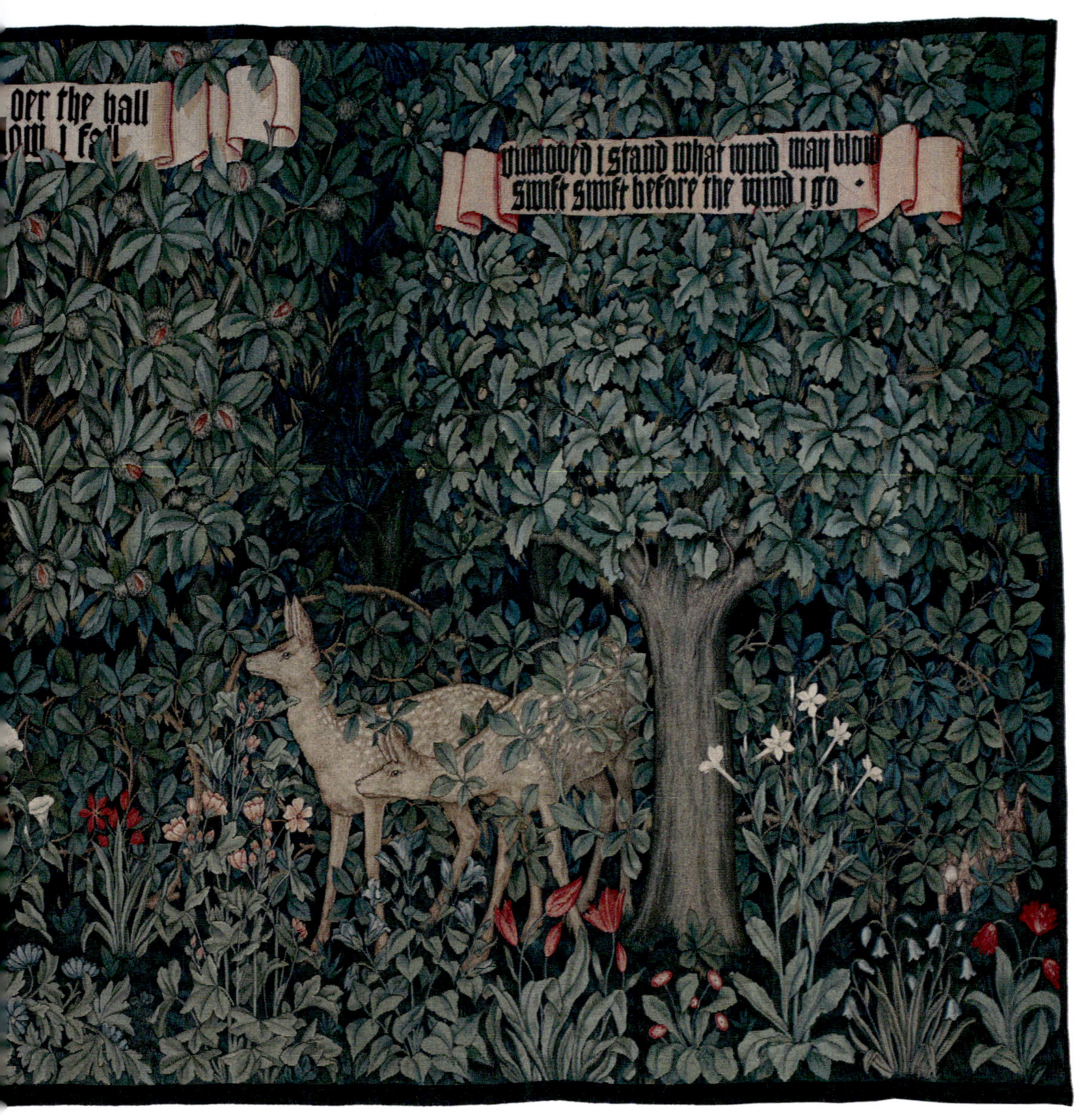

— 114 —
John Henry Dearle for Morris & Co., *Greenery*, 1892

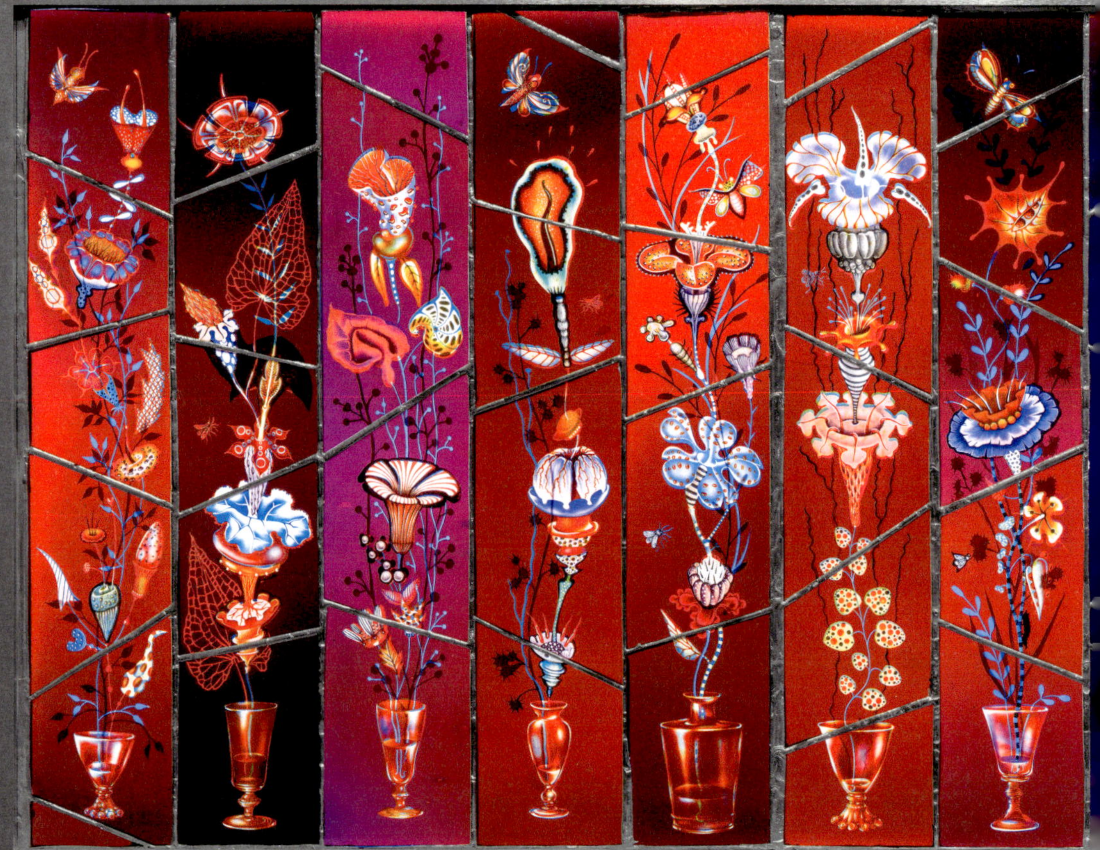

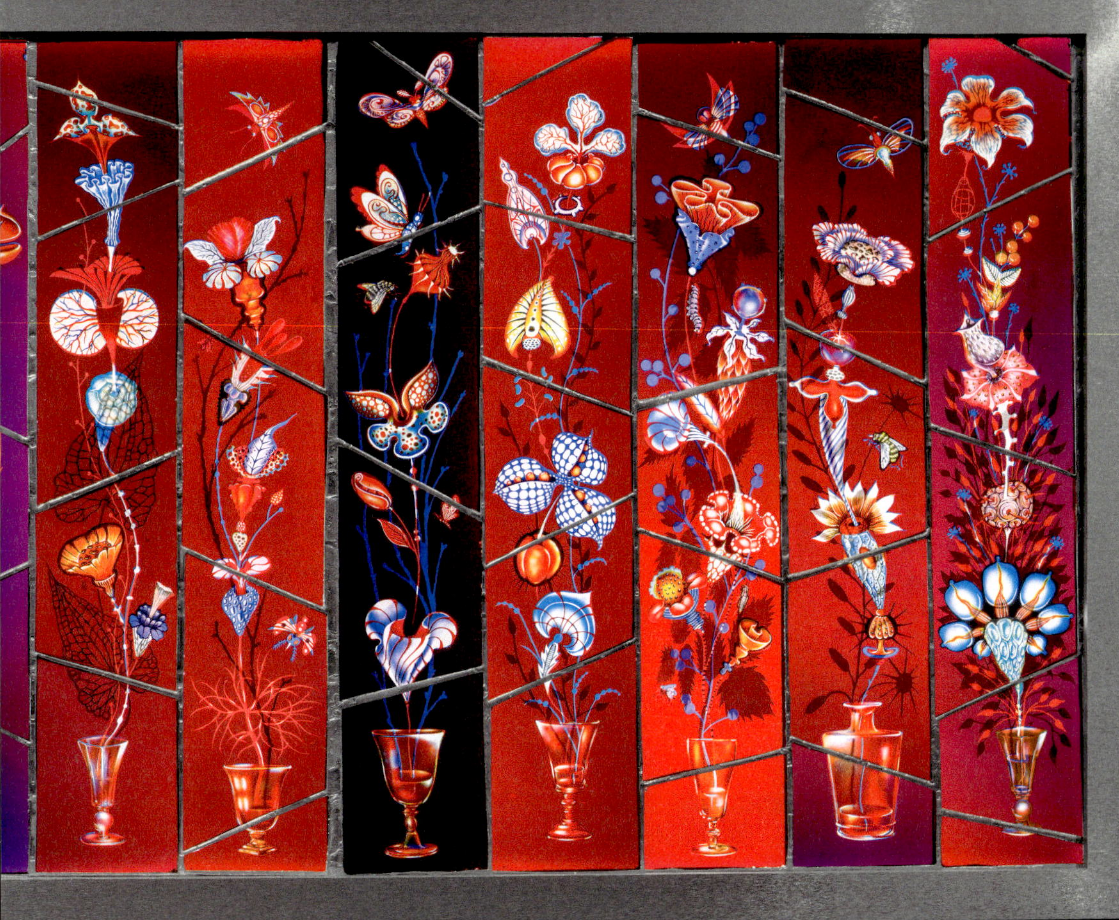

— 115 —

Judith Schaechter, *Cross Pollination*, 2019

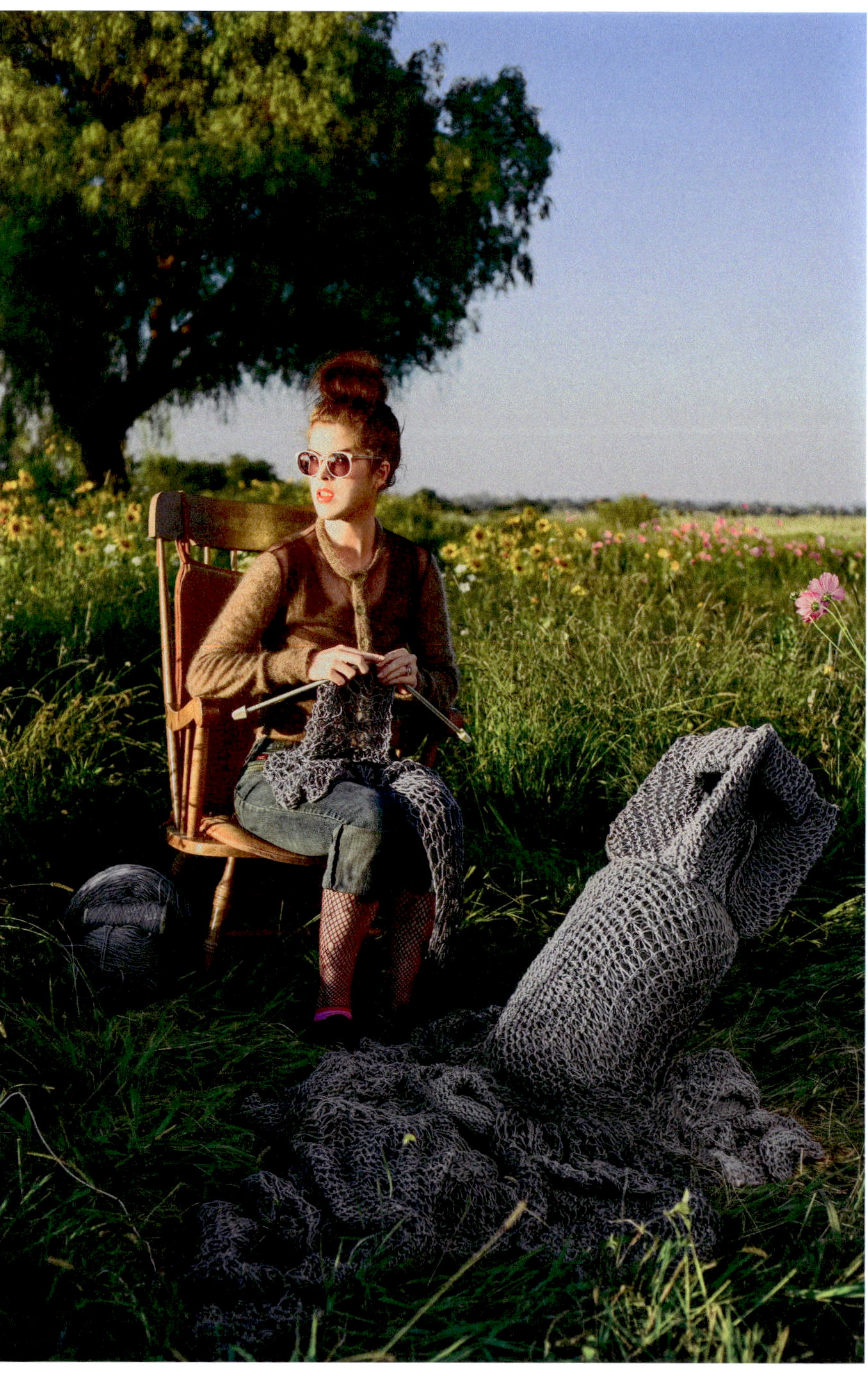

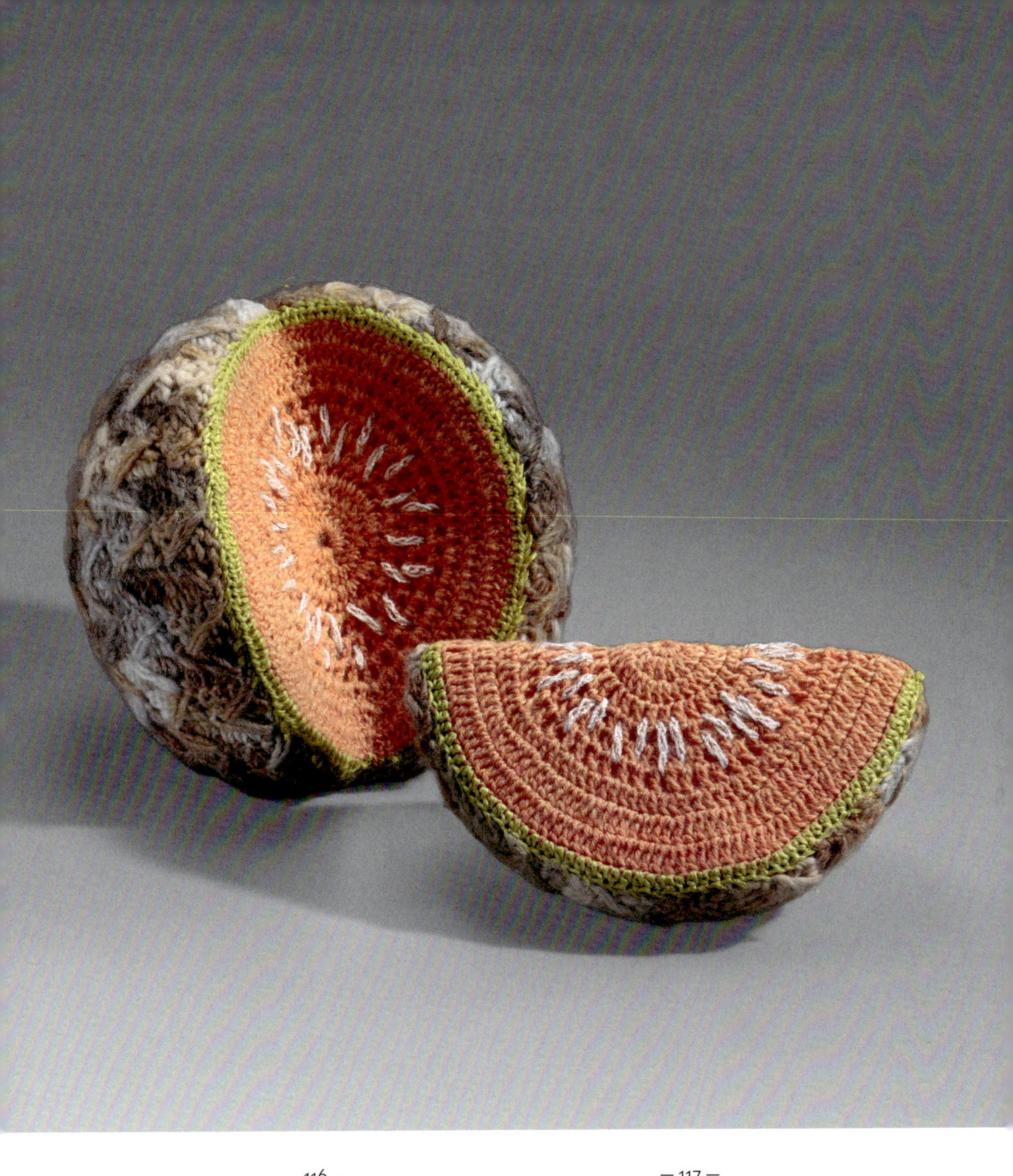

— 116 —
Daniela Edburg, *Killing Time*, 2010

— 117 —
Daniela Edburg, *The Melon*, 2011

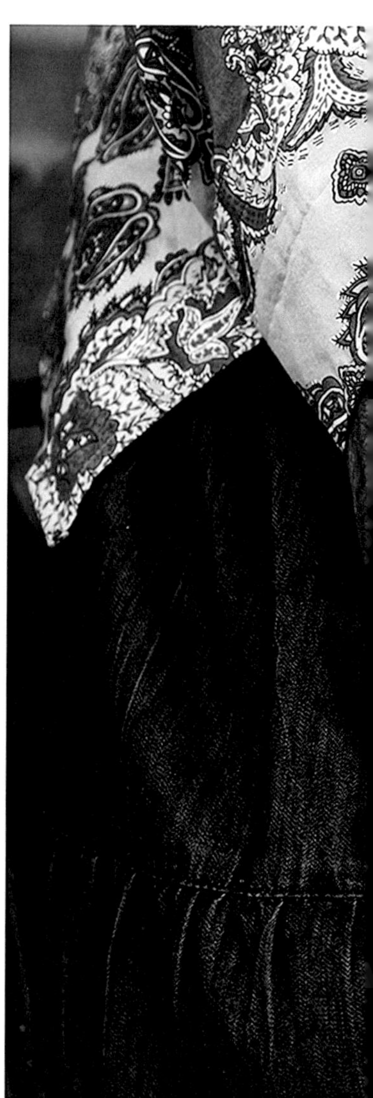

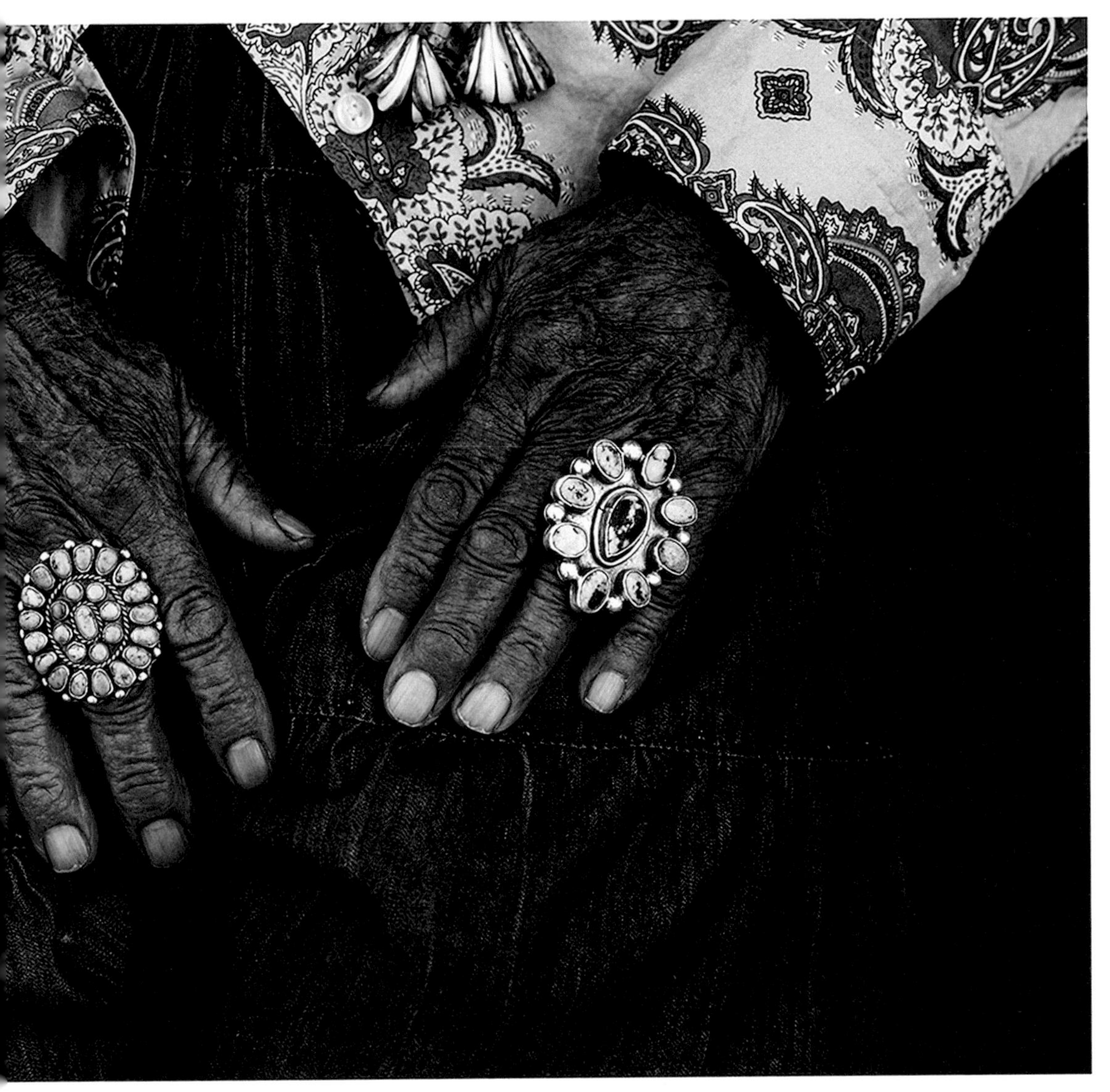

Dakota Mace, *Helen Nez, Diné Elder*, 2022

Garden Record

Peas, Onion Sets
...ttuce, Parsnips,
..., and Radish
...mber Hilled Dusted
...yhocks, Transplanted
...Sowed 50 ft Carrots
...Autumn Cup, Summer
...are beginning to

...on Apple & Rose
...sh, Peas & Catfish
...ock. One wolf growing
...re up except...
...& Beet.

...Seed for 6,000

...ow, Tomatoes,
...bagas, Mulched

...ocks & Garden
...Rose. ...
...lars from
...locating the
...Garden

...es
...wheat with
6000 □

1998 ~~Brad~~ (Garden Record)   1st snow 12-29 6 inches.   105

July 7 applied Henry Field's 19% Nit. Fert. to both Goldenglow — the Cucumber Hill and the #7 Tomato Plant, soon there is to be rain.

July 12 Dusted Tomato, Potato and Hollyhocks. Transplanted 8 Cabbage Plants.
July 17 Transplanted 17 Cabbage Plants Total 25.
18 Deer Juiced Apple & Rose.
20 The Black Hollyhocks are in bloom. Thinned Beets & Parsnips.
23 First Peas.
20 Humming Bird Feeder
25 Deer Juiced Apple & Rose. Side dressed Tomato Plants. 4 to go when ready. Dusted garden & Hollyhocks.
July 30 Side Dressed Nos. 6 & 7 Tomato Plants
1 First Summer Squash.
9 1st Cucumber. Side dressed last Tomatoes.
14 Deer Juiced Apple & Rose
21 Shortened vines of Autumn Cup Squash.
31 Picked 1st Tomatoes. (3)
Sept 6 Deer Juiced Apple & Rose
Sept 10 Picked 1st Big Beef Tomatoes. These are on stakes.
Sept 17 Light Frost on some Tomato Plants & Fruit.
Oct 19 Harvest 1 and 4 tenths bu. Beets. The Deer... with the harvest of 16 heads of Cabbage.
Oct 20 — 2 bu Potatoes. 2 bu Carrots. 60 ft row Onions Deer Juiced Apple Tree.

FURTHER READING

Alfrey, Nicholas, et al. *Art of the Garden: The Garden in British Art, 1800 to the Present Day*. London: Tate, 2004.

Berliner, Nancy. *The Emperor's Private Paradise*. Salem: Peabody Essex Museum, 2010.

Chivers, Ruth, ed. *Gardens of the Future: Unique Visions for a Changing World*. London: British Library, 2025.

Clément, Gilles. *Jardins, paysage et génie naturel*. Paris: Collège de France, 2012.

Cunas, Craig. *Fruitful Sites: Garden Culture in Ming Dynasty China*. Durham: Duke University Press, 1996.

Deliau, Phillippe, et al. *Dior: Enchanting Gardens*. New York: Rizzoli International Publications, Inc., 2025.

Dumas, Ann, and William H. Robinson. *Painting the Modern Garden: Monet to Matisse*. London: Royal Academy of Arts, 2015.

Farrar, Linda. *Gardens and Gardeners of the Ancient World: History, Myth, and Archaeology*. Oxford: Windgather Press, 2016.

Fenner, David, and Ethan Fenner. *The Art and Philosophy of the Garden*. Oxford: Oxford University Press, 2024.

Giesecke, Annette, and Naomi Jacobs. *Earth Perfect? Nature, Utopia, and the Garden*. London: Black Dog Publishing, 2012.

Goto, Seiko, and Takahiro Naka. *Japanese Gardens: Symbolism and Design*. London: Routledge, 2016.

Harrison, Robert Pogue. *Gardens: An Essay on the Human Condition*. Chicago: University of Chicago Press, 2008.

Hunt, John Dixon. *A World of Gardens*. London: Reaktion Books, 2012.

Kazemi, Farhad. *Jardins et Palais d'Orient*. Milan: Silvana editoriale, 2024.

Kincaid, Jamaica, and Kara Walker. *An encyclopedia of gardening for colored children*. New York: Farrar, Straus and Giroux, 2024.

Le Bon, Laurent. *Jardins*. Paris: Éditions de la Réunion des musées nationaux, 2017.

Mancoff, Debra N. *The Garden in Art*. London: Merrell Publishers, 2011.

Miller, Mara. *The Garden as an Art*. Albany: State University of New York Press, 1993.

Myers, K. Sara. *Ancient Roman Literary Gardens: Gender, Genre, and Geopoetics*. New York: Oxford University Press, 2024.

Ohlson, Nils. *Garten Eden: der Garten in der Kunst seit 1900*. Emden: Kunsthalle Emden, 2007.

Padon, Thomas. *Contemporary Photography and the Garden: Deceits & Fantasies*. New York: Harry N. Abrams, Inc., 2004.

Ross, Stephanie. *What Gardens Mean*. Chicago: University of Chicago Press, 1998.

Striolo, Carlotta, ed. *Eternal Spring: Gardens and Tapestries in the Renaissance*. Mechelen: Museum Hof van Buslyden, 2024.

Strong, Roy. *The Artist and the Garden*. New Haven: Yale University Press, 2000.

Tebbs, John, ed. *The Avant Gardens: Gardens Beyond Wild Expectations*. New York: Gestalten, 2023.

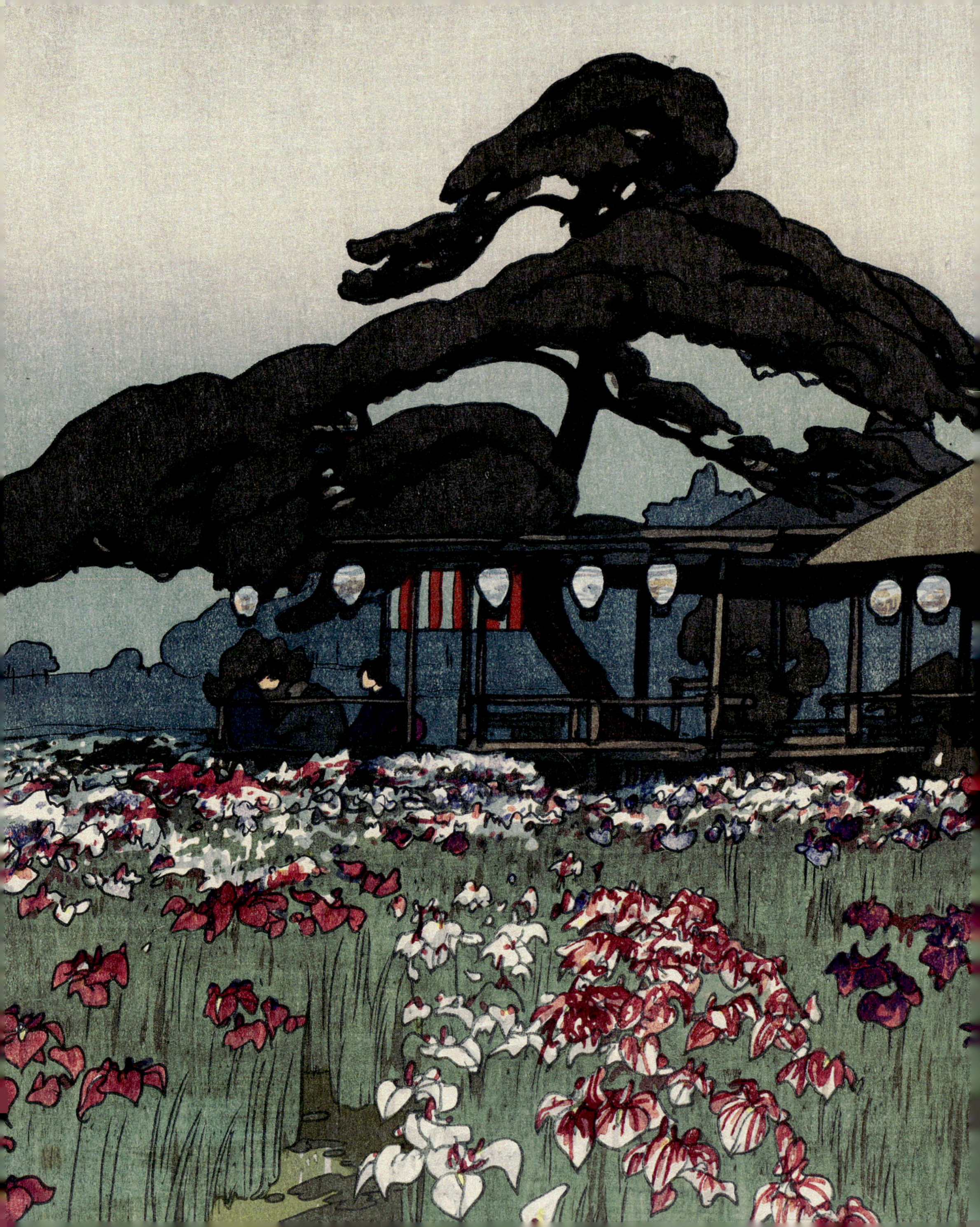

LIST OF ILLUSTRATIONS

10

Attributed to Chitarman
Indian, active about 1715–1760
Muhammad Shah in a garden,
about 1730–40
Ink, color, and gold on paper
38.6 × 43.4 cm (15³⁄₁₆ × 17¹⁄₁₆ in.)
Arthur Mason Knapp Fund, 26.283

11

Mary Nimmo Moran
American (born in Scotland),
1842–1899
A City Farm—New York, 1881
Etching
15 × 26 cm (5⅞ × 10¼ in.)
Gift of Sylvester Rosa Koehler, K1490

12

Milton Rogovin
American, 1909–2011
*Lower West Side, Buffalo
(Joe and Garden)*, 1974
Gelatin silver print
25.4 × 20.3 cm (10 × 8 in.)
Gift of Denise Jarvinen and
Pierre Cremieux, 2007.1032

13

Designed by Paul Poiret
(French, 1879–1944)
Illustrated by Georges Lepape
(French, 1887–1971)
"Les Jardins de Versailles -
Costume de Paul Poiret dans le
goût Louis XIV" (The gardens of
Versailles - an outfit by Paul Poiret
in the style of Louis XIV), 1913
Gazette du Bon Ton, volume 1, no. 4
Photomechanical lithograph
with hand-applied color (pochoir)
Transferred from the William Morris
Hunt Memorial Library, 2004.9.5

14

Justin Kimball
American, born in 1961
Phoenix, Arizona, from the series
Where We Find Ourselves, 1997
Chromogenic print
50.8 × 61 cm (20 × 24 in.)
Gift of Jeanne L. and Richard S.
Press. 2007.941

15

Edouard Vuillard
French, 1868–1940
Le jardin devant l'atelier
(The garden in front of the studio),
about 1901
Tempera on paper
68.1 × 49 cm (26¹³⁄₁₆ × 19⁵⁄₁₆ in.)
Helen and Alice Colburn Fund,
57.120a-b

16

Jean-François Millet
French, 1814–1875
Gardener with watering can,
about 1860
Graphite over black crayon on paper
26.4 × 21.4 cm (10⅜ × 8⁷⁄₁₆ in.)
Gift of Mrs. John Alden Carpenter,
63.2700

17

Amphora with Dionysos in
a vineyard, 540–530 BCE
Greek
Ceramic
H. 51.4 cm (20¼ in.)
Museum purchase with funds by
exchange from the Henry Lillie
Pierce Residuary Fund and Bartlett
Collection—Museum purchase
with funds from the Francis
Bartlett Donation of 1900, 63.952

18

Flo Perkins
American, born in 1951
87-Year-Old Cactus, 2009
Blown glass
H. 52.1 cm (20 ½ in.)
Gift of the artist in memory of her
father, Forbes Perkins, 2024.3911

19

Maeda Masao
Japanese, 1904–1974
Sand Garden, 1960
Woodblock print
63.1 × 46.5 cm (24¹³⁄₁₆ × 18⁵⁄₁₆ in.)
Asiatic Curator's Fund. 61.1116

20

Lois Conner
American, born in 1951
Xi Hu, Hangzhou, Zhejiang, China,
1998
Inkjet print
64.8 × 147.3 cm (25½ × 58 in.)
Museum purchase with funds
donated by Scott Offen, 2016.584

21

Yuan Yao
Chinese, active around 1740–80
Elegant gathering in a secluded
garden, mid-18th century
Ink and color on silk
232 × 50.7 cm (91⁵⁄₁₆ × 19¹⁵⁄₁₆ in.)
Julia Bradford Huntington James
Fund, 08.93–08.104

　　　LIST OF ILLUSTRATIONS

33
Andrew Raftery
September, Mowing, from *The Autobiography of a Garden on Twelve Engraved Plates,* 2009–16
Engraving transfer printed
on glazed white earthenware
Diam. 31.8 cm (12 ½ in.)
Otis Norcross Fund, 2019.510.9

34
Jacques Rigaud
French, 1681–1754
Vue de l'Orangerie de Versailles (View of the Orangerie of Versailles), 1720s
Black chalk, pen and gray ink, and brush with gray wash on paper
22.5 × 47.3 cm (8⅞ × 18⅝ in.)
Ernest Wadsworth Longfellow Fund, 2007.602

35
Elizabeth Talford Scott
American, 1916–2011
Flower Garden, 1989
Cotton plain weave, synthetic knits, cotton thread, glass beads and other media
144.8 × 111.8 cm (57 × 44 in.)
Museum purchase with funds donated by Suzanne Werber Dworsky, 2022.2011

36
Giovanni di Paolo
Italian, about 1399–1482
Madonna of Humility, about 1442
Tempera on panel
61.9 × 48.9 cm (24⅜ × 19¼ in.)
Maria Antoinette Evans Fund, 30.772

37
Carpet, about 1590–1600
Mughal
Cotton warp and weft with wool knotted pile
243 × 155 cm (95¹¹⁄₁₆ × 61 in.)
Gift of Mrs. Frederick L. Ames, in the name of Frederick L. Ames, 93.1480

38
Tile depicting the gateway to Paradise, about 1600
Ottoman
Fritware with polychrome decoration under clear glaze
67 × 70.2 cm (26⅜ × 27⅝ in.)
Gift of Mrs. Samuel D. Warren, 90.162

39
Elizabeth Courtis
English, 18th century
Sampler, 1796
Linen plain weave embroidered with silk
56.5 × 47 cm (22¼ × 18½ in.)
Gift of Mr. and Mrs. Berger in memory
of Susan Jeannette Westfall, 2003.432

40
Bowl with fish and lotuses, 1550–1295 BCE
Egyptian
Bichrome faience
Diam. 15.7 cm (6³⁄₁₆ in.)
William E. Nickerson Fund, 1977.619

41
Capital from La Charité-sur-Loire, about 1100–25
French
Limestone
62 × 68 × 42 cm
(24⁷⁄₁₆ × 26¾ × 16⁹⁄₁₆ in.)
Gift of Mr. and Mrs. Edward Jackson Holmes, 49.534

42
Fresco panel from Villa of the Contrada Bottaro, Pompeii, 14–62 CE
Roman
Fresco
190 × 143 cm (74¹³⁄₁₆ × 56⁵⁄₁₆ in.)
Ellen Frances Mason Fund, 33.499

43
Fountain basin with a reclining river god, 98–138 CE
Roman
Marble
69.2 × 88.6 × 72.5 cm
(27¼ × 34⅞ × 28⁹⁄₁₆ in.)
Museum purchase with funds by exchange from a Gift of Mr. And Mrs. Henry P. Kidder, a Gift of Thomas Gold Appleton, a Gift of Edward Jackson Holmes, a Gift of Mrs. Francis C. Lowell, Otis Norcross Fund, and a Gift of Edward Perry Warren, 2002.21

44
William Blake
English, 1757–1827
The Archangel Raphael with Adam and Eve, illustration to Milton's *Paradise Lost*, 1808
Black ink and watercolor with gold paint over graphite on paper
49.8 × 39.8 cm (19⅝ × 15¹¹⁄₁₆ in.)
Museum purchase with funds donated by contribution, 90.97

45
William Blake
The Temptation and Fall of Eve, illustration to Milton's *Paradise Lost*, 1808
Black ink and watercolor on paper
49.7 × 38.7 cm (19⁹⁄₁₆ × 15¼ in.)
Museum purchase with funds donated by contribution, 90.99

46
Attributed to Asnaku Melese
Ethiopian, active in Israel, 20th century
Pillow sham, 1990–2012
Cotton plain weave and twill, acrylic embroidery
35.6 × 40.6 cm (14 × 16 in.)
Gift of Judith Manelis, 2012.837

47
Funerary stele with paradisiacal motifs, 6th–7th century CE
Coptic
Limestone
58.5 × 42 cm (23¹⁄₁₆ × 16⁹⁄₁₆ in.)
Emily Esther Sears Fund, 04.1845

48
Erastus Salisbury Field
American, 1805–1900
The Garden of Eden, about 1860
Oil on canvas
88.26 × 116.52 cm (34¾ × 45⅞ in.)
Gift of Maxim Karolik for the M. and M. Karolik Collection of American Paintings, 1815–1865, 48.1027

49
Joyce J. Scott
American, born in 1948
Adam and Eve Being Cast from the Garden of Eden, 1981–82
Glass and metal beads, wire, and leather
48.3 × 31.8 cm (19 × 12½ in.)
The Daphne Farago Collection, 2012.1308

50
John Singer Sargent
American, 1856–1925
Villa di Marlia, Lucca: A Fountain, 1910
Watercolor, with wax resist, over graphite on paper
40.4 × 53.1 cm (15⅞ × 20⅞ in.)
The Hayden Collection—Charles Henry Hayden Fund, 12.233

51
John Singer Sargent
Villa di Marlia, Lucca: The Balustrade, 1910
Watercolor, with wax resist, over graphite on paper
40.2 × 52.8 cm (15¹³⁄₁₆ × 20¹³⁄₁₆ in.)
The Hayden Collection—Charles Henry Hayden Fund, 12.228

52
John Singer Sargent
Villa di Marlia, Lucca, 1910
Watercolor, with wax resist, over graphite on paper
40.5 × 53.2 cm (15¹⁵⁄₁₆ × 20¹⁵⁄₁₆ in.)
The Hayden Collection—Charles Henry Hayden Fund, 12.232

53
John Singer Sargent
Daphne, 1910
Watercolor, with wax resist, over graphite on paper
52.5 × 40.2 cm (20¹¹⁄₁₆ × 15¹³⁄₁₆ in.)
The Hayden Collection—Charles Henry Hayden Fund, 12.230

54
Master of the Gardens of Love
Netherlandish, active in 1440–1450
The Small Garden of Love, 1440–50
Engraving
8.5 × 19.9 cm (3⅜ × 7¹³⁄₁₆ in.)
Katherine E. Bullard Fund in memory of Francis Bullard, 65.594

55
Tyler Mitchell
American, born in 1995
Cage, 2022
Photograph, archival pigment print
127 × 101.6 cm (50 × 40 in.)
Private Collection

56
Pieter van der Heyden
(Netherlandish, about 1530–
after March 1572)
After Pieter Bruegel, the Elder
(Netherlandish, about 1525–1569)
Published by Hieronymus Cock
(Netherlandish, 1510–1570)
Spring, from the series
Four Seasons, 1570
Engraving and etching
22.9 × 28.8 cm (9 × 11⁵⁄₁₆ in.)
Seth K. Sweetser Fund, 33.557

57
Maria Auxiliadora da Silva
Brazilian, 1935–1974
Plantação (Plantation), 1971
Oil and mixed media on canvas
63.5 × 113 cm (25 × 44 ½ in.)
The John Axelrod Collection—
Frank B. Bemis Fund and Charles H.
Bayley Fund, 2011.1841

58
Katsushika Hokusai
Japanese, 1760–1849
The Cushion Pine at Aoyama,
from the series *Thirty-six Views
of Mount Fuji*, about 1830–31
Published by Nishimuraya Yohachi
(Eijudō)
Color woodblock print
25 × 37.7 cm (9¹³⁄₁₆ × 14¹³⁄₁₆ in.)
William Sturgis Bigelow
Collection, 11.17633

59
Jay Lynn Gomez
American, born in 1986
Resting, 2019
Acrylic and house paint on canvas
121.9 × 182.9 cm (48 × 72 in.)
James N. Krebs Purchase Fund for
21st Century Paintings, 2020.222

60
Barbara P. Norfleet
American, born in 1926
Anne Mazlish, 1987
Gelatin silver print
27.6 × 35.2 cm (10⅞ × 13⅞ in.)
Edwin E. Jack Fund, 2017.4472

61
Agostino Gallo
Italian, 1499–1570
*Le tredici giornate della vera
agricoltura & de piaceri della villa*
(The thirteen days of true
agriculture and the pleasures
of country life), 1566
Published in Venice by
Nicolò Bevilacqua
Bound volume, illustrated
with woodcuts
22.5 × 15 cm (8⅞ × 5⅞ in.)
Gift of Rumiko and Laurent
Adamowicz, 2023.1236

62
Tom Loeser
American born in 1956
Dig 23, 2015; reworked 2021
Spalted maple and shovel handles
167.6 × 67.3 × 94 cm
(66 × 26½ × 37 in.)
Anonymous gift, 2022.115

63
Ruth Bernhard
American (born in Germany),
1905–2006
Garden Hose, 1969
Gelatin silver print
34 × 26.4 cm (13⅜ × 10⅜ in.)
Polaroid Foundation Purchase
Fund, 1980.183

64
Plate, 1774
English (probably London)
Tin-glazed earthenware
23.1 × 2.6 cm (9 × 1 in.)
The Lloyd and Vivian Hawes
Collection, 2000.710

65
Wanda Gág
American, 1893–1946
Backyard Corner, 1930
Lithograph
26.5 × 32.8 cm (10⁷⁄₁₆ × 12¹⁵⁄₁₆ in.)
Gift of W. G. Russell Allen, 45.167

66
Attributed to Jan Cornelisz.
(Flemish, 17th century)
Woven by Jan Raes
(Flemish, 17th century)
Vertumnus as a Haymaker,
first half, 17th century
Wool and silk
528 × 343 cm (207⅞ × 135¹⁄₁₆ in.)
Gift of Mrs. William Dexter in
memory of her father and mother,
Mr. and Mrs. Bayard Thayer, 67.347

67
Attributed to Jan Cornelisz.
Woven by Jan Raes
*Vertumnus Throwing off His
Disguise*, first half, 17th century
Wool and silk
330 × 358 cm (129¹⁵⁄₁₆ × 140¹⁵⁄₁₆ in.)
Gift of Mrs. William Dexter in
memory of her father and mother,
Mr. and Mrs. Bayard Thayer, 67.348

68
Cupids gathering roses
in a garden, late 2nd to
mid-3rd century CE
Roman
Fine stone and glass tesserae
on terracotta panel
48.5 × 61.1 cm (19⅛ × 24¹⁄₁₆ in.)
Museum purchase with funds
donated by Jeffrey and Pamela
Dippel Choney, 2003.340

69
Willem van de Passe
Netherlandish, 1598?–before 1637
Martagon Pomponeum in *Hortus
Floridus* (A flowery garden), 1614–17
Bound volume, illustrated with
engravings
17.9 × 26.7 cm (7¹⁄₁₆ × 10½ in.)
William A. Sargent Fund, 2013.1486

70
Michael Mazur
American, 1935–2009
Tulip Book, 1991 and 2008
Pen, ink, and watercolor
27.9 × 35.6 cm (11 × 14 in.)
Gift of Gail Mazur, 2016.292

71
Kimathi Mafafo
South African, born in 1984
Umtwalo Wami III
(My burden III), 2019
Embroidery on canvas
53 × 73 cm (20⅞ × 28 ¾ in.)
Private Collection

72
Justin Kimball
American, born in 1961
Forest Road, Garden Record, from
the series *Pieces of String*, 2010
Archival pigment print
61 × 86.4 cm (24 × 34 in.)
Gift of Ralph and Nancy Segall,
2014.1776

73
Gustave Baumann
American, 1881–1971
Hoosier Garden, 1927, recut
and printed 1961
Woodcut
31.4 × 33.3 cm (12⅜ × 13⅛ in.)
The Leslie and Johanna Garfield
Collection—Partial gift of Leslie
and Johanna Garfield and Museum
purchase with funds from
the Charles H. Bayley Picture and
Painting Fund and John H. and
Ernestine A. Payne Fund, 2022.1394

74
Hilary Pecis
American, born in 1979
Hopie in the Garden, 2021
Acrylic on linen
188 × 162.6 cm (74 × 64 in.)
Gift of Federico Martin Castro
Debernardi, 2022.23

75
Anthony Green
British, born in 1939
*The Flower Arranger/Early
Summer*, 1982
Oil on board
171.5 × 171.5 cm (67½ × 67½ in.)
Sophie M. Friedman Fund
and museum purchase with
funds donated by Jean S. and
Frederic A. Sharf, 2007.9

76
Michael Mazur
Growth, 1996–97
Oil on canvas
92.1 × 97.2 cm (36¼ × 38¼ in.)
Gift of Barbara and Steven
Grossman in honor of Barbara
Stern Shapiro, 1998.225

77
Lilla Cabot Perry
American, 1848–1933
Monet in his garden, Giverny,
1890–95
Gelatin silver print
50.6 × 41.0 cm (19¹⁵⁄₁₆ × 16⅛ in.)
Source unidentified, 1990.307

78
Claude Monet
French, 1840–1926
Water Lilies, 1905
Oil on canvas
89.5 × 100.3 cm (35¼ × 39½ in.)
Gift of Edward Jackson Holmes,
39.804

90
Godefroi Holtzman
French, active 1780–1794
Pedal harp, about 1785
Painted maple, spruce
H. 156.8 cm (61¾ in.)
Leslie Lindsey Mason Collection,
18.30

91
Fan, 1740s
English
Painted paper leaf with carved
and pierced ivory sticks
W. 46 cm (18⅛ in.)
Oldham Collection, 1976.223

92
Christian Dior
French, 1905–1957
Evening dress, 1956
Silk plain weave (taffeta)
with warp print
L. 132 cm (51¹⁵⁄₁₆ in.)
Gift of Mrs. John P. Sturges,
1984.562a-b

93
Yves Saint Laurent (French
[born in Algeria], 1936–2008)
For House of Christian Dior
(French, founded 1946)
Day dress, 1958
Silk
L. 91 cm (35¹³⁄₁₆ in.)
Gift of Mrs. Cornelius Crane,
66.1071a-b

94
Hummingbird brooch and
earrings, about 1870
English
Gold, ruby, and taxidermied
hummingbirds
L. of brooch: 2.2 cm (⅞ in.)
Museum purchase with funds
donated anonymously and by
Joanne A. Herman, Susan B.
Kaplan, and Textile Curator's Fund,
2009.2347.1-3

95
Marjorie Schick
American, 1941–2017
In Henri's Garden, 2003
Painted canvas, wood, plastic
laminate, bronze rods, stitching
78.7 × 76.2 cm (31 × 30 in.)
Gift of Marjorie Schick and family,
courtesy of Helen Drutt, 2016.761.1-3

96
David Hilliard
American, born in 1964
Perennial, 2006
Archival pigment prints
Each 58.4 × 44.5 cm (23 × 17½ in.)
Museum purchase with funds
donated by Saundra B. Lane,
2022.1294.1-5.

97
Edouard Muller (French, 1823–1876)
Manufactured by Jules Defossé
(French, 1816–1889)
Jardin d'Armide (Garden of
Armide), about 1855
Block-printed paper, backed
with linen
3 × 2.13 m (9 ft. 8 in. × 8 ft. 8 in.)
Ernest Wadsworth Longfellow
Fund, 2020.304.1-7

98
Domestic scenes from an
opulent household palace,
third quarter, 18th century
Chinese
Ink, color, and gold on silk
40 × 37 cm (15¾ × 14⁹⁄₁₆ in.)
Charles Bain Hoyt Fund,
2002.602.9

99
Probably designed by Aqa Mirak
and Sultan Muhammad for
Shah Tahmasp (ruled 1524–1576)
Hunting carpet, about 1530
Safavid
Silk warp and weft with silk
knotted pile, with supplementary
metal-wrapped patterning wefts
480.1 × 225 cm (189 × 88⁹⁄₁₆ in.)
Museum purchase with funds
from the Centennial Purchase
Fund, John Goelet, and unre-
stricted textile purchase funds,
66.293

100
Joseph Constantine Stadler
(English [born in Germany], active
1780–1822)
After Peter Charles Henderson
(English, active 1799–1829)
The Blue Egyptian Water Lily,
1804, from *The Temple of Flora*,
1799–1807
Published by Robert John
Thornton (British, 1768–1837)
Aquatint, printed in color and
hand colored
51.9 × 39.7 cm (20⁷⁄₁₆ × 15⅝ in.)
Gift of the Estate of Mrs. James
Alden Marsh, 2012.10

101
Jim Dine
American, born in 1935
The Temple of Flora, Plate XIII:
Blue Egyptian Water Lily, 1984
Drypoint, engraving, and
electric tools
45.7 × 30.5 cm (18 × 12 in.)
Gift of Jim Dine, 1986.660

102
Birthday portrait of a lady,
late 18th century
Chinese
Ink, color, and gold on silk
340 × 154.5 cm (133⅞ × 60¹³⁄₁₆ in.)
Marshall H. Gould Fund, 2000.976

103
Sèvres Manufactory
(France, active since 18th century)
Decorated by Philippe Parpette
(active in 1755–1757, and 1773–
1806), Jacques-Nicolas Sisson
(active 1795–1845), and Gilbert
Drouet (active 1785–1825)
Gilded by Charles-Marie-Pierre
Boitel (active 1797–1822)
and Antoine-Gabriel Boulemier
(active 1803–1842)
Decoration designed by
Pierre-Joseph Redouté (French,
born in Flanders, 1759–1840)
Ice cream coolers from the
Services des plantes de la
Malmaison, 1803–04
Hard-paste porcelain
Each 31.9 × 23.5 cm (12⁹⁄₁₆ × 9¼ in.)
Gift of Mr. And Mrs. Henry R.
Kravis, 2001.250-251

104
Lemercier (French, 19th century)
After Pierre-Joseph Redouté
(French [born in Flanders],
1759–1840)
Albuca Minor, 1802
Stipple engraving, printed in
color and colored by hand
53.4 × 35.5 cm (21 × 14 in.)
Gift of Stephen Borkowski in
honor of Dominique H. Vasseur,
2007.794

105
Turcicum Frumentum from
De historia stirpium commentarii
insignes (On the history of plants),
1542
Written by Leonhart Fuchs
(German, 1501–1566)
Illustrated by Heinrich Füllmaurer
(German, 16th century) and
Albrecht Meyer (16th century)
Cut by Veit Rudolph Speckle
(16th century)
Printed by Michael Isingrin
(Swiss, 1500–1557)
Bound volume, illustrated
with woodcuts
38.7 × 26.7 cm (15¼ × 10½ in.)
Gift of W. G. Russell Allen, 38.655

106
Squash effigy dish, 650–850 CE
Maya
Earthenware
11.8 × 15.3 cm (4⅝ × 6 in.)
Gift of Alphonse Jax, 1972.902

107
Ansel Adams
American, 1902–1984
Rose and Driftwood,
San Francisco, about 1932
Gelatin silver print
22.9 × 28.9 cm (9 × 11⅜ in.)
The Lane Collection, 2018.2651

108
Vik Muniz
Brazilian, born in 1961
White Brazilian Orchid, after
Martin Johnson Heade, 2010
Chromogenic print
171.5 × 101.6 cm (67½ × 40 in.)
Museum purchase with funds
donated by Barbara L. and
Theodore B. Alfond through the
Acorn Foundation, 2012.3

109
Gregory Crewdson
American, born in 1962
Untitled, 1992
Chromogenic print
89.2 × 108.9 cm (35⅛ × 42⅞ in.)
Gift of Gregory Crewdson,
courtesy of Luhring Augustine,
1994.212

110
Gohar Dashti
Iranian, born in 1980
Untitled, from the series *Home*,
2017
Inkjet print
80 × 120 cm (31 ½ × 47 ¼ in.)
Private Collection

111
Graciela Iturbide
Mexican, born in 1942
Jardín botánico, Oaxaca, México
(Botanical garden, Oaxaca,
Mexico), 2002
Gelatin silver print
50.8 × 40.6 cm (20 × 16 in.)
Museum purchase with funds
donated by John and Cynthia
Reed, Charles H. Bayley Picture
and Painting Fund, Barbara M.
Marshall Fund, Lucy Dalbiac
Luard Fund, Horace W. Goldsmith
Foundation Fund for Photography,
Francis Welch Fund, and
Jane M. Rabb Fund for Film and
Photography, 2018.306

112
Harlan W. Butt
American, born in 1950
Extinction Vessel #6: Veneer, 2020
Enamel on copper, silver
30.5 × 11.4 × 11.4 cm
(12 × 4½ × 4½ in.)
Gift of The Enamel Arts
Foundation, 2024.2218

113
Mary Mattingly
American, born in 1978
Magnetic Field, 2023
Archival pigment print
50.8 × 50.8 cm (20 × 20 in.)
Linda C. Wisnewski Fund for
Photography, 2025.316

114
John Henry Dearle
(English, 1860–1932)
Designed for Morris & Co.
(English, active since 18th century)
Greenery, 1892
Wool and mohair
213.4 × 475.6 cm (7 × 15⅝ ft.)
Charles Potter Kling Fund and
Museum purchase with funds
donated anonymously and from
Jody and Tom Gill, Suzanne
Dworsky, Heidi Nitze, Mr. and
Mrs. E. Lee Perry, Ann Clarkeson,
Rita J. and Stanley H. Kaplan
Family Foundation, Inc., Lynne
Rickabaugh, Penny Vinik, Brigitte
Moufflet, Doris May, Mrs. I. W.
Colburn, Kathleen Kemper, and
Edith I. Welch, 2007.314

115
Judith Schaechter
American, born in 1961
Cross Pollination, 2019
Stained glass in lightbox
61 × 177.8 cm (24 × 70 in.)
The Wornick Fund for
Contemporary Craft, 2020.221

116
Daniela Edburg
American and Mexican,
born in 1975
Killing Time, from the *Knit Series*,
2010
Laser print
116.5 × 78.1 cm (45⅞ × 30¾ in.)
Gift of Leigh Braude-Borowski
and Marek Borowski, 2018.2212

117
Daniela Edburg
The Melon, 2011
Wool, cotton and synthetic yarns,
Styrofoam
20 × 20 × 20 cm (7⅞ × 7⅞ × 7⅞ in.)
Gift of Daniela Edburg, 2012.768

118
Dakota Mace
Diné (Navajo Nation), born in 1991
Helen Nez, Diné Elder,
from the series *Dahodiyinii*
(Sacred places), 2022
Digital archival print
61 × 76.2 cm (24 × 30 in.)
Gift of Donna and John Garcia

DETAILS
p. 2, fig. 48; p. 4, fig. 19; p. 6, fig. 27;
p. 8, fig. 6; p. 34, fig. 29; p. 64,
fig. 50; p. 92, fig. 65; p. 122, fig. 79;
p. 142, fig. 96; p. 164, fig. 100; p. 184,
fig. 114; p. 204, fig. 72; p. 206, fig. 5;
p. 218, fig. 56; p. 222, fig. 1.

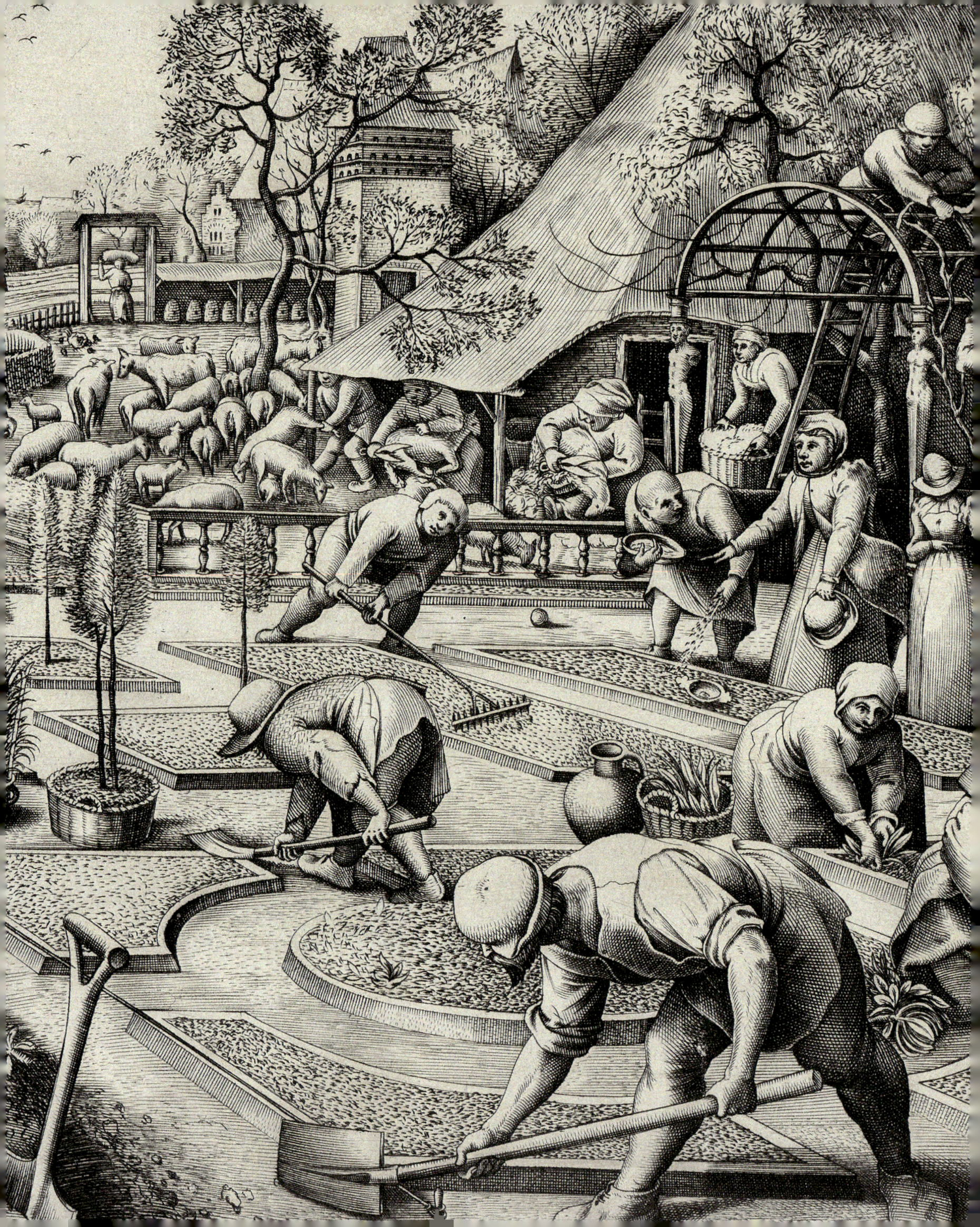

ACKNOWLEDGMENTS

Just as gardens require continued and shared care, so too do exhibitions; they are the sum of many individuals' efforts to arrive at an enduring, larger good. *Gardens and Imagination* and the exhibition it accompanies were the result of an effort across the entire museum in an innovative collaborative project. We thank Matthew Teitelbaum, Ann and Graham Gund Director emeritus, and current Ann and Graham Gund Director Pierre Terjanian for encouraging us to gather works from across the entire collection to explore a cross-departmental topic of great hopefulness and complexity. Angie Morrow, Senior Director of Exhibitons, and Ethan Lasser, John Moors Cabot Chair, Art of the Americas, convened a group of curators to talk through different collections-based ideas; we thank Denise Doxey, Norma Jean Calderwood Curator of Ancient Egyptian, Nubian, and Near Eastern Art; Kristen Gresh, Estrellita and Yousuf Karsh Senior Curator of Photographs; Erica Hirshler, Croll Senior Curator of American Paintings; Jared Katz, Pappalardo Curator of Musical Instruments; and Edward Saywell, Chair, Prints and Drawings, for the early brainstorming sessions that resulted in this collaboration. We thank Kelly Hays for supporting the exhibition's strategic aspects and encouraging us in all stages of its planning.

Colleagues across all museum departments generously spent time with us and offered suggestions that helped shape the exhibition in countless ways, in our weekly standing meeting, in conversations over lunch and coffee, and in front of artworks throughout the museum. We extend thanks to all of our MFA curatorial colleagues, especially Ian Alteveer, Beal Family Chair, Department of Contemporary Art; Lawrence Berman, John F. Cogan Jr. and Mary L. Cornille Chair, Art of Ancient Egypt, Nubia and the Near East; Layla Bermeo, Kristin and Roger Servison Curator of Paintings, Art of the Americas; Marietta Cambareri, Senior Curator of European Sculpture and Jetskalina H. Phillips Curator of Judaica; Anastasia Christophilopoulou, George D. and Margo Behrakis Chair, Art of Ancient Greece and Rome; Nonie Gadsen, Katharine Lane Weems Senior Curator of American Decorative Arts and Sculpture; Katie Hanson, William and Ann Elfers Curator of Paintings, Art of Europe; Anne Havinga, Estrellita and Yousuf Karsh Chair, Department of Photography; Carmen Hermo, Lorraine and Alan Bressler Curator of Contemporary Art; Michelle Millar Fisher, Ronald C. and Anita L. Wornick Curator of Contemporary Decorative Arts; Anne Nishimura Morse, William and Helen Pounds Senior Curator of Japanese Art; Patrick Murphy, Lia and William Poorvu Associate Curator of Prints and Drawings; Simona di Nepi, Charles and Lynn Schusterman Curator of Judaica; Lucía Abramovich Sánchez, Carolyn and Peter Lynch Associate Curator of American Decorative Arts and Sculpture; Phoebe Segal, Mary Bryce Comstock Senior Curator of Greek and Roman Art; Emily Stoehrer, Rita J. Kaplan and Susan B. Kaplan Senior Curator of Jewelry; Jennifer Swope, David and Roberta Logie Curator of Textiles; theo tyson, Curator of Fashion Arts; Sarah Thompson, Terrie and Bradley Bloom Curator of Japanese Prints; Marina Tyquiengco, Ellyn McColgan Associate Curator of Native American Art; Laura Weinstein, Ananda Coomaraswamy Curator of South Asian and Islamic Art; Benjamin Weiss, Leonard A. Lauder Senior Curator of Visual Culture; Julia Welch, Arthur K. Solomon Assistant Curator of Paintings; and Christina YuYu, Matsutaro Shoriki Chair, Art of Asia. In the library and archives, we thank Jordan Barnes, Hee Jung Lee, Paul McAlpine, and Maureen Melton. Angie Simonds, volunteer in the

department of Asian art, was a crucial interlocutor on the MFA's Japanese Garden. In conservation and collections care, Meghan Anderson; Brett Angell; Lisa Ceccarini; Jacki Elgar, Pamela and Peter Voss Head of Asian Conservation; Abigail Hykin, Robert P. and Carol T. Henderson Head of Objects Conservation; Alison Luxner; Rhona MacBeth, Rose-Marie and Eijk van Otterloo Director of Conservation and Scientific Research, Head of Paintings Conservation; Annette Manick; Eve Mayberger; Kimberly McParland; Meredith Montague; Andrew Nelson; Greg Porter; Christine Storti; and Joel Thompson. In exhibitions and design, we thank Nick Pioggia. On our media team, we extend appreciation to Sarah Cowen, Jared Medeiros, and George Scharoun. In publications, Hope Stockton kept our catalogue on track in all ways. We wish also to warmly thank our fall 2025 Pathways Intern, Sophie Sundaram.

Beyond the walls of the MFA, we benefited enormously from support from many colleagues who shared their collections, expertise, and knowledge with us. We are grateful to the lenders to the *Framing Nature* exhibition, who kindly offered works that expanded our exhibition's thematic approach: Deborah Glasser, Azita Bina-Seibel and Elmar Seibel, and Richard and Lucille Spagnuolo. Sean Gilsdorf, Administrative Director of the Committee for Medieval

Studies and Lecturer on Medieval Studies at Harvard University, provided much-appreciated access to additional library resources that enhanced the exhibition's research framework. Lihong Liu, Sally Michelson Davidson Professor of Chinese Arts and Cultures & Assistant Professor of History of Art at the University of Michigan, provided feedback on the concept and checklist. We express our very deepest gratitude to Anatole Tchikine, Curator of Rare Books, Dumbarton Oaks Research Library and Collection, who served as scientific advisor for the show and set us thinking about gardens as artworks in their own terms.

Lastly, we would like to thank MFA colleagues who played especially important roles in this exhibition's development and who deserve recognition for their collegiality, thoughtfulness, and kindness. Nancy Berliner, Wu Tung Senior Curator of Chinese Art, shared early feedback that shaped the exhibition's direction in substantial ways. Samantha Fleischman, summer 2025 Pathways Intern and MA student at the Bard Graduate Center, was a key team member whose excellent feedback only improved the exhibition's concepts and checklist. Rachel Nicholson, Barbara and Theodore Alfond Director of Interpretation, was instrumental in refining the exhibition's concept and audience experience, pushing us always in wise directions. In a show where design and concept were so intricately connected, Keith Crippen, Director of Design, always steered us beautifully and well. Kat Bossi, Project Manager, worked tirelessly behind the scenes to ensure the project stayed on track and in good stead.

Generous support for this exhibition is provided by Penny Vinik. Additional support is provided by the Laura and Tait Nielsen Exhibition Fund, the James & Virginia Welch Foundation, the Loring Textile Gallery Exhibition Fund, the Wendy Lipsey Ecker and Family Exhibition and Publication Fund for Fashion, Textiles and Jewelry, the Patricia B. Jacoby Exhibition Fund, and the Ellen and Robert Jaffe Fund. This publication is made possible with generous support from the MFA Associates/Senior Associates Tribute Fund in Memory of Past Members. Additional support is provided by the Anne Poulet European Decorative Arts and Sculpture Publication Fund.

ELIZABETH DOSPĔL WILLIAMS
Penny Vinik Chair of Fashion, Textiles, and Jewelry

KAREN E. HAAS
Lane Senior Curator of Photographs

COURTNEY LEIGH HARRIS
Associate Curator of Decorative Arts and Sculpture

MEGHAN MELVIN
Ruth and Carl J. Shapiro Senior Curator of Prints and Drawings

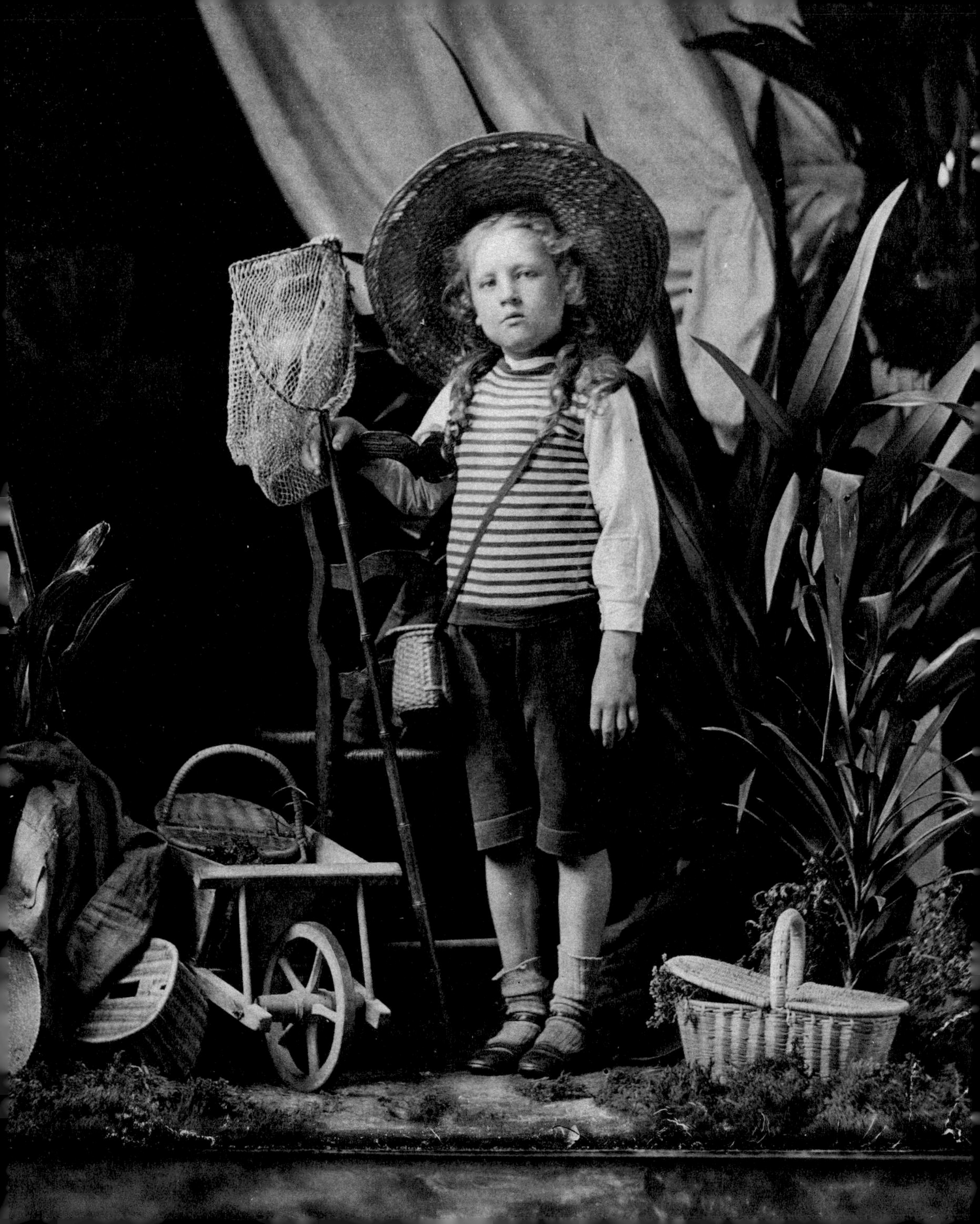

PHOTOGRAPHY CREDITS

fig. 13: © 2026 Artists Rights
Society (ARS), New York /
ADAGP, Paris

fig. 24: © Barbara Westman

fig. 27: © 1979 Nancy Crasco

fig. 29: © 2026 Artists Rights
Society (ARS), New York /
DACS, London

fig. 49: © The Joyce J Scott Art
Trust, Courtesy Goya
Contemporary Gallery and TALP.
Reproduced with permission

fig. 55: © Tyler Mitchell

fig. 59: © Ramiro Gomez

fig. 60: © 1987 Barbara P. Norfleet

fig. 62: © Thomas Loeser

fig. 63: Reproduced with permission
of the Ruth Bernhard Archive,
Princeton University Art Museum.
© Trustees of Princeton University

figs. 70 & 76: © 2026 Estate of
Michael Mazur / Artists Rights
Society (ARS), New York

fig. 71: Image courtesy of the artist
and EBONY/CURATED.

fig. 73: © Ann Baumann Trust

fig. 74: © Hilary Pecis

fig. 75: © Anthony Green

fig. 80: © 2026 Imogen
Cunningham Trust,
www.ImogenCunningham.com

fig. 82: © Claudio Eshun
(aka Don Claude)

fig. 84: © Anna Fárová

fig. 85: © Estate of Shiro Kuramata

fig. 89: Reproduced with
permission

figs. 87, 92 & 93: Courtesy
Christian Dior Couture

fig. 96: © David Hilliard. Courtesy
of the artist and Yancey
Richardson, New York

fig. 97: Courtesy of Carolle
Thibaut-Pomerantz

fig. 101: © 2025 Jim Dine / Artists
Rights Society (ARS), New York

fig. 107: © The Ansel Adams
Publishing Rights Trust

fig. 108: © 2026 Vik Muniz /
Licensed by VAGA at Artists
Rights Society (ARS), NY

fig. 109: Courtesy of
Gregory Crewdson & Luhring
Augustine Gallery

fig. 110: © Gohar Dashti. Courtesy
of the artist.

fig. 111: © Graciela Iturbide

fig. 112: © harlanwbutt.com

fig. 113: © Mary Mattingly,
Courtesy Robert Mann Gallery

fig. 115: © Judith Schaechter

figs. 116 & 117: © Daniela Edburg

fig. 118: Courtesy of the artist.
© Dakota Mace

MFÆBoston

MFA Publications
Museum of Fine Arts, Boston
465 Huntington Avenue
Boston, Massachusetts 02115
mfa.org/publications

Published in conjunction with the exhibition *Framing Nature: Gardens and Imagination*, organized by the Museum of Fine Arts, Boston, March 15–June 28, 2026.

Generous support for this exhibition is provided by Penny Vinik. Additional support is provided by the Laura and Tait Nielsen Exhibition Fund, the James & Virginia Welch Foundation, the Loring Textile Gallery Exhibition Fund, the Wendy Lipsey Ecker and Family Exhibition and Publication Fund for Fashion, Textiles and Jewelry, the Patricia B. Jacoby Exhibition Fund, and the Ellen and Robert Jaffe Fund.

This publication is made possible with generous support from the MFA Associates/Senior Associates Tribute Fund in Memory of Past Members. Additional support is provided by the Anne Poulet European Decorative Arts and Sculpture Publication Fund.

While the objects in this publication necessarily represent only a small portion of the MFA's holdings, information about approximately 400,000 objects is available to the public worldwide. To learn more about the MFA's collections, including provenance, publication, and exhibition history, kindly visit mfa.org/collections.

For a complete listing of MFA publications, please contact the publisher at the above address, or call 617 369 4233.

Cover art: Gustave Baumann, *Hoosier Garden*, 1927, fig. 73
Endpapers: John Henry Dearle for Morris & Co., *Greenery* (detail), 1892, fig. 114

Illustrations in this book were photographed by the Imaging Studios, Museum of Fine Arts, Boston, except where otherwise noted.

Edited by Hope Stockton
Proofread by Jessica Altholz Eber
Design and production by Julia Ma, Miko McGinty, Inc.
Typeset in Romie, Edgar, and Mallory
by Tina Henderson, Miko McGinty, Inc.
Printed on GardaMatt Ultra 150gsm
Printed and bound at Trifolio S.r.l.

Distributed by
ARTBOOK | D.A.P.
75 Broad Street, Suite 630
New York, New York 10004
artbook.com

FIRST EDITION

Printed and bound in Italy
This book was printed on acid-free paper.

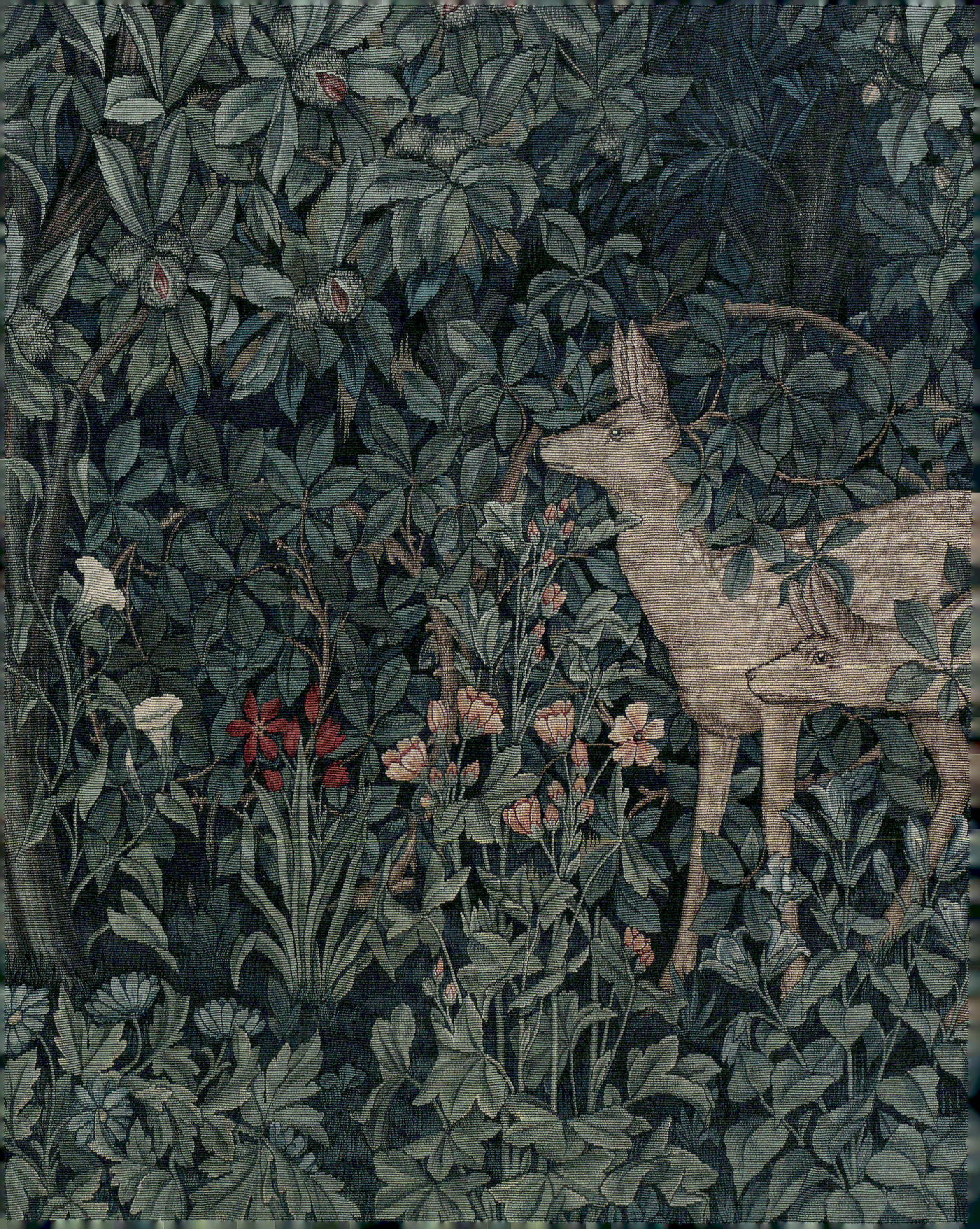